THE PRINCE OF
SOUTH WACO

Books by Tony Castro

Chicano Power:
The Emergence of Mexican America

Mickey Mantle:
America's Prodigal Son

The Prince of South Waco:
American Dreams and Great Expectations

THE PRINCE OF SOUTH WACO

American Dreams and Great Expectations

TONY CASTRO

iUniverse, Inc.
Bloomington

THE PRINCE OF SOUTH WACO
American Dreams and Great Expectations

iUniverse books may be ordered through booksellers or by contacting:

iUniverse
1663 Liberty Drive
Bloomington, IN 47403
www.iuniverse.com
1-800-Authors (1-800-288-4677)

ISBN: 978-1-4759-8388-3 (sc)
ISBN: 978-1-4759-8390-6 (hc)
ISBN: 978-1-4759-8389-0 (e)

Library of Congress Control Number: 2013905873

Printed in the United States of America

iUniverse rev. date: 5/22/2013

For Renee
The Fairest of Them All

TABLE OF CONTENTS

Love is patient. Love is kind. Love is not jealous. It does not brag, and it is not proud. Love is not rude, is not selfish, and does not become angry easily. Love does not remember wrongs done against it. Love is not happy with evil, but is happy with truth. Love bears all things, believes all things, hopes all things, endures all things. Love never fails.
1Corinthians 13:4-7

PROLOGUE

A noble heart cannot suspect in others the pettiness
and malice that it has never felt.

– Jean Racine

Patricia O'Neal lived in a majestic white shingle Queen Anne Victorian style house that evoked a romantic, wistful sense of another time, much as I suppose she did in my young mind. The O'Neal house, as many of us called it, sat on almost two hundred acres of land, most of it stretching the better part of a mile from South Third Street eastward to the Brazos River in the southernmost part of Waco. Most of us knew of no other house like it in town, at least not on a plantation-sized spread this large, and certainly nothing approaching it in our part of town, which was suitably called South Waco. There was a longing sense of romance and the Old South about the house. Perhaps it was just the mood created by the large front porch that resembled an inviting, grand veranda of a Dixie-era mansion, something like the mythical Tara in *Gone With the Wind*. The O'Neal house was an easy eye-grabber to anyone driving on South Third, a lonely, two-lane farm-to-market road with gravel shoulders. It wasn't difficult to imagine late afternoon and early evening breezes turning the porch into a family retreat, especially during our scorching Texas summers. In the evenings you could sometimes see Patricia sitting on the porch listening to crickets or perhaps enchanted by the night sky filled with fireflies and day-dreaming of a fairy ring of toadstools.

On that same farm-to-market road, several stone throws south of the O'Neal house, sat a less distinguished structure: Gurley Elementary, which was situated in a rural setting with dairies and black farmland that was still cultivated with crops like cotton, corn, and sugar cane. The school had been named after a prominent early settler, Davis R. Gurley, an Alabama transplant who had been a Confederate officer and adjutant general of the state, not to mention a high priest of the Masonic lodge in Waco. To my knowledge, no Confederate or Masonic flag ever hung from the flagpole in front of the school, not that anyone would have objected, I suppose. Almost a century after the Civil War, this was still part of the Old South. It was easier to find photographs of Confederate President Jefferson Davis and General Robert E. Lee than of Abraham Lincoln or General Ulysses S. Grant hanging on the walls of local Dixie die-hards, including some teachers. In fact, for a few years a small portrait of Lee adorned a wall at Gurley Elementary, which Patricia attended, as did almost every grade school-age child in our part of South Waco. Each weekday morning, most of us were driven to school along South Third Street, passing Patricia's house framed by early sunlight like a picture postcard. Whenever we passed it on the way to school, my younger sister strained from the back seat to catch just a glimpse of the house, which reminded her of a storybook home in which a princess might live. My sister envied that picturesque porch and would have memories of it for the rest of her life. I harbored no such grand illusion of the house. My fascination with the home was simply Patricia and the memory of her that I would carry for eternity.

It would not be until years later that I would learn about the unique history of Patricia's house, a history that would help me finally come to a personal reckoning with my hometown as well as with myself. As a youth, I had not recognized that the house sat apart from the rest of our surrounding community. Growing up there, I also don't think I ever truly understood that South Waco was literally on the wrong side of the railroad tracks that divided the city. I suppose I knew South Waco only for what I saw it at the time – a collection of working class neighborhoods ingrained in Texas values: conservative, God-fearing, and with an up-from the bootstraps mentality.

Like many towns and cities in the South, Waco was also segregated and followed the Jim Crow laws that had been enacted in the South after the Civil War. They mandated what textbooks would describe as *de jure* racial segregation in all public facilities. Separate public drinking fountains, restrooms, and accommodations existed for whites and blacks, or "coloreds" as the signs usually read. This extended to segregated schools. The U. S. Supreme Court's historic 1954 *Brown v. Board of Education* decision had struck down so-called "separate but equal" public schools in America, but only in theory. Not surprisingly, it would be years before Waco, like many communities in the country, actually began reluctantly complying with the law of the land.

What I would learn years later too, as would Patricia, is just how much her house, this great, white Victorian home many of us admired so much, symbolized the racial divide that existed in Waco. In back of her home stood a row of wood-frame cabins or outbuildings that by the mid-1950s were all shuttered and no longer in use. To a child, they appeared to be empty storage sheds or perhaps dilapidated servants' quarters, and, in a sense, they were. Those tiny cabins had been slave quarters dating back to the 19th century when the original owner of Patricia's beautiful Victorian house had also been among Waco's many slave-owners.

In the mid-1800s, the fertile land surrounding Waco in Central Texas attracted countless settlers from the Deep South who introduced slavery into the area. The 1860 Census was the last time the federal government took a count of the South's vast slave population, and the greatest rate of increase in a state's slave population appears to have been in Texas where the number of slaves more than tripled from

58,000 in 1850 to 182,566 in 1860. By 1860, slaves made up almost forty percent of the population of Waco and surrounding McLennan County. There was a white population of 3,799 and a slave population of 2,404, which was worth more than a million dollars in currency of that time. In 1950s South Waco, our neighborhood adjoined a large but overlooked black community that remained as a racial and cultural island where plantations with slaves had once existed. The children who lived there attended segregated, all black schools in East Waco. By comparison, East Waco made South Waco appear upscale. East Waco was a virtual no-man's land secluded on the other side of the Brazos River, which early Spanish explorers had named the *Rio de los Brazos de Dios,* "the River of the Arms of God."

Four decades earlier, an almost unspeakable act of violence occurred in Waco that would forever link it to the tragic annals of the racial divide that later consumed the South. Jesse Washington, a seventeen-year-old African American farmhand who may have been mentally retarded, was convicted of raping and murdering a white woman on the outskirts of Waco. His trial on May 15, 1916, lasted all of four minutes, and a jury of twelve white men found him guilty and sentenced him to death. But just minutes after his conviction, an angry mob seized the young man without resistance from the authorities. Members of the mob put a chain around his neck and dragged him to the downtown square surrounding City Hall. There, at the base of a tree, the mob castrated an already physically brutalized Washington, threw him onto a pile of wooden boxes, doused it with coal oil, and set it ablaze. With the chain secured over a tree limb, Washington was hoisted above the flame to the delight of the angry crowd. When Washington tried to climb the hot chain, other mob members yanked at his hands and cut off his fingers to keep him from resisting. According to reports, a mob of some 16,000 cheered and roared as the writhing youth was repeatedly lowered into the flame for over an hour. When he was dead, the mob tore his body apart, keeping fingers and teeth as souvenirs and dragging other body parts around the streets of Waco. The killing drew national outrage with the *Nation,* the *New Republic* and the *New*

York Times condemning the lynching. But no charges were ever brought against those involved, even though lynching had long been outlawed. Instead, the lynching was celebrated on postcards.

Growing up in Waco almost half a century later, the only Washington I knew of was the father of our country. It may not have been so much that Jesse Washington had been forgotten as that new generations in his hometown had never heard of him. I'm certain we would all have been mortified by the horrific accounts of his death, but it wasn't something that was in our history books, nor taught in our schools. Maybe the people of Waco, those who might have known of it, would have wanted to forget about this act of savagery or wanted to erase it from their memories. But what couldn't be removed from the mindset were lynchings, which along with hangings had been a fact of life in Texas. Between 1882 and 1968, there were 352 lynchings of African American men in the state. It is also estimated that at least 597 Mexicans were hanged between 1848 and 1928 in the Southwest. It was no wonder then that lynchings were as much a part of the popular American culture of the West as was Texas. Rare was the Hollywood western of that time that didn't include a hanging of some cattle rustler or outlaw who hadn't outrun the posse. I remember one cowboy film in particular, in which the big advertisements in the newspaper had featured actor Randolph Scott's Stetson-covered head about to go into a broad noose. It was one of his most popular cowboy movies, and other kids my age must have seen it was well.

And although they may not have been found in our local histories, stories of lynchings and hangings were part of the local lore, even among young children. When I was five, my parents enrolled me in kindergarten at the First Baptist Church of Waco where they assumed I would be taught to speak English. Until then, I spoke only Spanish. It was the language my parents spoke at home, the language I spoke with my relatives, and the language I would have spoken with my friends had I had any, which I didn't, outside a small group of cousins, who all spoke Spanish as well. Looking back, it was strange that I had not been exposed to English beyond the specialized language of baseball, cowboy westerns, and the country music that my parents listened to on the radio. However, none of those were really the language of children, certainly when there weren't other children to speak to or play with on a daily basis. I don't know exactly why that was. Perhaps it was because I had been sick so often from as early as I can remember and had been hospitalized numerous times for an assortment of illnesses. From our windows, I would watch other children, including our neighbors' young sons and daughters playing outside, and I wished I could join them. My parents, however, kept reminding me of how sick I could easily become and how awful it was in the hospital with all the shots that I dreaded. So kindergarten was my first true exposure to the world of other children and the experience of learning. Every day I sat in wonderment listening to the teacher and the stories she read. I didn't understand them, but it was easy to pretend I did. All the other children would giggle and laugh at the stories, and so would I.

Our teacher, I suppose, might have easily assumed that I was simply another shy child because I do not ever recall saying a word in class. I also did not participate in any of the activities except drawing, finger-painting, and the games we played at recess. At some point at recess, our games invariably drifted to playing cowboys and Indians and cowboys and cattle rustlers. We used imaginary six-shooters formed by pointing our forefingers, and we galloped around pretending to ride our horses. An old oak tree dominated one corner of the playground with a large sandbox underneath it. Two long, thick ropes hung from a tree branch and could be reached easily from the sandbox. The ropes were meant for rope climbing, but we put them to better uses for our games of cowboys and rustlers. We had shaped a noose from the ends of the ropes, and whoever happened to be the rustlers would be hanged the way they did it in the movies. They wouldn't really be hanged, of course, though the nooses would be placed around their necks. But it was all make-believe. No one was ever hurt, and it all seemed innocent enough until the week that my cousin Gloria came to visit from Houston and spent the day with me in kindergarten.

Gloria was the daughter of my Uncle Lupe, one of my father's brothers, and she and I were inseparable when our families visited each other several times a year. The day she joined me at kindergarten was no different, and maybe that is why the dynamics changed on the playground. We were playing alone in the huge sandbox under the shady tree when my classmates ran toward us. They were whooping and hollering the way we always did when we played cowboys. I don't think they understood that we didn't want to play because they grabbed us as if Gloria and I were pretending to be the cattle rustlers. They next thing I knew they were strapping the nooses around our necks. I was accustomed to playing hang-the-rustler, but Gloria wasn't. And she panicked. She screamed and fought trying to escape, and her fear was infectious. Suddenly I was frightened, more because she was than any other reason. She was hysterical, breaking into tears as I tried in vain to assure her that there was nothing to fear.

"It's okay, Gloria," I said in Spanish. "They're just playing."

"No! It's real! They're going to hang us!" she screamed. "Don't you hear what they're saying?"

I strained to listen to what my classmates were hollering.

"Hang the Mexicans!" They shouted. "Hang the Mexicans!"

It sounded just like all other times we played. "Hang the rustlers!" we would yell. Or: "Hang the murderers!"

But this was new. I didn't know who the Mexicans were.

"That's us!" cried Gloria. "We're the Mexicans!"

PART ONE:
The Prince of South Waco

So we beat on, boats against the current,
borne back ceaselessly into the past.

– F. Scott Fitzgerald, The Great Gatsby

How often can anyone say that the moment they first saw someone was the instant their existence changed forever? The Bible cites Moses at the burning bush, the annunciation of Mary by the angel Gabriel, and the resurrection of Jesus among others. For Francis Scott Key in the American Revolution, the sight of Old Glory still billowing at Fort McHenry offered inspiration. For some in the decade that I came of age, the moment of personal enlightenment may have been seeing Elvis. To be sure, true revelation is rare. But when it happens, the few fortunate souls are left in a new awakening and, as the saying in the South went, smiling through the apocalypse.

At the age of eleven, I had only a murky notion of what the apocalypse was, but I was smiling all the time and constantly thinking about Patricia O'Neal. It began on an early spring day when she entered my life in the most unexpected of ways. We were on the edge of our elementary school playground near the end of recess where I was playing catch with a friend and she was displaying a perfect, if tentative, pirouette on *pointe* for her own set of admiring classmates nearby. Patricia was standing on a concrete walkway holding on to a handrail as if it were a ballet barre. As she let go of the handrail, she seemed to spring to her toes with a small hop. Then, raising one foot up and balancing on her other leg, she spun completely around herself and turned a second pirouette. Her girlfriends jumped up and down, sharing in the small triumph of her achievement. From what they were saying amid their laughter and squeals of joy, I could hear Patricia telling her friends she was studying pointe and how it was one of the most demanding skills for all ballerinas. I tried to absorb everything about her. She wore a silky, pink summer dress and what appeared to be ballet slippers, and her long blonde hair was pulled back into a ponytail that left her sensitive face aglow. Her muted slate hazel eyes caught mine, and she smiled when she saw me staring at her. That's when, in the delight of self-forgetfulness or the justice of the sports gods, the baseball I was gripping firmly just fell out of my hand. However, I couldn't stop staring at her; and, as I tried to pick up the ball, I dropped it again. The baseball rolled away, and Patricia smiled a second time and tried to pretend she hadn't seen my clumsiness.

"What's up with you, man, you can't even hold on to a ball today?" my friend Johnny Silva yelled, as he came over to pick up the ball. He saw that my eyes were glued on Patricia.

"It's just Patty O'Neal," he said.

"I've never seen her before, Johnny." At least I couldn't recall ever seeing her.

"Yeah, you have," he said. "She's a sixth grader, and she's been at Gurley her whole life. Stay away from her."

And we were fifth graders, which might have also explained why I didn't remember ever seeing her. They say there's a time you notice girls not for being girls but for being, well, *girls*. It's when brain chemistry kicks off the irrational behavior and flaky thinking of teenagers. I wasn't quite a teenager, but for weeks I had noticed my body changing in ways that I didn't quite understand. When I mentioned this to my father, he had smiled and said it was part of becoming a man and that we would talk about it soon. When I brought it up to my mother, she made the sign of the cross, blessing herself. Then she said to talk to my father. Couldn't anyone understand why Patricia O'Neal made me feel the way I did?

When recess ended, I watched Patricia walk back into the school building. She seemed weightless and sylph-like. She walked with incredibly erect posture, her shoulders back and flat stomach in, and long strides guided by her toes in a slight outward motion. It was a warm late spring Texas day, but I was cold and trembling. I was also breaking out in goose bumps as my body was taken over by a sensation that I had never experienced. The more I tried to stop thinking about Patricia, the more I was consumed by thoughts of her. Her pirouette replayed over and over in my mind, leaving me dizzy and light-headed. Could this be what it was like to have a heart attack? Had I died and was this young ballerina an angel? But eleven-year-old boys don't have heart attacks, do they? I didn't understand what I was feeling because for the first time in my young life, I'd fallen unabashedly, head-over-heels in love. What a time to suddenly feel like all my strength had been drained from my young body. A term paper was due tomorrow. There was a big math test Friday. Most importantly to me, Little League tryouts were in less than a week. But all I could think or care about was Patricia O'Neal. Patricia O'Neal springing to her toes on a hop and turning a pirouette. Patricia O'Neal smiling at me, as I couldn't hold on to the baseball. My mind was one big canvass painted with Patricia O'Neal and her lovely, delicate face that had been indelibly and forever imprinted on my consciousness.

I paid no attention in class the rest of the day, thinking about Patricia and wondering what Johnny meant when he warned me to stay away from her. Of course, if anyone knew these things, it was Johnny Silva. He was possibly the smartest kid in our class, not to mention without doubt being the best athlete and the most popular, too. He always had a smile on his face, and he had an enthusiasm for everything he did that was infectious. Teachers knew that if they ever wanted the boys in class to do something they didn't like, such as square dancing at recess on a rainy winter day, all they had to do was get Johnny involved. We all then became square dancing fools. Johnny's precocious wisdom about life also came from having an older brother, Junior, who had the newspaper route in the neighborhood and, with that income, the best baseball card collection around. Junior Silva had been the first kid with prize New York Yankee rookie Tony Kubek's card, and the previous fall he had cornered the market on Topps' special 1957 World Series cards of Mickey Mantle and Hank Aaron mirroring their lefty and righty batting stances.

"Why did you tell me to stay away from Patricia O'Neal?" I finally asked Johnny as we walked home together from school that afternoon. We lived a block apart and always walked home together along a creek that took us past a golf course, under a bridge on Garden Drive, and through a cemetery where hobos sometimes camped out, eating wild blackberries growing in the brush and catching crawfish in the waterbed.

"Because, Tony, that's what Mrs. Redding said." Mrs. Redding was the Gurley Elementary School principal who favored Johnny, whom we all called "Mrs. Redding's pet," and I was puzzled as to why she would have said this to him. What could be so wrong about Patricia?

"Mrs. Redding? Honest? She said to stay away from Patricia O'Neal?"

"Well, no, she didn't say to stay away from *her.*"

"Who then? Who did she say to stay away from, Johnny?"

We walked a while along the creek bank before Johnny would answer. He seemed embarrassed and uncomfortable that we were even talking about this. "Mrs. Redding said to stay away from white girls," he said.

"Mrs. Redding told you that? When?"

"One day when I was helping out in her office." Johnny sometimes sorted papers and opened mail in the principal's office as well as ran errands for Mrs. Redding. There were times when he returned to class bearing the latest rumors about students who were being suspended or, worse, expelled and whose parents had been called in for meetings with the principal. Johnny also knew the gossip about the teachers. One teacher's husband had been arrested for drunk driving, he said. Another teacher had been served at school with divorce papers. He said the sixth-grade teacher, Mrs. Seals, received mail at the school from the fan club for Raymond Burr, the handsome Hollywood star of the popular *Perry Mason* television show. Junior Silva had also attended our elementary school, and Mrs. Redding often asked Johnny how his older brother was doing in high school.

"The last time I helped in the office I told Mrs. Redding that Junior had a girlfriend, and that they talk on the phone every night," Johnny said. "I thought she'd be happy to know that."

"So how did white girls come up?"

"Mrs. Redding asked who Junior's girlfriend was," said Johnny, "and I told her."

"So what's the deal with that?"

"She's white," Johnny said.

"So why does that matter?"

"Oh, you know," he said "Some people don't like to see white girls with Mexican guys."

"Mrs. Redding said that?"

"When I told her who it was, she made a face," he said. "Then she said to tell Junior that he should stay away from white girls. She said I should, too. That people who don't stay with their own kind can get into a lot of trouble."

But then Johnny Silva didn't really like girls. Not in that way. Of course, if you did like girls, you didn't admit to it. Johnny, though, had seen the way I looked at Patricia on the playground and how I had appeared completely befuddled and confused in the moments afterward. It was a secret I would keep to myself, even as I tried to steal glimpses of her every chance I could in the coming days. Fifth graders ate lunch before the sixth graders, so each day I would be the last fifth grader in the cafeteria, taking my time cleaning off my tray until the last second possible just to see her when she walked in for lunch. Our recess periods were also staggered, and I would purposely hang out with some of the sixth grade boys near the playground entrance to the school, talking baseball and about our Little League teams, just to catch a glance of her as she went back inside.

Patricia was the first thought in my head every morning and the last image on my mind when I fell asleep. My mom often complained that my bedroom was a place of worship to my hero, Mickey Mantle, and not to God. Maybe she was right. I did have a crucifix on a wall, but it was dwarfed in size by two large posters. One was a photograph of Joe DiMaggio, my father's favorite baseball player, and the other was of Mickey Mantle, who was my hero and the player who had succeeded DiMaggio in centerfield for the Yankees. Each evening my nightly prayers that began with "Now I lay me down to sleep..." ended with a special request that God watch over Mickey Mantle, who had bad legs and was often injured. The night after I first saw Patricia, she jumped ahead of Mickey in my prayers to God.

I was so obsessed with Patricia that I imagined that one day, under circumstances even I couldn't foresee happening, she would be transferred to our classroom. Maybe she would be demoted one grade. Maybe they would find out she was allergic to something in the sixth grade classroom. I wanted to will it so much that I started getting headaches thinking about it. Then one afternoon, Patricia appeared like a vision standing at the door of my classroom. She was with her teacher, Mrs. Seals, and our fifth-grade teacher, Mrs. Johnson, who both surveyed our room as if looking for something. Over the next few minutes they called several boys to the front of the class and asked them to stand tall and straight back-to-back with Patricia. She was unusually tall for her age, possibly five feet six inches, maybe even taller, and she towered over all the boys. Everyone, that is, except Gene Liggett and myself, though we both stood just a bit shorter than Patricia as well. A few minutes later, Gene and I had joined Patricia and the two teachers in the cafeteria, which also doubled as an auditorium. There Mrs. Seals explained that she had been put in charge of organizing and directing the school's year-end May Fete show that would be performed on a special night in front of parents and guests. Then she got down to business:

"Do either of you two boys know how to waltz?"

Gene said he had taken dance lessons, which delighted Mrs. Seals. She asked him to partner with Patricia in a waltz and turned her attention to a record player that was on top of an upright piano in a corner of the cafeteria. From it *Around the World*, the theme tune from a popular movie of the same name, began to play. Both Patricia and Gene appeared uncomfortable. She kept looking at the floor and averting her eyes, and I realized for the first time just how shy she was. To be honest, the only thing I really knew about Patricia, besides that she loved ballet, was that she was smart and kind of a bookworm. She loved to read, a classmate of hers named Skipper had told me. A bookworm like myself, wow, I thought: How more perfect could she be?

Watching Patricia and Gene dance, I felt like I might have blown it in not speaking up. I had taken dance lessons myself, though this wasn't something to brag about. What boy would? My parents had forced me to take dance lessons as a favor for my father's boss at the Veterans Administration Hospital. His boss' daughter operated a new junior cotillion in dance and etiquette in North Waco, and she had run into the age-old problem encountered by all cotillions: Not having enough boys as partners for the girls. I didn't want to do this, but my father bribed me with a new Mickey Mantle autograph model baseball glove. What a deal. My dad got to please his boss, and I received the benefits of society cotillion graces for free, not to mention new baseball equipment.

Now, as I watched her dance, it was impossible not to be struck by Patricia's grace and how she moved so naturally. Soon, though, I found watching Mrs. Seals much more interesting. She didn't appear happy with what she saw on the makeshift dance floor. Gene seemed

7

stiff, and he might just as well have been dancing alone because he showed no connection with Patricia. You also couldn't really tell if he was leading her or the other way around. But, then, Gene always wore a look of disdain for everything. Mrs. Seals didn't even wait for the song to end before she stopped the music and turned to me.

"Tony, let's see how you dance with Patty?"

I wasted no time in taking Patricia's right hand in my left, and I carefully placed my other hand on her back, realizing immediately that she had an extremely high waist and incredibly long legs. A frightening thought occurred: Was I going to look ridiculously short? Was she going to wear high heels in the show? Would I look like one of the Munchkins with Dorothy? Thankfully, the music began again, and I was leading Patricia effortlessly for the next few minutes. We exchanged looks and smiles. I relaxed, but I could tell she wanted to say something.

"Is something wrong?" I asked. Was I holding her the wrong way?

"I'm not going to break," she said. She smiled shyly and avoided my eyes. "You can hold my hand a little tighter."

I firmed up my grip and felt her hand tighten as well.

"I think that will help you to lead me." She was right, and it felt nice to hold her hand. When I firmed my hold on her waist she smiled again.

"You'll tell me when I do something wrong?" I asked.

She nodded. This time her eyes locked with mine for a moment. "Only if you promise to tell me when *I'm* doing something wrong."

Up close I saw that she had the most captivating eyes I had ever seen and that they, too, were showing approval. As I guided her with long, flowing movements and turns across the dance floor in the cafeteria, I also caught a glance of Mrs. Seals from the corner of my eyes. She was beaming. So was Mrs. Johnson.

"Where did you learn to dance like that?" Mrs. Seals demanded playfully afterward, though I don't think she really wanted an answer. I wasn't about to tell anyone that I took fancy cotillion lessons, and the only answer that I would have given her was that my mother often watched *The Arthur Murray Party* on television. "It must be that Latin blood," she said. "But you have saved us."

I wasn't sure what Mrs. Seals meant either about the Latin blood or saving anyone. But I suppose that if she had to come to the fifth grade classroom to find a partner for Patricia, then that meant that all the boys in the sixth grade had struck out. Where were they going to find a kid in the fifth or sixth grades that they could teach to waltz in four weeks and then perform on stage in front of every parent of every student in the school? I wasn't sure I was even up to it and probably would have said I couldn't do it or didn't want to do it if hadn't been that I would be dancing with Patricia.

Mrs. Johnson gave me a big hug. She explained that I would need to wear a white dinner jacket and tuxedo pants and wondered if my parents would be able to rent those for me? Of course, I told her. They had rented a tuxedo for me for several evening banquets I had attended with them at the Roosevelt Hotel downtown. I usually felt out of place at those things because I was the only kid there; but the food was always great, and sometimes I actually listened to the speeches. One night one of those speakers was a reporter for The Associated Press in Dallas who would leave a lasting impression on me. His name was Jules Loh, and he gave me his business card, which he may have later regretted. Every two weeks or so, I would write a letter asking him about his work as a reporter. He was always kind enough to answer, sometimes in great detail.

"Really, you've worn a tux before?" Mrs. Johnson asked. "Are you teaching dancing at night?" Her joke caused an eruption of laughter among us. "I'm going to get you to teach my husband to dance," she said. "I'll shame him into learning to waltz."

At that point, I would have done anything to repay my teacher for helping me live out a dream. Over the coming days, Patricia and I practiced each afternoon on the auditorium stage where we would be dancing in the show, with Mrs. Seals choreographing some of the movements to keep us at the front of the stage. Mrs. Seals seemed to go out of her way to compliment me on my manners and on how I led

Patricia in the waltz almost the same way every time we danced. It made me thankful for what I had learned at cotillion on how to behave in formal social situations and on how to dance the waltz as it was taught without improvising any fancy or complicated movements.

I was still nervous around Patricia, though, and we didn't say much beyond what dance partners say to one another: She liked when I moved with her in a particular way, and she again told me more than once that her hand wouldn't break if I held it firmer. A few times we found ourselves holding hands during rehearsal breaks. I tried not to make a big thing over it, and usually we were able to joke about things as we watched other students practice their own routines. It was playful banter, and over several days we were becoming friendly and close. We were both in our school's scouting troops. I was in Cub Scouts; Patricia was in the Girls Scout Brownies. It was also apparent that Patricia and I had been at Gurley for several years, though in different grades. I just couldn't recall ever seeing her before that day on the playground. Then a thought struck me: Had she been on that parade float that I wanted to forget from the third grade? I was one of seven third-graders dressed up as dwarfs on a school float that had traveled along Austin Avenue downtown in the city's Christmas parade. Had Patricia been the girl who played Snow White, waving to the crowds lining the city's main street? I couldn't remember, possibly because I had wanted to forget the experience of being dressed up as a silly dwarf. I vaguely remembered that Russell York, a kid two grades ahead of me, had been chosen for the role of the prince. But for the life of me, I couldn't place Patricia as Snow White. Maybe I didn't want to. How could I face her? Me, a dwarf, Dopey at that, wanting to be with Snow White?

It was easier fantasizing about being her prince charming in a waltz. When she talked to me, it was impossible not to look longingly into her eyes. Sometimes she would glance away, and I would stare at her bangs. They were extremely long, I realized, and they were curled so as to fall on her forehead in soft, gentle waves that flattered her face. Patricia told me she dreamed of being a ballerina. She had been in ballet lessons for some time, but she had only recently started studying the art of *pointe.*

"*Pointe?*" I knew nothing about ballet, and I don't think anyone else at our school did either.

"It's also called 'toe.' It means on the tips of the toes," she explained. What was so memorable is the way she would say these things to me and her speech pattern. She would say them to me, slowly, as if she truly wanted me to understand ballet. And she would look for a reaction in my face or in my eyes to know that I had, in fact, understood some of these finer points of ballet, something most eleven-year-old boys could give a hoot about. "You have to have special shoes to do it," she said. "They're called toe shoes."

"I bet you're good at it," I said.

"Oh, it's hard. "

"Yeah, but I bet you'll be great at it." I couldn't imagine anything she couldn't be excellent at.

As she smiled, more shyly than I had ever seen her do before, she bent her head, slightly embarrassed that I would have so much confidence in her.

"Thank you." Her voice had become breathless and almost a whisper. "That's why I'm studying both ballet and toe."

"They have special classes just for toe?" I could not recall ever having been this interested in anyone else's life.

"Yes, but you can't start toe until you're twelve," she said.

"Why is that?"

"Because you can hurt your feet," she said, telling me that she had only turned twelve only earlier that month, on April 3, a date I would immediately memorize. "The muscles and bones in your feet need to be strong enough, so that's why you can't start studying toe too early."

I could not have imagined this being any better than it was. But a part of me was frightened of losing that moment. I felt that if I blinked, it would all be gone. But I blinked, and she was still there. The more Patricia and I practiced dancing, the more Mrs. Seals kept telling us things to boost our confidence. She said that we looked like "a princess and her prince." Those were her exact words. She said our waltz would be the finale of the program, and that she had been bragging to the faculty how impressive we were and that our dance would be the showstopper. Patricia squeezed my hand when we heard this. I could tell that she was becoming more comfortable around me. One afternoon, as we sat on a piano bench during a break, she slipped her shoes off and flexed her toes for just a few moments. Her toenails were painted pink, and her feet were like the rest of her: Elegant and fine-boned, and her graceful high arches accentuated her narrow heels and slender ankles. When she noticed I was staring, Patricia smiled and nudged me. It was time to practice again.

Several teachers and the principal soon came to watch us dance, and their enthusiastic applause told us they were both surprised and extremely pleased. Mrs. Redding was the only one not smiling. In fact, she had a grim scowl on her face, apparently having seen something she didn't like. We learned what it was the next day. That Friday Mrs. Seals, who until then had been wildly supportive, informed Patricia and me of a major change in our waltz. She didn't tell us why, but Gene would now be dancing the waltz with us in a threesome. It didn't make sense, but what could we say? It seemed unheard of, and even Mrs. Seals seemed puzzled about how this would work. If going from a duet in a waltz to a threesome seemed awkward, the new choreography was even stranger and felt forced. It called for Gene and me to stand on opposite sides of the stage, with Patricia starting alone in the center. She was to start with a series of pirouettes leading her to Gene who would waltz with her for a few moments, leading her to the other side of the stage where I would become Patricia's partner. We were to alternate dancing with Patricia, and eventually she would finish the waltz with Gene. It all felt awkward and poorly planned. The only thing that made it even seem worthwhile was the fact that I would still be dancing part of the time with Patricia and seeing her every day.

Then on Saturday, my world started really falling apart. I woke up that morning with an itchy rash of spots and symptoms that looked like I had the chicken pox. Kids with the chicken pox usually have to stay home and miss a week of school or more. Any other time, this would have been a godsend. But for once, I couldn't wait to go to school every day and had even wished the weekends would pass more quickly. In bed that morning, I looked at the cross over a side of my headboard and asked God to please take my chicken pox away and give them to someone else, someone more deserving like Gene Liggett. God was listening. On Monday, I felt better, and it appeared I might not have had chicken pox. Monday was also a school holiday, and on Tuesday my parents called my teacher and informed her I was under the weather but likely would be back in school in a day or two. Sure enough, I was back in school Thursday morning and couldn't wait for our dance rehearsal that afternoon, but I never made it to the cafeteria. Mrs. Seals came to my classroom and asked me to join her in the school library. She appeared upset, as if something was wrong; and she began with an apology. She was sorry to have to tell me this, she said, but there had been another change in the waltz. The waltz was now going to be a duet again, but Patricia would be dancing it with Gene, not me.

Suddenly, I felt like I was going to be sick, far worse than the chicken pox. I wanted to say something, but I couldn't. I was stunned and devastated. I wanted to ask why, but kids just didn't do those kinds of things in that day.

"The good news is that we have a new modern dance that we think only you with your exceptional talent can do," Mrs. Seals said, unconvincingly. "And we're going to make that our new show finale. I know you'll do a terrific job, Tony. You'll be upstaging Patty and Gene."

But I didn't want to upstage Patty. Who would want to? I listened as Mrs. Seals told me how wonderful I was going to be in this new dance and that we would get started on it right away. But it all felt empty and meaningless, and I didn't really believe any of what she was saying. I didn't know what to say or how to react. Oh, I knew the way I wanted to react. But if I learned anything from the special tutor who had helping me with my speech and learning problems when I was younger, it was that challenges in life reveal character – and that, when under pressure, I had to rise above being petty. It was at those times especially, she had taught me, that I had to rein in my emotions.

"Who will be my partner?" I asked. It was all I could do to hope that this would be another dance with Patricia, and Mrs. Seals seemed relieved that I appeared to be taking the bad news so well.

"You won't have a partner. You will be dancing solo," she said. "It'll be fabulous. You'll be representing the incredible energy of the atomic age and the future. I'm so excited about this, and I think everyone else is, too. I know you'll be great and that you'll send us out with a wallop."

The only walloping I knew, though, was the walloping I felt. I wanted to die. I didn't want to do any of this, but I knew it was now too late to back out. I also felt that maybe, just maybe, Gene would come down with chicken pox or might just be so nervous and awful that Mrs. Seals would have to change her mind and replace him with me. I couldn't wait to go home and, when I did get home that afternoon, I locked myself in my room and cried like a baby. I couldn't stop tearing up because everything that just a few days ago had been like a dream now seemed like a hopeless nightmare. My head was racing as I ran through a mental checklist of what I could possibly have done differently. Could I have danced with Patricia better? Surely, I couldn't have lost my place to Gene, fair and square. Gene? The most uncoordinated boy in class, the last kid always chosen at recess for sports teams, even after most of the girls? No chance. I had seen how he danced with Patricia. More importantly, Mrs. Seals had seen it, too and didn't like it. Could I have talked to Mrs. Seals? But what would I have said? Maybe if I hadn't gotten sick. Maybe if I had gotten to know Patricia better I could now call her and ask if she knew why this had happened.

The telephone rang in the hallway of our home, and I rushed to answer it, thinking in my wildest imagination it could be Patricia. Then I recognized Johnny's voice. He had not gone to school that day, and I hoped I hadn't gotten him sick.

"Johnny, did I give you the chicken pox?" I felt guilty that I might have, if that's what I'd had.

"Nah, I have a cold," he said. "But, hey, I heard you won't be dancing with Patty O'Neal."

"Who did you hear that from?" I was angry that people were gossiping about my misfortune, and I was surprised that Johnny, who hadn't been at school that day, already knew.

"Everybody knows," he said. "Man, what did I tell you? Going after white girls will get you in trouble."

"I'm not in trouble, Johnny. And I wasn't going after her. We're friends."

"Man, everyone knows you like her," he said. "Even Mrs. Redding. Junior says she's a racist. Do you know what that is?"

I wasn't really sure, but I was learning fast.

"I bet you the moment Mrs. Redding saw you holding Patty O'Neal in your arms, she went nuts," Johnny said. "She saw *Beauty and the Beast*, man. Patty O'Neal's like delicate white china, and, I don't think you realize just how dark you really are, man. There are colored people who aren't as dark as you."

As soon as I got off the phone, I went to my parents' bedroom where my mother had a tall, empire floor mirror. I tore off my clothes and stood in front of the mirror, seeing myself totally naked from head to foot perhaps for the first time in my life. I was brown but not just one shade of it. I guess I had always thought of myself as being a smooth but light palomino color, though I don't know why. Maybe I saw myself as being a lighter shade of brown than I actually was because of my mother's fair skin coloring. My mother's family, the Segovias, were Spaniards who identified themselves as Europeans and not as Mexicans. Perhaps I had been overlooking the fact that my father's family, the Castros, had dark, *mestizo* features – a mixture of Spaniard and Mayan bloodlines. My younger sister had taken after our mother's side of the family. She was tan-skinned, only a couple of shades darker than mom. Now looking at myself critically, it was obvious that I was much, much darker. While my chest, abdomen, and legs were a caramel color, my face, neck, arms and hands were a deep mocha, part of it hereditary but part also from the long summers of playing all day under the scorching Texas sun. In fact, the mahogany wood decorating the edges of my mother's mirror was only slightly darker than my skin. I often spent so much time out in the sun during the summers that my mother called me "*lagartijo*," Spanish for lizard. For the first time in my life, I guess, I realized just how "Mexican" I did look.

Mexican, though, was not a word that I had ever said of myself. Not that I could remember. Do kids ever really focus on race and ethnicity on their own? I know I didn't, and I don't think the friends I grew up with did either. Maybe we were just so young and naïve that being white or brown or black was not uppermost in our minds. We judged each other on an entirely different set of values. Were we fair, loyal, and honest with one another? Did we respect each other's parents and homes when we visited? Did we cheat in class? Did we help others with schoolwork, understanding the homework, not doing it for them, when they asked for help or when we thought it was needed? Perhaps it was because we were all so much alike and so homogenized, like the milk we all drank, that race and ethnicity rarely, if ever, came up. But now it had. The closest thing to an ethnic identity I'd had until then was a Mexican folkloric dance troupe that Johnny and I had been forced to join by our mothers, but it had been a brief experience. Raymond Aleman, the teenage son of one of my mom's best friends, fancied himself a dance troupe impresario and needed boys to fill out his troupe. However, he quickly grew tired of our silliness and the fact that at practices Johnny and I often would pull the large sombrero off his head and send it flying through the air.

I hadn't cared about dancing the *Mexican Hat Dance*, but the waltz with Patricia was another matter. And being denied that chance had shocked and humiliated me. When my mother got home from work late that afternoon, she immediately sensed something was wrong. Of course, my swollen eyes from an afternoon of crying might have been a dead giveaway. I started crying again when I told her what had happened at school and that Johnny said that now everyone in class knew and that it was because Patricia was white and I was not. I didn't understand, and this was something that nothing I could do would change. My mom tried to hold back her own tears but couldn't.

"Why should it make any difference?" I kept saying to my mother as I cuddled in her arms like an overgrown baby. "Why should it matter?"

"*Dios mío,* maybe it's for the best," she said, stroking the back of my head, as she had when I was a child.

"No, mommy. Shouldn't I be judged on who I am? Shouldn't it be about who's the best?"

"Maybe it's as it should be, *mijo,*" she said. She was resigned to an inevitability I was too young to understand. "Maybe it's as it should be."

We both cried and, afterward, my mother suggested that we not mention this to my father.

"It's not something he'll want to hear," she said.

My father had strange priorities in life. They were God, family, and baseball, though not necessarily in that order. He was the son of a coal miner who in 1901, at the age of thirteen, had first emigrated to Texas, helping his family settle safely in Webb County near the Mexican border in South Texas. My grandfather, Jose Angel Castro, then returned to Mexico during the Mexican Revolution. There he joined General Francisco "Pancho" Villa's División del Norte and fought with the rebel army in battles throughout the northern part of the country. He crossed the border into Texas several times from 1910 to 1915, according to records, to aid his family and that of Anacieto Guevara, who were from the same village outside Saltillo in the state of Coahuila. When he returned to Texas for good, it was to recover from battle wounds during the revolution that had shattered a leg. He was nursed to health by both my grandmother's family and the Guevaras, including their teenage daughter Catarina. In 1917, Jose Angel Castro, by then twenty-nine, married sixteen-year-old Catarina Guevara, who gave birth to my father the following year. My grandfather supported his young family as well as his mother and two younger sisters, working the silver and coal mines in South Texas until the Depression slowly choked all work and opportunity. A teenager by then, my father left home in 1934 to work in the Civil Conservation Corps created by Franklin Roosevelt's New Deal. After that, he had enlisted in the army, and the experience defined his adult life, as it did for many men of his generation. He served with distinction in World War II where he was seriously wounded in the Battle of the Bulge. After spending months recuperating in a European military hospital, he returned home with a patriotic entitlement of being an American. His legacy from the war was the same as it was for many other returning veterans: Schooling on the G. I. Bill and the pursuit of whatever piece of the American Dream that he could find. As a young child, I often marched around the house wearing my father's army dress uniform cap flopping around my head and his dog tags rattling from my neck. He spoke Spanish with my mother and with me, but that was almost the extent of his ethnic identification. Nothing made him angrier than hearing any of his Hispanic friends say, "*somos mejicanos*" that "we are Mexicans," because he maintained that only those living in Mexico were "*mejicanos*."

"We are American, and never let anyone tell you differently," he lectured me on more than one occasion. "I have a gut full of shrapnel to prove that."

Maybe that explains why, after a tornado in 1953 that killed one hundred and forty four people and virtually destroyed our home near the devastated downtown area, my father moved us to a house in an almost exclusively white working class community in the southernmost part of Waco. Until then, we had lived on South Fourth Street, just a block east of Baylor University. At a young age, I had traversed the campus almost daily, walking with my mother several blocks to the local market or to take the bus downtown. I found the campus hypnotic: Ivy growing up some of the aging brick buildings; bronze statues of important men dotting the landscaped lawns; book-laden students walking purposefully; bells from a tall tower tolling and chiming throughout the day. I would miss all this when we moved deeper into South Waco, where I would come to understand more of the racial realities of that time. In the lore that the country produced about Texas, people generally overlooked the fact that Texas was part of the South, more so than the Southwest.

For almost all of my elementary school years, I was one of just a handful of Hispanic students in my class that also included Johnny Silva, though he seemed only vaguely Mexican. He was light-skinned, he couldn't speak Spanish, and in all the years I visited his home I don't think I ever heard anything but English coming out of his family's mouths. In the neighborhood and at school, we were like anyone else. We participated in Cub Scouts, Boys Scouts, Little League, and the Soap Box Derby. Although Johnny and I were Roman Catholics, we regularly joined our friends in attending the Wednesday night prayer meetings at the local Baptist church as well as its summer Vacation Bible School. When Walt Disney's popular *Davy Crockett: King of the Wild Frontier* was released in the mid-1950s, both Johnny and I saw the film with several friends. We cheered for Davy and the Texans at scenes of the Battle of the Alamo and booed the Mexican army, leaving the theater in tears over the slaughter but with pride in the Texas honor for which the Alamo heroes had sacrificed their lives.

If you had asked my father, he would have said he had raised his son to stand with the defenders of the Alamo, to not complain about my lot in life, and to die like a soldier. So my mother was right. What had happened to me at school was not something we wanted to tell my father. We knew how he would react. My father was a stickler for discipline, humility, and sacrifice. He had a bad temper, which he unfortunately lost occasionally, so much so that well-intended acts of behavior modification sometimes became belt lashes of physical cruelty and abuse. More than once in those young years, I crawled away whimpering, terrified, and begging that he stop hitting me. Perhaps that accounted for the fact that my sleep was often disrupted by nightmares, and it was rare that I would sleep though the night. My father was also not much for disobedience of authority, and he was likely to feel that if the teachers had removed me from dancing with Patricia, then it must have been that they didn't think I was the best person to waltz with her. My father could be that way. He didn't take kindly to rebels, outlaws, or defiance. So that night, we said nothing about it.

The best thing that might have been said about my father at this time, and no, I'm not being too harsh, was that my mother had fallen in love with him. I once asked her why, and she said:

"I loved your father and he took me away from all the unhappiness I had growing up in my own home."

Of course, that was something you might have heard from a lot of women of her time. Maybe even for years to come, as well.

My mother had been raised in a house that that revolved around my grandmother, Concepción, who was known as Concha. They lived in Rosebud, which in the 1930s and 1940s was a farming hub about thirty miles outside Waco. They had family money or pretended to; no one in my family was ever quite sure about that. Concha Rivera fancied herself being of Spanish nobility with no *mestizo* blood in her family. Doña Concha is the only name I ever knew my grandmother by, and she maintained that her Spanish ancestors had arrived in the New World in 1604 and that her family moved northward toward the U.S.-Mexico border. In 1767, Doña Concha's fifth great-grandfather received some two thousand acres of land just south of the border from the King of Spain, which her family slowly sold off. A newlywed, Doña Concha Segovia moved to Texas with husband Francisco shortly after the Mexican Revolution and started a large family in which my mother had the misfortune of being the oldest daughter. It was a misfortune because as soon as she could walk she began her young life's indenturement of helping her grandmother, *Ama Grande*, mom called her, in the task of raising the flock of Segovia children that seemed to grow larger every other year. As the oldest girl aiding with the housework, my mom had no real childhood of her own and no formal education to match. She was kept home from school to help raise her younger siblings Florencia, Jesus, and Francisco, while her mother and father spent all day behind closed doors in their bedroom. That ended when Francisco was shot to death under circumstances no one in the family ever wanted to talk about much, but Doña Concha wasn't alone for long. She soon remarried and began raising a second family.

When my mother met my father, she knew little about the world except the life of a domestic in her own home. When she first told me this, I could not help but be reminded of the story of Cinderella. My father was the first man other than her brothers to whom she had ever spoken to, and she became devoted to him, even against her mother's wishes.

"*Qué quieres hacer con ese mejicano negro?*" Doña Concha demanded. This is what my mother recalled. "What do you want with that black Mexican?"

My father's family had extremely dark complexions. In photographs from that period, his father looks as if he could be mistaken for being black, as did some of his brothers and sisters. My father's skin had more of a dark reddish tone, much like that of Native Americans, which sometimes led my friends to wonder if he was an American Indian.

"Your father looks like the Navajos from New Mexico," one of my neighbors was fond of telling me.

He was right. I actually thought my father looked more like Allie Reynolds, a pitcher with the Yankees of the early 1950s who was Native American and had the nickname "Super Chief."

It said a lot for my father, who had just returned from the New Deal's Civil Conservation Corps service, that he didn't ask for my mother's hand in marriage but simply informed my grandmother of their plans.

"You are a bold young man," Doña Concha said to him. "I hope that boldness comes with money to feed and clothe my daughter."

"*Qué chingada princesa,*" my dad said he had muttered about my grandmother under his breath at the time. That became his private nickname for Doña Concha: *La chingada princesa*, a nickname I would hear him blurt out whenever he was angry with her, which was often.

"I was afraid that I had married into a family of witches," he once said. I couldn't have been more than six or seven at the time.

"Witches, you mean like witches and warlocks?" I couldn't understand why he would say that.

"They're *brujas* and *brujeros*," he said.

"How do you know?" How could he seem so certain?

"Because I have *curanderos* and *curanderas* in my family, too," he said. "They are like cousins in all that dark mysticism."

"You mean all the *estafiate* and *yerba buena*?" My aunts on both sides of my family were always brewing teas and other potions. "Like Doña Juana?"

"Never speak ill of Doña Juana," dad said, speaking of his great aunt. "She saved your life."

"She did?" I'd never heard this before. "How? With witchcraft?"

My dad looked at me as if he wished he had never started this conversation.

"With magic," he said. "Good magic."

When he was drafted and sent overseas, my father wouldn't hear of his new bride returning to live with her family. He insisted that my mother stay with his family. My mother said it was her first opportunity to feel that she was an equal to those in the same household.

"Your father's sisters became as close to me as my own family," my mother said many years later. "As far as I'm concerned they are my sisters."

When my father returned from the war, he was stationed at army bases in Palacios on the Gulf Coast and Abilene in West Central Texas. As a child, I would be entertained by my mom's stories of their brief life at Camp Hulen in Palacios and how she and my father often took strolls hand-in-hand in the light showers that were a daily occurrence. She also loved to sing, in particular one love song about true love without lies, nor wrong:

"Por vivir en quinto patio/ desprecias mis besos/ un carino verdadero/ sin mentiras ni maldad."

My mother spoke no English at the time, which would seem like an overwhelmingly intimidating situation for a young, attractive woman in an English-speaking society, made more so by the fact that she had few friends there and was usually alone when my father was playing soldier. But she managed somehow. Later, when my father was transferred to another base, my mother took care of closing up their apartment and taking a bus alone from Palacios to Abilene. When her bus arrived several hours late, my father wasn't at the terminal to meet her. He had gone to the movies, leaving her to fend for herself. Thankfully a soldier who had known them in Palacios was at the terminal and stayed with her until my father finally showed up.

"I wasn't scared," my mother told me. "I felt safe. There were American soldiers all around me."

My grandmother finally accepted my father after he and my mother returned to his family's home in Rosebud. When my dad found little opportunity there for returning soldiers, he and my mom moved to Waco, followed soon by Doña Concha when she learned that she would be a grandmother. She was at Providence Hospital in Waco when I was born, and she later insisted that my parents visit her several times a week. Knowing my father and his genuine dislike of my grandmother, I can only imagine he did so grudgingly. When Doña Concha converted the front of her house into a small café, my father found it a useful excuse to limit the visits to Sundays and holidays when the tiny restaurant was closed. But my grandmother was shrewd. She bought one of the first television sets in Waco, and it was there where I would retreat on Saturdays to watch TV westerns like *The Roy Rogers Show*. Doña Concha's television was also the source of humor she would never live down. She once called and insisted that my parents bring me over to watch a football game being televised from Rosebud. It was New Year's Day, and the game was the Rose Bowl.

"Oh, well, it sounded like they were saying Rosebud," said Doña Concha. "The place where they're playing looks like it could be Rosebud, doesn't it?"

Yeah, Pasadena, California. The only thing Rosebud had in common with Pasadena, home of the Rose Bowl, was that both were in the United States. And, despite her Spanish roots, Doña Concha was quite proud of her American heritage. The Fourth of July, though, was always an unusual celebration. Most Americans grow up celebrating that day; but my earliest memory of the country's most patriotic day was commemorating it in mourning, possibly because I was spending it at Doña Concha's home. Doña Concepción Rivera de Segovia Veracruz was an eccentric by most standards. She was always exquisitely dressed, sometimes with a mantilla covering her pristinely coiffed hair pulled back into a bun; and she always wore stiletto pumps, even into her 60s, that the other women in my family usually wore only at weddings.

"It's the day my family honors a great distant uncle," she told me once as she prepared her house for a commemoration of a deceased loved one on a day most other people were barbecuing and playing at the park. "He's the reason the King of Spain gave my family land here in the new world." And then she dropped the words that would make any American child stop whatever they were playing and listen.

"George Washington himself mourned him for giving his life for this country," she said.

It would be years before I got the story about this distant relative, as she knew it, from my grandmother. Even then I had to tread carefully between fact and misunderstanding. Her Rose Bowl's confusion with Rosebud was always on my mind. What can I say? She was hard of hearing and had high ambitions for a place in Central Texas that later became a virtual ghost town.

I would learn that the distant relative from the American Revolution was a Spaniard named Don Juan de Miralles Trailhon, who according to one history book was King Carlos III's envoy to the interim colonial government. Another history described him as a merchant, a smuggler, and possibly a pirate who delivered arms and supplies to Washington's ragtag army. Born in Alicante Valenciana, Spain, on July 23, 1713, Miralles reportedly led Spain from neutrality into open support of the colonial revolt, in exchange for control of Florida, something that his untimely death apparently kept from being fulfilled. According to several accounts, Miralles fell ill with a deadly fever while on a visit to Washington's camp in Morristown, New Jersey, where he died on April 28, 1780. He was given Roman Catholic burial rites by a Spanish priest and mourned by Washington, other officers, and members of the Continental Congress.

In his memoirs and letters, Washington was more explicit about Miralles' role, specifically that he was acting undercover so as to conceal Spain's participation and support. According to Washington, an elaborate ruse had created the impression at the time that Miralles had been shipwrecked near the American coast and sought assistance, though he carried letters from the governor of Havana.

"The truth is, however, that Miralles was an unofficial agent of the Spanish government, and was introduced in this way, that he might obtain a knowledge of the affairs of the United States, and communicate it to the ministers of the Spanish court," Washington wrote. "It was uncertain how far he acted under the immediate authority of the Spanish government... Congress showed every mark of respect to this agent, which was due to his personal character, but carefully avoided treating with him in any public capacity, except through the intervention of the French minister."

Back, in my childhood days, however, I accepted my grandmother's story as just that, a story that entertained me on those days when it was easy to dismiss the things she said. Fortunately, my grandmother's refrigerator was stocked with beer, so my father hid his chuckles and sipped his suds. This was the man that both my mother and I knew we couldn't be honest with about me not dancing the waltz in the end-of-school show. We just couldn't tell him the truth. Instead, I told my father I was going to be Atomic Man in the school show.

What I didn't tell him was that I would be dancing in tights and looking absurd in a costume my mom would design with a red cape among other things. My mother was a seamstress and, when she wasn't working at a clothing factory, she was making dresses at home for teenage girls. She had the uncanny ability to make formal and evening dresses and even wedding gowns with makeshift patterns or from an image in a magazine - and often very quickly. A sewing machine, it seemed, was always running in our house. Mothers whose daughters needed dresses for their First Communions, their proms, or some special occasion routinely sought out my mom. Sometimes she made the dresses for entire bridal parties. It meant that our house was often filled with young women trying on fluffy confections of white silk and linen and tulle. Unfortunately, my mother had no reservation about demanding that I help and in the most embarrassing of ways. I was her model on whom she would regularly try out these dresses for making adjustments or aligning the hems. I was tall, skinny, and about the size of many of the girls who would come to our house to have their measurements taken or to be fitted for a dress. My younger sister was still too young and short, and my mother would either shame me by saying that if she didn't finish a dress, she wouldn't get paid or by bribing me with a commission off her sale. At times, I had to put on a full show for mothers who came alone to check on their daughters' dresses. On those days, I would have to try on the dresses with satin high heels. It never occurred to these mothers that I was a boy modeling their daughters' gowns, and I think some of them assumed I was a gangly girl with a short boyish hairstyle. One woman who had several daughters and was over at our house every few weeks, checking out mom's progress on prom and bridesmaids dresses, would often admire my high cheekbones and say she wished her girls had my long eyelashes. Once, Barbarita Ortiz, a pretty girl in her late teens and a regular client, was at our house when mom was using me to show another customer the progress on her daughter's prom dress. Barbarita kept staring at me thinking she recognized me. She should have. We knew each other from church, but apparently it didn't register.

"Señora Castro, I didn't know you had two daughters," she said to mom who smiled back at her but luckily didn't bother to correct Barbarita.

"Mom," I protested after everyone left. "They think I'm a girl!"

"Let them think what they want, they pay good money," she said. "*Es porque tienes nalgas como una muchacha.* It's because you have butt cheeks like a girl."

Just what you want to hear when you're a young, insecure boy.

It was my greatest fear that one of my friends would come knocking on our door when my mom was trying on a gown on me. I could just imagine trying to live that down. But it never happened. My friends all knew my mom as someone who didn't put up with foolishness. She could hear our conversations going on at the other end of our house or out in the yard, and her angry voice could quickly make itself present if she heard anyone using profanity. She would give anyone misbehaving a look out of the corner of her eyes, and she would purse her lips to show her annoyance.

My friends weren't aware of it, but I always knew she could be even more disapproving. From the time I was young enough to understand, my mom would correct any bad behavior by threatening me in the harshest manner known to any boy. *"Te voy a capar si no lo haces,"* she would say. Translated literally, she was saying: "I'm going to castrate you if you don't do it." Honest, she said those things to me. And very dramatically. She would stiffen her hand in the shape of a blade and then she would make a chopping motion with the side of the palm, as if she were cutting sausage or some private part. *Te voy a capar.* Was it any wonder that I became the best-behaved boy in my school?

Of course, she had mastered controlling the men in the family by practicing on my father. Any time they argued, my mother pulled out what I came to call "the nun card." When my father returned from action in World War II, my mother found in his belongings a small photograph of him with a nun who had been one of his nurses in a European military hospital. The photograph was seemingly innocent enough except in the mind of a devout but suspicious Roman Catholic housewife.

"And it's not just any nun," my mom would tell anyone who would listen. "But Antonio," she always called him by his full given name, "is with his German sweetheart!"

And she would make the sign of the cross, as if asking God's forgiveness on this seemingly adulterous and sacrilegious situation. I don't know how many times I saw her do this, thousands, no doubt, because she did it every time my father did anything to cross her, which was often. Worse, a copy of the photograph always seemed to be handy for her to show around. "This right here," she would start. "This is the kind of war your father was in. He spent the war in Europe with her, his little German! And a nun, at that! In the name of the Father, Son, and Holy Ghost."

Amen.

So I could understand why my father might think my mom was a *bruja*. She had unique powers over him. Many years later I would understand she had powers over even the men, the *brujeros*, in her family. My Uncle Raul, or Roy, as he liked to be called, Doña Concha's oldest child, went to his grave refusing to see or talk to my mother, his sister, for almost the last decade of his life.

"He was telling people that I was a witch and was using witchcraft to slowly kill him," mom told me in her own last days. "I don't know where he got the idea I was a witch. I always thought it was Raul who was into black magic or the Rosicrucians."

Mom, even her loved ones said, had special powers, so I had no doubt she could turn me into Atomic Man for the school show where I was no longer waltzing with Patricia. If I had known then, though, about the extent of those powers, I would have asked for so much more. As it was, this was now the lowest point of my life. I couldn't think of anything worse that had happened to me in my young life, unless it was the fire in the cemetery. In the third grade, Johnny and I had experimented with smoking cigarettes. We lit up several times while walking home along the creek through the cemetery that was covered by brush and dry weeds. That all ended the hot spring afternoon when we were surprised by a fire engine just as we stepped out of the cemetery. Several firemen jumped out of the fire truck and ran toward us, waving us away. When we looked back at where other firefighters were headed, we saw why they were there. The cemetery was ablaze in flames, and black smoke billowed up into the sky. Johnny and I were frightened that we would get blamed for the fire and ran home, half expecting that the police would coming knocking on our doors. They never did, and Johnny and I never mentioned it again. Nor did we ever light up even once. My mom, though, suspected something about the fire. How could she not? My clothes smelled of smoke she said when I got home, and she quickly washed them.

"You have the luck of a gypsy," she said. It was close to what she said to me one day when I tried on the Atomic Man costume she was making. She said, "You should have been a gypsy."

I wasn't sure what she meant. I was reminded of the carnival that would come to town once or twice a year, setting up tents next to the Circle Drive-In on LaSalle Avenue. It was a regular ritual for my family as was the soap opera that my parents would play out. My father was always drawn to the gypsy fortune-tellers, and my mother would insist that he hand over his wallet to her before we even set foot on the grounds. Fearing that the gypsies would pick my dad's pocket, she would hold on to the wallet and dole out whatever money we spent. The big attraction for me was the freak shows with the tattooed men, the fire-eaters, the sword-swallowers, and the bearded ladies. And now, as the Atomic Man, I guess I could join them. In the coming days, though, I would realize that nobody knew exactly what the Atomic Man was. Mrs. Seals was making up the choreography to my new dance number as we went along, and it changed every day. Worse still, I was practicing alone, nowhere near the other people in the show and, of course, nowhere near Patricia, except once. On that occasion, we looked at each other briefly and exchanged smiles. That day was also the closest I showed any disagreement with the decision that had been made. I approached Mrs. Johnson and shared my unhappiness that Gene was dancing with Patricia.

"It was better when Patricia and I were waltzing alone – everyone said so," I said to Mrs. Johnson. "There was magic. Isn't that what Mrs. Seals said one time? That there was magic between us? Why didn't anyone ask us what we wanted?"

Mrs. Johnson bit her lip uncomfortably, and some of her lipstick smeared off on her front teeth. She knew this wasn't right.

"I don't know what to tell you, Tony," she said. "I don't think Patricia is any happier about it than you are. She's a wonderful dancer, and I'm sure she would want the partner who makes her look best.

But it's done. I'm sorry. And right now you have to do what is best for the show."

And what was best for the show was for me to look silly and ridiculous. I had gone from wearing a tuxedo and waltzing with Patricia to dancing with a six-foot tall rocket ship while dressed in red tights, a red dancer's top and cape with a matching mask and cap that made me feel like a clown.

"Think of it this way," said Johnny, trying to console me. "In that stupid costume, no one will know it's you."

On the night of the show, I walked on to one of the wings of the stage just as Patricia and Gene were preparing to start their waltz. Patricia looked dreamlike in her innocent beauty, and I thought myself fortunate, after all that had happened, just to be backstage to catch this moment. She wore a ball gown that recalled a countryside manor scene out of Jane Austen, and Mrs. Seals had been right: Patricia was a princess. When their waltz began, I imagined myself being the one who was holding her hand and her waist and dancing with her. I was so immersed in that thought that I lost track of time. Before I knew it, their waltz was over and, as I quickly took my place on stage, I caught one last look of Patricia as she left. I was hoping she would look back, but she didn't. For all I knew, she now didn't even know I existed.

Then I became Atomic Man, surrounded by a foggy cloud of smoke created by the dry ice and hot water that Mrs. Seals brought in to heighten the illusion. Ella Fitzgerald's (We're Having A) Heat Wave boomed from the sound system, and I wondered if the audience might not know what to make of seeing a kid in tights gyrating and dancing like an Indian medicine man or an atomic warlock around a giant rocket ship that was in the center of the stage. My friend Ardie Meeker had given me an idea that I used for choreographing my so-called modern dance. Ardie loved to pretend he was Elvis Presley, and he had lip-synced to Hound Dog and other Elvis songs at a couple of parties in the neighborhood. So he showed me how I should imitate Elvis swivel-hipping around the rocket ship, and that's what I tried to do. Whatever I did in those silly tights must have worked because as soon as the music ended, I heard a thunderous ovation. Elvis disguised as Atomic Man had brought the house down. Perhaps it was applause for the entire show, but maybe I had done something right and deserving of attention.

I just know that as it ended, I felt a terrible sadness and emptiness. This had all started on such a high and with so much promise. It had started as an answer to my prayer of being with Patricia, and now it was over and would soon be forgotten. The thought exhausted me, and I wanted to just walk into the night and lose myself. Then, as I started to walk off-stage, a hand tapped me gently on the shoulder.

Patricia stood behind me, still dressed in her waltz gown but covered in a gorgeous red velvet cape. Her eyes danced the way I remembered from our practice sessions, and she wore a smile that suggested she knew more than you thought she should. The stage lights had been darkened, and it was loud and hectic around us, so she leaned very close to me. She looked beautiful and smelled of lilacs: Sweet heaven on a perfect spring day.

"Tony, you were great!" she said. "You were so good!" She was wearing stage makeup, but it only seemed to accentuate her angelic face. I couldn't believe it. She actually had come back, when she could have been gone, just to acknowledge that she had seen me perform. At that moment, I felt an ocean of emotions wanting to express themselves, and maybe I should have said more than I did.

"You were great too," I said. "You are a wonderful dancer, Patricia."

It was becoming noisier around us, making it harder to hear ourselves, so Patricia drew even closer and whispered in my ear.

"Thank you," she said softly. She turned to leave, then came back and whispered one more time: "Good night."

Years later, a Judy Garland quote would remind me of what that moment would mean to me. *For it was not into my ear you whispered, but into my heart. It was not my lips you kissed, but my soul.*

Patricia and I, however, had not been alone. In the darkness and the shadows, someone apparently saw a silhouette of us and of our faces

31

coming together and mistook our innocent moment as a passionate embrace. The next day my classroom was abuzz with gossip.

"They're saying you and Patty O'Neal were kissing after the show," Johnny said to me the next morning. "Were you?"

"No, that's not true, Johnny," I protested. "It's not. We were just talking." I briefly trembled and shuddered to think what could happen if anyone believed this rumor, and I was afraid that it could get Patricia in trouble. "What should I do, Johnny?"

"I keep telling you, man," he said. "Stay away from her."

Fortunately, nothing came of the gossip. At least, no one else said anything more to me about it, but I kept getting looks, especially from the sixth-grade boys who had a chip on their shoulders to start with. That spring, our teachers arranged a softball game between the sixth grade and the fifth grade boys, and we had destroyed them, which didn't surprise anyone. Johnny's uncle Wallace and my uncle Angel were co-owners of the Waco Missions, a semi-professional baseball team made up of over-the-hill minor leaguers and prospects along with ringers from the local Baylor University varsity team. At the time, almost every city and big town in Texas and throughout the South fielded strong semi-pro teams that would play on weekends from spring until the fall. Our uncles' team played at Katy Park, a professional baseball stadium that had been abandoned by a Class B minor league team belonging to the Pittsburgh Pirates when it relocated from Waco. Katy Park was famous for having hosted Babe Ruth, Lou Gehrig, and the Yankees in a 1929 exhibition game. According to legend, though hung over from a night of drinking and entertaining a string of women in his room at the Raleigh Hotel, Ruth hit a prodigious home run over centerfield that carried almost six hundred feet.

The Waco Missions practiced almost every evening, which in the Texas summers could last until almost eight o'clock. When Johnny and I weren't at Little League practice, we would slip over to the semi-pro team's workout. Near the end of the workouts, we would take batting practice with several former minor leaguers who were always willing to give us tips not just on hitting but on fielding, pitching, and base-running. Johnny and I would share these tips with our friends, most of them in our same grade year, and the result was a team beyond its years in talent. What had made that spring's win over the sixth-graders so special to me, at least, was that Patricia had watched the game with some girlfriends from under the shade of a big elm. It had been just a few days after I first noticed her, and I was glad she could see me doing more than just drop a ball.

The school year would end in a few days, and I didn't know when I would see Patricia again. Maybe not until I got to junior high school in a year. And perhaps that would be different. So on the last day of school, I took my parents' camera to school to snap pictures of my classmates, and Mrs. Johnson arranged for me to also take a picture of Patricia with her best friend. My photograph of Patricia, taken in a garden in front of the school, turned out to be a portrait of a lovely young woman smiling mysteriously, filled with mixture of innocence and sensuality. My neighbor Roland, a graphic artist with a black and white processing room, enlarged the photograph and said it was an unusual picture. He liked it and said the picture was as special as the girl in it. For almost two years, Roland had been giving Ardie Meeker and me drawing lessons in his little studio. He had shown us how to handle pencils and produce a controlled variety of lines, values, and textures. Most recently, we had been working on preliminary sketching and practicing drawing people's faces from pictures in magazines and newspapers.

"This would be a perfect picture to use as a model for drawing a portrait," he said. "Her face is wonderful. And those eyes, there's just a trace of an Asian lilt on the ends, isn't there?"

"Asian? No," I protested. "She's American."

Roland roared.

"I know. But look at the eyes, the ends of the eyes, and nothing else. See how they go up just so? It's part of what gives her that little smile even when she's not smiling. She's not really smiling, but the eyes lead you to think she is."

"She's beautiful, don't you think?" Boy, I had it bad for her.

"Of course, she is," he said. "But you have more than just a picture of your friend here. You have something that transcends that. It's the face of a girl about to become a young woman, and the picture captures both innocence and a coquettishness that tell the story. You should see if you could draw that."

I studied the picture more closely and tried to imagine it as a drawing. Over the coming weeks, I must have started a pencil drawing several dozen times and thrown each one away. I had drawn faces before, but they had all been anonymous faces of people I didn't know. This one was different, I knew, and I was almost too frightened to try.

Roland finally helped me figure out how to draw her.

"Are you in love with her?" He saw that I was embarrassed and didn't know what to say. "It's okay to admit it. She's someone you care about, right?"

"Yeah, she is, more than anything else in the world," I said. "I think about her every waking moment, and I dream about her when I'm asleep."

Roland let out a bellowing laugh that reverberated throughout his house. "Okay, well, then that makes drawing her easy."

I looked at him incredulously. "How can you say that? I'm afraid I'll mess up."

"It makes it easy because what you'll be doing is drawing the young woman you love," he said. "If she's in your mind and in your thoughts the way you say she is, then she'll come out in your drawing."

I started drawing her, but I also began writing poetry that I hoped to give to Patricia the next time I had a chance.

I steal glimpses when I pass you,
Small Polaroids that quickly fade
Into the sepia blurriness
Of a moment's antiquity.
I take those glimmers of shy smiles
And mature girlishness,

Of worried dedication and its frowns
And collect them like tiny shards
Of glass that sparkle with the sun
And make each minute brighter
Than the day before.
Did our innocence waltz
To a different beat?
Is that what they never saw?
I wanted to memorize your face:
Is the sepia of old photographs
Like the paleness of your hair
And those frail, soft features –
Do they stare at me through time's muted light
Like your hazel eyes that I wish
Would cross my own and lock tightly
Forever before the moment passed?
I have never been in love –
That's what I now have learned.
I never cared for anyone
Until I fell in love with you.

Writing a poem to her seemed much easier than trying to talk to her. I simply wasn't good at small talk. It wasn't just that I was incredibly shy and introverted. I also had a speech impediment growing up, a lisp and a slight stutter, along with mild dyslexia that made reading correctly almost impossible. This wasn't helped by the fact that I grew up speaking Spanish at home with my parents, with relatives on weekends when we all got together at my maternal grandmother's house, and with my fraternal grandparents when they babysat me on Friday and Saturday nights. I didn't start learning English until well into the second grade. That was startling, considering my father's avowed Americanism. I think he assumed that English would be taught as part of sending me to school at two different kindergartens that I attended, including the one at First Baptist Church. But it wasn't. It was not until the second grade when my teacher Mrs. Coker's increasing frustration with my poor work led to the discovery that I wasn't slow mentally, as she and others had suspected. I just didn't understand the language. I had trouble pronouncing simple words, so I didn't participate in class, and I couldn't read when called upon. It was my classmate Ronnie Barber who finally spoke up on my behalf.

"He doesn't understand English," he told the teacher one day, "because he really only speaks Spanish."

Mrs. Coker was flabbergasted.

"How then do *you* communicate with him?" she demanded of Ronnie.

"Well, ma'm, he understands baseball, so that's what we talk about. If you explain things to him using baseball words, he'll understand you."

That wasn't completely true. I knew the lyrics to most of the Hank Williams songs that my parents played endlessly on their record player when they weren't listening to country music on the radio. From the time I was about three years old, much to the delight of my parents, I would entertain them in the evenings with my own renditions of Hank Williams. I spoke each word perfectly, having learned them phonetically by just listening to the music, but I had no idea what the words nor the songs meant. I was also under the strictest of commands from my parents that I was not supposed to sing or speak these words at school. I guess they didn't want me saying things to the teacher like "Hey, good lookin'," "Honey, do you love me, huh?" "I heard you cryin' in your sleep," or "Son of a gun, we'll have good fun on the bayou."

Otherwise, I understood a few words, but I had no sense of the language. Children usually grow up listening to sounds and words that they imitate. In my early years, there had been no English around me to hear and mimic. By the time I was introduced to it at the age of five, the experience was overwhelming and complicated by the dyslexia that led to me transposing syllables except on single syllable words. I had staggered through my first and second grades mostly with Ronnie's help. We had attended Sul Ross Elementary together in the first grade, and then his family moved near mine when we started the second grade. A little girl named Donna Oliver who sat next to me had also helped me muddle through. She tried to help me correct my lisp and stutter. She would also show me her handwritten homework, usually just a few sentences done in large printed letters, which I would copy.

Soon my parents and I were in the principal's office talking to Mrs. Redding and Mrs. Coker about my predicament. Their initial suggestion was to place me in a Special Education class where I could hopefully learn enough English to be placed back in the second grade. My mother broke into tears. Special Education, in the 1950s, consisted of classes made up almost exclusively of mentally retarded students. Students and parents alike were aware of Special Education classrooms and their students who wore those tragic and empty expressions of being intellectually slow. My father eyed me with anger and contempt that his son could be this stupid. I shuddered to think what could happen at home that night. Thankfully, Mrs. Coker offered a solution. Baylor University had a special department that corrected speech problems and also taught English to non-English speakers, and she offered to seek their help. Within a few days, I was spending several hours each afternoon working with a speech therapist who focused on my stutter and lisp. A graduate speech therapy student who was also specializing in English instruction and literature soon joined her, and she eventually took over as my tutor.

Miss Taylor, the graduate student, became a savior. She quickly picked up on the fact that I liked baseball, so she began teaching me English by having me read the player biographical information on the back of baseball trading cards. She also taught me to read phonetically and to recognize vowels within syllables and their unique sounds. Learning this, for instance, kept me from butchering a word like "bicycle" into "bicacyl," which is a common transposition among dyslexic kids. She showed me exercises for relaxing my lips, mouth, and larynx. Most importantly, Miss Taylor discovered that I didn't stutter when I spoke Spanish, only when I spoke English – and that the stuttering disappeared as I became less frightened of not knowing the language and more comfortable and confident in my use of it. She moved on to having me read from a new magazine, *Sports Illustrated*. Using our second-grade reading book, she taught me to pace my reading aloud by controlling my breath from my diaphragm. Each week she also brought me a new book that we would read together. It began with children's books, but that summer she began coming to my home and the reading got harder. Miss Taylor continued working with me in the third and fourth grades, by which time my reading skills had improved so much that we read *The Old Man and the Sea*, *The Great Gatsby*, *Wuthering Heights* and many more, books that I should not have been reading for several years. It wasn't easy. She gave me a pocket dictionary, and sometimes I spent as much time in the dictionary as I did in the novels. But books were a new world that I had fallen in love with and which had become my refuge. In the fourth grade, Miss Taylor showed me how to keep a journal and instructed me to start writing in a diary each day. Most nights I would spend at least an hour documenting my day's activities that I thought were important. In April of my fifth grade, those entries were almost entirely about Patricia.

Miss Taylor was also a Greek Studies major at Baylor, and she introduced me to a verse of ancient Greek that she said would help any time my lisp threatened to raise its ugly head. It was impossible to recite this verse and maintain a lisp, she said. The verse was the first few lines from the opening passage of *The Odyssey*:

andra moi ennepe, mousa,
polutropon, hos mala polla planchthe,
epei Troies hieron ptoliethron epersen

Sing in me muse, and through me tell the story of that man so skilled in the art of contending... I memorized the passage and began using it, successfully, as a crutch. It became my silent mantra I would call upon when I felt nervous, which I learned was often the trigger for what was left of the lisp and stutter. Once, without thinking, I muttered it aloud before a test, and Johnny Silva heard me.

"Hey, man," he said, believing I might be using the Latin I had learned as an altar boy at church, "if you're praying, say a Hail Mary for me."

As the time grew near for her to graduate from Baylor, Miss Taylor sensed my apprehension about her leaving to return to South Carolina. She was going home to be with her ailing mother and to teach school there. She would also be joining her fiancé, who had gone to the Air Force Academy and was now a fighter pilot stationed in Charleston. In her final days at Baylor, we spent an entire afternoon just walking around the campus, talking.

"Do you know," she said, "that there are students here at this school that haven't read some of the books you've been reading?"

I found that hard to believe. "How can they be in college then?"

"It's a long story," she said, "but it's often done. People read comic books that have been made about important novels. Or they read cheat notes that tell them the story. It's not the same thing."

"I wouldn't do that," I said. Miss Taylor had taught me far more than how to read. In doing so, I had also learned about altruism, tolerance, love, peace, and honor.

"I know. That's why I'm telling you this," she said. "You don't have to. You can read any book from cover to cover. And you don't need me to do it."

Reading books, though, was not the same thing as talking to people, which still overwhelmed and intimidated me. It was easier if there was a reason for talking to someone, like when Patricia and I were thrown together to dance and coordinate our waltz movements. But to start cold and from scratch was frightening. Miss Taylor suggested that I might conquer my fear by going door-to-door selling magazines or anything that would force me into initiating a conversation. She ordered some White Cloverine Brand salve in small tin cans that she said her younger brother sometimes sold in South Carolina. The trick, she said, was to approach nice old ladies, many of whom she said swore by White Cloverine. It was true. In the summer after my fourth grade, I netted almost $150 selling White Cloverine salve to old ladies in my neighborhood and at church. In the summer after the fifth grade, my profit was just over $200. But to show up at Patricia's house hawking White Cloverine? No way.

However, I did telephone Patricia's home several times that summer. No one ever answered the phone, not even in the early evenings. At Bible school at the local Baptist church, a girl who was in same grade as Patricia told me she thought the O'Neals were on a long summer vacation. Patricia had been in Disneyland that summer, I would later learn, on a vacation she and her brother Michael had paid for by selling vegetables from their garden. Each summer day, they would man a makeshift stand in front of their house on Third Street, selling okra, corn, tomatoes, and other vegetables, for theirs was no ordinary garden. Their father planted vegetables on no less than three acres of their land that yielded far more food than their family could use. "One day, someone asked daddy why he planted such a large garden," Patricia later would tell me, "and he said he had to have something big enough to turn the tractor around."

But that summer, I had no idea where Patricia was, and I wanted desperately to communicate with her. Roland saw how miserable I was, and he offered a suggestion. He cut a rose from his wife's garden, wrapped it in beautiful gift paper for me, and said I should take it to Patricia. If she was gone, he said, I should leave it with a note. That afternoon I rode my bike in 100-plus degree Texas summer weather to Patricia's house. I was nervous as I turned from Garden Drive on to Third Street, as much over the apprehension of seeing Patricia, as being aware of how dangerous that street could be. Farmers and truckers used it as a shortcut to the Marlin Highway, often with no regard to the speed limits. In the third grade, one of my classmates, a little girl named Dolores Ann Bohn, was crushed to death by a big construction gravel truck as she crossed Third Street, almost in front of Patricia's house, on her way to school. Dolores had been very popular, and her death devastated all of us. For some of us there was also the trauma of seeing someone so young in a casket for the first time.

No one was home at Patricia's that day, and it appeared from the secured house that the family might not be coming back any time soon. I didn't know much about Patricia's family. Years later I would learn that her mother, Ethel Ruth Weinmann O'Neal, was from a German background. When Patricia was in the Brownies, Mrs. O'Neal was head of the troop, and she was president of the Gurley PTA when Patricia was in the sixth grade. Patricia's father was Irish and had grown up in Waco. While in the Air Force, Francis Marion O'Neal moved his family to Dallas, Knoxville, Tennessee, and Greenville, South Carolina, before resettling in Waco. By then Patricia was in the second grade and had come to resemble her father's family to the point that as a little girl she would often come across old ladies in Waco who would say, "You're one of the O'Neal girls, aren't you? You look just like your aunt Wanda when she was your age."

Houses can look different when you're up close to them than from the road, and at first I wasn't even certain that I was at the right house. I rode my bike to their next-door neighbor's home and asked if this was where the O'Neal family lived. The neighbor said it was, so I biked back to Patricia's and sat for a while on the front steps. I looked out at the big yard, imagining that this was where she had grown up playing outdoors, riding horses from their stables, and fishing from the Brazos. In back I saw for the first time the small houses that looked like servants quarters that were now all shuttered. The sky had become overcast, and then the most unusual thing happened for a hot summer day in Texas. It started raining. I had no choice but to return to the porch where I waited out the storm. I had my journal with me, and I wrote Patricia a note telling her I had come by and wanted to give her this rose. I tore out the page and left the note and the rose inside their screen door and hoped it would be there when she returned.

The sun glowed more brightly than ever when the rain stopped, and the sunlight had an unusual hue to it. I biked down the driveway to the street where the sky appeared more normal. That's when I turned back to look at the house and realized why the sun had shone in an almost blinding brightness there. Patricia's house was sitting at the end of a new rainbow.

Around this time I happened to meet a young couple whose love affair was an inspiration I desperately needed. Actually, the first time I met Arthur Fuentes, who was a local sports legend in my hometown, he looked startled and quickly shook his head when I referred to him as a hero.

"I just play sports," he said. 'Heroes are people who are doing fantastic things in saving people's lives, like the scientists who find cures for polio and other diseases."

It was in the 1950s, the age for the polio plague in America and about that time when vaccines for the disease had only recently been discovered, alleviating fears in a nation in which polio had crippled tens of thousands. I was the batboy for the semi-professional baseball team that my uncle owned, and Arthur had joined the team as a "ringer" to play against a professional team from the Mexican Leagues that had come to town. I was blown away by what Arthur said. But he was a hero, no matter what he said, and he had been a star in three sports at University High School. Actually there were a lot of athletic stars in Waco high schools at the time, but none of the others had a name like Arthur Fuentes.

In fact, until he came along, there had never been anyone like Arthur Fuentes.

Arthur Fuentes was a sports hero at a time when there was a scarcity of sports stars in Texas, in the nation for that matter, who were Hispanic and born in this country. I knew of none, and I followed sports religiously. There certainly weren't any American-born Latino athletes playing at any of the major colleges, and that's where Arthur was headed. He had just received a full baseball scholarship to Baylor where he would be the first Mexican American athlete to letter in a varsity sport.

But it was not only in sports where Fuentes blazed a trail. In high school he fell in love with the girl he would eventually marry, Barbara Grace Matheson. She was blonde and Anglo, and not unlike Patricia. I wanted to know everything I could about their courtship and what kind of opposition they might have run into, but how do you ask someone you barely know about something so personal? How had they overcome the obvious obstacles that they likely faced? They had become engaged and married while they were at Baylor, and they were a rarity. McLennan County, of which Waco is a part, keeps no record of marriages between Latino men and Anglo women. Most places in the country don't either. It is believed among locals, however, that Arthur and Barbara's marriage may have been among the first, if not the first, between a Hispanic and an Anglo in Waco.

That summer, I got to know Arthur well enough to finally ask. Arthur's response was as romantic as it was simple.

"I love her," he said. "She loves me. Love can conquer all."

Arthur's answer was what I needed to throw myself back into finishing the portrait of Patricia. I had accumulated several sketches for the portrait because all but one had flaws that made the drawing unacceptable. I was having difficulty because Patricia had a square jaw line that made her delicate chin appear even smaller. My photograph had also captured Patricia with her head tilting just so and accentuating a long, incredibly slender and straight neck. There was also a problem getting the nose right. Patricia had almost a pixie nose, and creating the right impression on a flat surface proved to be both troublesome and frustrating. I had been afraid that the eyes were going to be the most challenging to capture, but Roland had been right. There truly was a slight lift on the ends of her eyes that made them so distinct. Almost Asian eyes on a porcelain skin, I think, is the way Roland described them. Roland also had me cheat a little.

"Doesn't your Patricia look just a little like a young Audrey Hepburn with blonde hair?" he said when he handed me a close-up picture of the actress that he had cut out of a magazine.

She did, a little. It was remarkable really. Patricia did have Audrey Hepburn eyes.

I finished the portrait just as summer was ending, but I had no idea if anyone would know who it was until one day when Ardie returned from vacation and went to Roland's house for an art lesson.

Ardie knew immediately.

"That's that Patty girl from the sixth grade who danced with Gene Liggett in the school May Fete, isn't it?" he said. "Weren't you supposed to dance with her? What happened with that?"

Your friends, of course, are usually the ones whose observations cut the deepest. But they can also lift you up with just a few kind words.

"Tony, you should enter the drawing in the county art contest," Ardie said. "It could win. Really. It's that good."

And it did. The portrait won first place among student drawings for my age at the annual Heart of Texas Rodeo and Fair art show, and news quickly got back to my school. Mrs. Seals was no longer the sixth grade teacher. Her replacement, Mrs. Alexander, asked me to bring the drawing to school so that it could be placed on display in the library. Roland framed it for me, and the librarian gave it prominent display. To my surprise and relief, it appeared that few people could recognize the subject in the portrait. But then, like Mrs. Seals and Patricia's classmates, many of the people who would have known the subject of the portrait were no longer at the school.

"Who is this mysterious girl in your drawing?" Mrs. Alexander asked one day after she had seen the portrait.

"It's Patricia O'Neal, a girl from last year's sixth grade," I told her.

Mrs. Alexander's eyes lit up, and she shook her head in disbelief. "That's Patty O'Neal? Oh, my. That's her? I heard about the two of you."

"You heard what?" How could she have heard, I wondered, and from whom?

Mrs. Alexander smiled coyly and then gave me the shame gesture, rubbing one index finger down the other index finger as if in admonishment.

I spent much of that afternoon talking to Mrs. Alexander about Patricia, about our dance that hadn't happened and about what really happened backstage. She seemed fascinated by the story and said she would try to find out just why, after we appeared to click so well together as dancers, we were split up. Mrs. Alexander also took great delight in the special interest in Greek, Latin, and the theater that I had developed through Miss Taylor. Mrs. Alexander even wrote a letter of recommendation for me to get into a special classics study program at Baylor as well as to get accepted into the Baylor Children's Theater Workshop. Over the next two years, I would read both *The Iliad* and *The Odyssey* in the original Greek, and I would continue with the Latin that I started learning from my parish priest. But I think it saddened Mrs. Alexander, a Baylor alumnus, to learn that for all the work that Baylor and its teachers had done in helping me overcome my learning and reading disabilities that I had my sights on attending Harvard. I had already written several letters to Harvard asking about their admissions, for a catalog of the university, and how someone such as myself could best prepare himself in seeking acceptance some day.

"That's a completely different world than the one you know," Mrs. Alexander said to me one day. "Why would you want to go so far away?"

"I guess I would just like to see the other world," I said. "What if it's better than the world I've known?"

I never could have talked to another teacher the way I spoke with her, but my classmates and I had discovered that Mrs. Alexander was someone we could open up to. She took an interest in each of us and sometimes dropped that day's study plan just to ask us what was on our minds: From the rebelliousness of rock 'n' roll music and all the new movies to the excitement of the space program, the frightening nuclear testing, and the rise of Fidel Castro. Mrs. Alexander was the first teacher I remember who seriously wanted to hear her students' opinions instead of just talking about her own.

"We live in a democracy," she used to say, "and you need to learn to make your voices heard."

Democracy was a big topic for us in the sixth grade, possibly because of what was happening just ninety miles off the Florida shore with the Cuban revolution. There was also the emergence of Fidel Castro and the way he first came to the attention of most Americans, especially if you should happen to share the same surname. As it turned out, that year Fidel's early military campaign and victories in Cuba made me the most popular kid at Gurley Elementary. The day that Castro's uprising came to prominence in the news media, the principal Mrs. Redding made a surprise visit to my classroom. She asked me to stand up, and there in front of all my classmates, she carried on about this heroic man she likened to the American revolutionaries and how he was a model for democracy and patriotism.

Was I related to Fidel, my principal wanted to know. I had no idea. I had never heard my family speak of him. I explained to her that my family was Mexican and Spanish, and that Fidel Castro was Cuban. I would remember the principal's next words for years as if they were tattooed on my skin: "Oh, I'm sure you're related from back in Spain somehow."

Over the following days, sometimes I did wish I was related to Fidel so that I could brag to anyone who asked if I was – and there were many – and tell them that, yes, he's my long distant uncle or something. All that changed one day, however, when Mrs. Redding returned to my classroom and informed us all that Fidel hadn't been the hero she and everyone thought he was. Instead, she said, Fidel Castro was a communist.

"Fidel Castro," she said, "turns out to be an infidel."

My classmates felt sorry for me. I might be related to a communist; and in the 1950s, there was no worse thing you could be in America than a communist. Hollywood black balled directors and actors suspected of being communists. The country was caught in the vice of a Red Scare, and a demagogue U.S. senator even held congressional hearings to ferret out communists throughout America, especially those in high positions. Fidel Castro was no longer my long lost relative, and I tried to put him out of my mind, though it was difficult. The disastrous Bay of Pigs invasion kept him front and center in the news, as did his visits to New York and the United Nations. Then the Cuban Missile Crisis had us all checking out bomb shelters in our neighborhoods as we feared there might soon be guided missiles sent to destroy our cities from tiny neighboring Cuba.

Fortunately, there were always thoughts about Patricia to which

I could escape. Over the coming weeks, Mrs. Alexander and I had several long conversations that were sparked by her curiosity about me and, more specifically, about my infatuation with Patricia. I asked her if she had learned why Patricia and I had been split up as dance partners, and she said she hadn't gotten a clear answer. There was also a big coincidence behind her interest in Patricia. It turned out that her husband taught at South Junior High School where Patricia was a seventh grader. Patricia was either a student of his or he had checked on her because Mrs. Alexander began updating me on Patricia. I was thankful for the information and, for a while, thought Mrs. Alexander was trying to help me in preparing for my pursuit of Patricia the next year. But as time went on, I realized that maybe there as another motivation. Slowly, her updates on Patricia became almost warnings.

"You know, you're so young and you show so much promise as an artist," she said one afternoon. "One day you're going to have a lot of girls throwing themselves at you. And Patty O'Neal is not what you want, not really. She's not the kind of girl you want to end up with."

"The kind of girl?" That really upset me, and I told Mrs. Alexander so. "Is this about her being white and me being Mexican?"

She gave me a long explanation but became exasperated when it seemed obvious to her that she wasn't changing my mind.

"Don't you get it, Tony? You're not supposed to be together." Her words hung in the air. Even Mrs. Alexander thought it. Wow. If I couldn't turn to someone like her for unconditional trust and support, where could I turn? "I'm just so afraid that you're only going to get hurt, not just emotionally but physically, too."

What I would hear from Mrs. Alexander over the coming weeks was a no-holds-barred primer on race relations in Texas and an introduction to a racial-ethnic divide I had no idea existed. We had not progressed enough by the middle of the twentieth century anywhere near the point where interracial relationships were widely accepted in the state, she told me. Lynchings of Mexican men for associating with white women, once commonplace in parts of Texas, were no longer the issue. But there were frequent reports of violence by groups of white men against inter-racial couples involving Mexican men and white women. Usually the violence was only directed against the Mexican man, but sometimes the white woman became a victim as well. In those instances, she said, the violence wasn't only a beating but sometimes was sexual. Everything she said made my stomach turn uncomfortably. Why would people do that to one another? Maybe at another time and at another place, things would change. But until that day, Mrs. Alexander feared, all I was doing was potentially jeopardizing my well-being and safety as well as that of Patricia.

In making her point on the issue, Mrs. Alexander even recruited Mrs. Teague, my third grade teacher with whom I had been unusually close. It was in Mrs. Teague's class where I had finally begun catching up with my eight- and nine-year-old peers in our schoolwork. Miss Taylor, who was still working with me on correcting my learning disabilities, would occasionally visit with Mrs. Teague. Together, they devised a study plan that evidently did wonders for me. At some point in the spring semester, all the third-graders took standardized IQ tests that were routinely administered then. Those test scores were often circulated among teachers in implementing what unfortunately became student tracking and placement programs. The brightest students were identified on the basis of those tests, and teachers and administrators closely monitored their future work and school progress. A few weeks after we took those tests, I was taken into an empty classroom and given the identical test again, with both Mrs. Teague and Mrs. Redding observing. I had no idea why I was the only one taking the test a second time until days later.

"Some people just thought there was a mistake with the first test," Mrs. Teague told me.

"What kind of mistake?" Had they thought I cheated?

"Oh, it's nothing to worry about. You did even better on the second test," she said.

Had they been considering placing me in special education again?

The next day, my parents were summoned to school for a special parent-teacher meeting with Mrs. Teague and Mrs. Redding. That previous night, after receiving the telephone call asking for the meeting, my dad had been angry with me, warning that I had better not be misbehaving because I knew what that would mean. Yeah, my dad was not above taking a belt to my behind. That put his fear in me, though it was nothing compared to what my mom could do. Remember? *Te voy a capar.* My father still appeared unhappy when I saw him and mom come into the principal's office where I was already waiting. Mrs. Teague had brought me to the office in case anyone needed to talk to me. Waiting in the outer office lined with teachers' mailboxes and office machines, I dreaded what would happen afterward. Much to my surprise, though, my father came out of the meeting smiling with my mom wiping away tears, not tears of sadness but of happiness. That night, when he came home from work, my father told me what my mom already had tipped me off to. On the IQ test, my dad said, I had scored off the charts, at least for the kids in recent memory at Gurley. I wanted to know what I had scored, but he wouldn't tell me. I begged.

"Is it more than a hundred?" I pleaded. From the kids at school, who all talked about IQs, I knew that one hundred would put me in an average range, which as a third grader was all I wanted to be.

My dad, beaming with pride, nodded.

"Is it close to one hundred twenty? You know, twice Babe Ruth's home run record." Inevitably, my mind always went back to baseball.

"*Mucho más alto,*" my mom said. Much, much higher.

I didn't know what to think.

"Joe DiMaggio's hitting streak record," dad said, alluding to DiMaggio's fifty-six games with at least a hit in 1941.

"Fifty-six? My IQ is only fifty-six!" My God! That *would* put me in Special Ed.

My dad laughed. "Now add to that the first score you threw out," he said.

Add one hundred to fifty-six. One hundred fifty-six? Were they serious?

"You can't tell anyone," mom said. "You shouldn't even know. I don't know why your father told you."

"Do you know what that means?" dad asked.

"That I'm not stupid!" I yelled.

"It means," said dad, "that you have to go to college."

College? Good lord, I just wanted to get out of grade school. But it also meant that Mrs. Teague and all the other teachers I had in the coming years at Gurley took special interest in me and in my grades. Mrs. Teague would call our home once every couple of weeks to talk to my parents, even after I was out of the third grade. But none of the teachers took as much of a day-to-day interest as Mrs. Alexander had during the sixth grade.

"You're a smart kid. You're going to go far in life," she said to me in one of those talks about my obsession with Patricia. "But you're going to be judged more harshly than if you were white. This is puppy love, and you'll be in love again many more times. Some people aren't going to like that you succeed. Don't give them any more reasons for hurting you or those you care about. Because they will."

Those are powerfully persuasive words of warning to a twelve-year-old boy, even a precocious twelve-year-old. No one else had ever told me the sexual and racial reality of the world I lived in. Certainly not my father, nor my uncles. It had never occurred to me that no one in my extended family had married outside their ethnic group. They never talked about race, not that I could remember. My Uncle Angel once had talked about Jews in a strange, awkward way. I had been showing him some of my new baseball cards, and we had stopped at one that didn't seem particularly important. But out of the clear blue, he wondered if the player was Jewish. I wasn't certain what being Jewish meant. I mean, it wasn't like being a righty or a southpaw, so why should being Jewish matter. And at Mass, at gospel readings around Easter, didn't they talk about Jesus being the King of the Jews, so why should there be a big deal about a ball player being a Jew? But being white or being Mexican, that wasn't anything I recall any of my relatives dwelling on, and certainly not about marriages between the two. We did have a neighbor, a postal worker who happened to be Mexican, who was married to an Anglo woman. But they were much younger than my parents and didn't socialize with them. I had gone to their house a few times to sell them White Cloverine salve, and they bought a couple of tins. They had a baby, and they appeared to be happy. Had they experienced this hell that Mrs. Alexander described? Did I dare ask them? It just didn't seem important. Besides, wouldn't my world change in the next ten to fifteen years? Couldn't people change in my lifetime?

In the following weeks, I purposely steered clear of any conversations with Mrs. Alexander, and I think she knew that she had only disappointed and frustrated me more than she had helped me. She had made me even more suspicious about adults than I had ever been. But I could avoid her only so long. One day, she walked over to my desk and handed me a slip of paper with a name on it.

"Do you know her or her family?" she wondered.

I looked at the name printed in large letters on the slip of paper: Lidia Montemayor. "I don't know her," I said. "My parents might know her family. I don't know."

"You need to meet her." Mrs. Alexander said it as if she knew something I didn't. "She goes to South Junior, and she's beautiful and brilliant."

"How do you know about her?" I asked.

"My husband teaches one of her classes." She could tell that I didn't look convinced. "And I've seen her myself. On days when I've picked him up after school, we've driven past her as she's walked home from school."

"You have? Why?" This was absurd. My sixth grade teacher was following girls she thought would be "right" for me?

She had no answer, but I knew why. Mrs. Alexander now saw me as some kind of prematurely sexually conscious young man, a red-hot young Latin, and she was trying to find a new object for my attention, perhaps a target that wouldn't get me hurt or killed.

"I don't know," I said, handing her back the slip of paper.

51

"No, you keep it. And check her out yourself when you start South Junior. And she's a lot prettier than Patty O'Neal."

I shook my head. "It's not because she's pretty that I'm crazy about Patricia," I said. "It's more. There's a beauty in her heart and in her soul. I know. It's touched me. If I believe in anything, I believe in her. Look, Mrs. Alexander, I go to church regularly, Bible School in the summers. I'm an altar boy at two Masses each Sunday, and I hear God preached all around me. But you know what? I don't really believe any of that. I don't have that kind of faith. But Patricia? There's something truly divine about her. I hope that some day she might feel the same way about me. I don't know. I just know this: I love her, and one day, no matter what anybody says, there will be a way for us to be together."

For once, I had silenced Mrs. Alexander, and I think I even saw tears beginning to well in her eyes. But she held them back, and then she stung me the way only adults and their logic can.

"Will Patty remember you?" she asked. "When's the last time you talked to her? How can you be sure she will feel the same way about you? And how do you know she doesn't have a boyfriend. How will you ever win her over?"

I didn't know. I just had the blind faith that I would. And I vowed then, that one day when I made it in life, I wouldn't be just good. I wouldn't be just brilliant. I would be the greatest thing that ever was in whatever I chose to do. I had read somewhere that the great Ted Williams, always combative with the sportswriters in Boston, had once boasted that if you work hard and you become the best, how could the world deny you. So, too, if I could become the best, the best journalist, of my time, how could the world deny me being allowed, at long last, to have that dance with Patricia? So, for now, as the sixth grade school year wound down, I threw myself into Little League baseball where I quickly met my best friend of the next few years. He played on an opposing team, and in a big game he had made a great catch in centerfield on a ball I'd hit that looked like it was going to be a home run. He caught the ball against the fence as I had rounded first base and was almost to second. When I saw that he had taken away a possible homer, I slowed down approaching second base and kicked the dirt around it in disgust, like DiMaggio in the 1947 World Series after Brooklyn's Al Gionfriddo robbed him in a great play. It was one of the highlights they always showed on television at World Series time.

We introduced ourselves after the game, and we hit it off right away. My Gionfriddo's name was Dick McCall. I would learn later that he was the son of the vice president of Baylor University and the younger brother of the student council president at South Junior. We connected again the first day of junior high school as we both dealt with the overwhelming intimidation of our new environment. It didn't seem to matter that we came from two extremes in backgrounds. He was from a long line of educators, and I would be the first in my family to even graduate from high school. But we both loved sports and literature, especially Hemingway and Fitzgerald. One of Dick's sisters had recently represented Baylor in the G.E. *College Bowl*, a popular Sunday afternoon TV show of brainiacs. At lunch and whenever we had free time, he and I would play a variation of the game ourselves, trying to stump each other with academic trivia. But in those early days in junior high, we were consumed with acclimating to a schedule of getting to several classes on time, each with a different teacher, while fending off the traditional harassment from eighth and ninth graders. It was chaotic, but I made sure to keep a folded copy of the poem I'd written for Patricia with me. I knew we were bound to run into one another, and I had practiced in my mind numerous times what I would say when I gave her the poem.

Then on one of those first days at my new school, I saw her. Patricia was at the bottom of a stairwell on the first floor of the old junior high school building. She and Linda McMahan, her girlfriend from Gurley with whom I had photographed her at the end of their sixth grade, were walking upstairs. Dick and I were walking down from the second floor after our last class before lunch, and I tried slowing down so that she and I could meet. Patricia had her long hair hanging loose, with soft curls on the end, and it bounced and flowed as she moved. She looked almost unchanged since the last time I had seen her, though she may have been an inch or two taller than I remembered, and she now wore glasses. We were about to reach the same place in the stairwell when several students ran hurriedly between us, blocking our view of each other. I stopped, though, and turned to continue looking at her as she walked up the stairs. Dick had slowed down as well and couldn't help but see that my attention was completely on Patricia.

"That's Patty O'Neal," he said as he rejoined me. "She's in the eighth grade."

"You know her?"

"Yeah, a little," he said. "She goes steady with a friend of mine from RAs."

She goes steady. She goes steady? Now *there* was a showstopper. I swallowed hard and pretended it didn't matter. "RA's. What's RA's?"

"Royal Ambassadors," he said. "It's a group of guys, junior high, some high school, that my dad made me join. It's nothing. Mostly a lot of snotty kids from North Waco. But my friend's okay."

"Your friend... How long has he been going steady with Patricia?"

"A while. They're real tight. You know?"

No, I didn't know. The curiosity was already killing me, but I didn't really want to know. "Is your friend a good guy? He's not one of those snotty kids, is he?"

"No, he's great," said Dick. "You'd like him."

Yeah, I could just imagine becoming good friends with the guy going steady with Patricia.

"And Patricia – is she happy? With your friend, I mean?"

"Yeah, from the best that I can tell," Dick said. "I see them together a lot. They're crazy about each other."

Dick and I walked down a long, yellow hallway in the basement to the gymnasium where we were heading to sign up for seventh grade football. Dick, though, saw that I had become quiet and withdrawn. His face grew long, seemingly wanting to share in what was troubling me. Football was now the last thing on my mind. An eighth grader who was the star of the ninth grade team passed us in the hall, running and hollering. From the gym ahead, we could hear other football players yelling and carrying on, their adrenaline and testosterone on overdrive. Dick wanted to say something, I could tell, but he left me to my thoughts a little longer. He was too smart, though, not to figure out that my drastic mood change had something to do with having seen Patricia.

"I want to scream at the top of my lungs," I said when we got to the gym.

Dick laughed. "Go ahead," he said. "You'll fit in with all these nutty jocks."

I didn't scream. I was a brooder, I guess, not a screamer. I remembered some line from a T. S. Eliot poem that Miss Taylor had me read once. *This is the way the world ends. This is the way the world ends. This is the way the world ends: Not with a bang but a whimper.* Was this all delusional? Why had I believed so passionately and so obsessively that I could rule the world and win Patricia? Had Mrs. Alexander been right? Is it possible that Patricia might not even remember me? And what would I do when I did face all those obstacles ahead that Mrs. Alexander warned about? Could I really fight for Patricia and win her in a world I didn't understand, a world whose rules of right and wrong were kept secret, brought out only when it was feared you might upset the order of things? Who had I been kidding except myself? There are people who feel oppressed, sad-assed, and sorry for themselves. I wasn't one of them. But for this moment, at least, I wanted to dwell in that kind of self-obsessed pity. I was nothing more, I felt, than the anonymous Atomic Man full of harmless fake smoke and hopelessly trapped inside an emotional garden maze without a clue of how to get out.

"Do you know Patty?" Dick asked at last. "I mean, you called her Patricia, so you know who she is, right?"

I didn't immediately reply, until Dick pressed for a friend's answer with a look of realization. "My God! Do you have a crush on her?"

I collected myself and, trying to break out of my funk and brace emotionally for a long year ahead, buried the heartbreak I was feeling deep in my soul. I stared heavenward but saw only a yellow ceiling.

Andra moi ennepe, mousa, polutropon. I even made a sign of the cross and said a silent Hail Mary. But there would be no answered prayer, not any time soon. When a moment is missed, I had come to learn even at my young age, it is gone, possibly forever, and no amount of beating on against the current will bring it back, short of a miracle.

"She went to my elementary school," I finally said to Dick. "And when she was in the sixth grade, she danced..." I was having troubled clearing my throat. "She danced a waltz in our school show at the end of the year. You should have seen her. She was terrific. She was amazing. She was wonderful. She was a princess."

Dick suspected there might be more.

"I mean, did she dance that waltz with you? Were you her prince?"

I tossed that around in my head for a moment.

"Me? Her prince? The prince of south Waco? Fat chance," I said. "That would have been a miracle. I wish I had been so lucky."

"Well, I believe in miracles," Dick said. "Don't you?"

Patricia and I had had our waltz in my mind, but that would be my own private treasure to keep, to remember, and to inspire for that day when the world would finally change. You only fall in love for the first time once. And if it's strong enough, and you believe in rainbows and miracles, maybe it can last forever.

PART TWO:
Fathers and Sons

My mother was the most religious woman I knew in my young life. She had committed herself to Jesus Christ, and I wonder if she should not have become a nun. She carried a rosary almost everywhere she went, and her hushed prayers over each bead in the strand carried the loving devotion of a true believer. My mother's most prized possession that I knew of was a *Niño Dios* that was displayed on an altar in an alcove in our home. This was a ceramic doll-like baby Jesus with blue eyes that was dressed in a white silk gown that my mother regularly cleaned and ironed. My mother prayed to the *Niño Dios* daily, and twice a year my family hosted annual venerations of the image following a centuries-old tradition that had begun in Mexico. On Christmas Eve, friends and neighbors would come to our home or to my grandmother's house to take part in what was known as "putting the child to bed." These guests would sing lullabies while the *Niño Díos* was carried around the house for everyone to worship and kiss the image. When they finished, the *Niño Díos* was laid in a manger where he would stay until Candlemas on February 2 when everyone again gathered to commemorate the end of the Christmas season. On that day, my mother and grandmother would take the *Niño Díos* to Mass to be blessed by a priest who later would come to our home to participate in a celebration with tamales, *buñuelos* and hot chocolate.

As early as I can remember, I would accompany my mother to church for rosary during the week and to confession every Saturday. But my first real recollection of being with her in church is the Sunday morning I accompanied her to Mass and Communion. Perhaps I had never paid attention to the detailing of the ornate, gothic-styled Roman Catholic Church that was around the corner from my grandfather's house near the Brazos River. On that day, I was especially drawn to the church's high walls that were covered with larger than life-sized paintings depicting the Stations of the Cross.

Then my eyes focused on an alcove at the far end of the communion rail where my mother had knelt awaiting Communion.

"Mommy, mommy," I said, tugging on her black mantilla.

She tried hushing me with the castrating sidelong glance that has worked disciplinary wonders for mothers with their misbehaving sons from the beginning of time, but my four-year-old boy's eyes were focused on the alcove as I tugged and whispered again:

"Mommy, mommy."

She looked down the rail lined with other communicants and saw the priest moving nearer, mumbling the words, "Body of Christ" and then popping white unleavened wafers into the mouths of the faithful.

"What, Tonito?" she said.

"Who's that?" I pointed to an oversized crucifix sprouting high above the side altar that was stacked with a funeral pyre of burning red-vase votive candles.

"Jesus," she said. "That's Jesus on the cross. Now be quiet."

She walked solemn-faced back to the second-row pew with me at her side. She knelt and waited for the wafer to melt in her mouth when she felt my tug on the *mantilla* once again.

"Mommy, mommy," I whispered. "Why?"

She swallowed hard, almost choking on the communion wafer.

"Why what, Tonito?"

I was pointing at the crucifix.

"Why is he on the cross?"

"Because they crucified him," she said, close to losing her patience. "Now, please, Tonito, you have to be quiet."

I stared with a look of horror at the writhing wretch hanging from his bloodied hands.

"Mommy," I said. "How old was he?"

"Thirty-three. He was thirty-three years old. Please, Tonito, you must be quiet."

Thirty-three. I couldn't even count that high.

Then I tugged on my mother's *mantilla* one last time.

"Mommy, is this Jesus the same as the *baby* Jesus, the *Niño Dios?*" I pointed to a nativity manager to the side of the altar.

"Yes," she said. "It's baby Jesus."

Moments later, the quiet of the church was shattered by a young boy's screams as I ran down the center aisle toward the entrance.

"They've killed baby Jesus!" I wailed and sobbed. "They've killed the baby Jesus!"

Man's inhumanity to man can be a difficult lesson to learn first-hand, especially for children. Older people don't do much better, perhaps because so often it is they who have been responsible for it. In the coming years, as my life's religious baptism continued, I would come to appreciate the hypocrisy of living in the heart of the Bible Belt. Waco promoters billed it as being "the Heart of Texas." Years later, when I would inform a friend of that, he suggested that there was nothing wrong with my home state that a coronary transplant wouldn't help correct. But in those early years, I didn't see that side of it. I saw home. I felt loved. And, as much as anyone else, I also heard all those admonishments to love one's fellow man that originated from the pulpits every Sunday.

From what I overheard as a young boy, my mother's relationship with God revolved largely around my father. I remember her praying to God for help in keeping my father away from a woman named Jerri. Apparently Jerri was my father's lover and, as I would learn years later, the mother of at least one illegitimate child, a son who looked more like my dad as a teenager than I ever did, and possibly a daughter as well. My father had carried on with Jerri in the evenings when he was supposedly in classes paid by the G.I. Bill. Instead my father spent much of his free time hustling pool and evidently met Jerri at a billiard parlor where she was a barmaid. In the 1940s and 1950s, downtown Waco was dotted by several underground pool halls in dive bars that existed below the sidewalks on Austin Avenue, the city's main drag. It was not difficult for my mother to figure out where my father was each night. He would leave home in slacks, a sport coat, and tie, smelling of Gillette After Shave Skin Bracer. In the mornings, I would see my mother hanging the same coat that now smelled of smoke and cheap perfume.

The only time I ever recall my mother complaining directly to my father about the affair was on a Sunday afternoon when he went into his oversized army footlocker trunk and pulled out a handgun. He didn't seem to mind me watching him checking it and an ammunition clip and returning it to a black leather holster. Minutes later, with my mother trailing behind screaming at him, my dad walked out of the house and to his car, a 1942 Chevrolet sedan. I was also chasing him and, standing on the car's running board, saw my dad stash the weapon into a side panel under the dashboard while my parents continued to quarrel.

"You're going to get killed over that woman!" my mom cried. "He'll kill you."

I don't recall my father saying anything. He drove off instead. I assumed Jerri had a husband at the time because she had other children about the same age as those she bore my father. I never met my father's other children, though I strongly suspect they attended junior high school with me. The son looked like a miniature of my father, down to the thick wavy hair that I didn't have. The daughter was in music class with me and often used to tease me that her mother knew my father when they had been young.

"What is your mother's name?" I asked her one day.

"Jerri," she said. "Ask your dad if he remembers Jerri."

"I will," I said, lying. "And your father - did my dad know your father, too?"

"I don't think so," she said. "I didn't even know my father. He was killed in a fight when my mom was pregnant with me."

I began wondering if my father had killed Jerri's husband. I remembered the day my dad had stormed out of the house with his pistol, stuffed it in what he thought was a secret spot in his car, and sped away. He had returned, obviously, and he was still alive. I made a mental note to ask him whether he had gunned down this man. It wasn't like it was out of character for him. It was also difficult to think of my father as a rebel and an outlaw. But then each generation denies its links to the previous, doesn't it. Defiance was something more associated in the restless young men of my generation than my father's. Maybe it had its seeds in James Dean's *Rebel Without a Cause* or when Marlon Brando's character in *The Wild One* was asked what he was rebelling against and he replied, "Whatcha got?" I suppose I had ideal role models for how I felt growing up. The negative experience over my dance with Patricia in elementary school and what would be the first of the "white girl speeches" from many adults in my youth had shot open an incredible emotional wound within me. It also created a tumultuous sense of not belonging, nor wanting to be a part of a society, in which the ultimate measure of a person's worth was the color of his skin. What Mrs. Redding and all the well-intentioned people who warned me of the personal dangers that came with wanting a white girl like Patricia didn't realize, was that deep within my heart, I knew my place. It just wasn't where *they* thought it should be.

Perhaps I sometimes over-reacted at being told who I was and who

I should be with. In my early days at South Junior, I was called out of my homeroom by the school's speech teacher who was coordinating the presentation of the school's princesses for a big show in the auditorium. In the seventh grade, I was a relatively tall kid for my age, and I possibly looked taller because I was so lanky. I also happened to wear a suit to school one day early that first semester because my parents were taking me out of class to attend the funeral of a family friend. A teenage kid showing up at school in a suit draws attention to himself that he had just as soon avoid.

Mrs. Newman, the speech teacher, told me she had seen me dressed up that day and that she was looking for properly attired boys in suits or sport coats to escort the princesses at the show. About a dozen girls, the princesses, were practicing their walks on the stage behind the speech teacher. They were all cute, pretty girls in the ninth and eighth grades. I surveyed them hoping to see Patricia, but she was not among them. Those princesses couldn't have been more beautiful than Patricia, and that upset me a little. For that matter, I hadn't seen anyone at South Junior who was as lovely as she.

"Will you be able to escort one of the princesses?" Mrs. Newman wanted to know.

I felt like telling her that the only princess I would escort was Patricia, but I knew that wouldn't be smart.

"I don't know," I said. "Who would I escort?"

"Anita Canales," she said. I didn't know who Anita was, but I assumed she was the only Hispanic girl on stage. *My kind*, in other words. I didn't mean to be rebellious. I don't think I did. But this would be a start.

"No, I don't think I'm interested," I said. "I'll just watch the show in the audience."

At a loss for words, Mrs. Newman just glared at me. The gall of a seventh grader saying no to such a request from a well-respected teacher had to be unimaginable. Dick couldn't believe I had actually turned down the teacher's request.

"Mrs. Newman will make your life living hell if you ever take speech," Dick said. "She's got a lot of power here."

"I don't care," I said.

"And how could you turn down Anita Canales? Have you ever seen her? She's hot."

Okay, so my retaliation for all the "white girls" speeches got the better of me sometimes. Anita Canales *was* hot. I should have escorted her. Dick was much smarter than me at understanding the politics of the world.

"Man, if you'd have escorted Anita Canales, other girls would have noticed you," he said. "Who knows who you might have met. Why would you do that?"

Word got around. I quickly gained the reputation that, although academically a home run slugger, I was arrogant personally and defensive to the point of pugnacity. I was the uppity seventh grader who refused to escort Anita Canales. When I met Anita a few weeks later, she demanded to know why.

"I don't have a good reason that I could tell you and that you would understand," I said.

"Well, can you give me a bad reason?" She appeared more angry than hurt.

I mulled it over for a moment. "I thought," I said, "that you should have been escorted by someone in your own grade."

I had been at South Junior a few weeks when the first sock hop was held. For an hour, our Crackerjack box of a gymnasium filled up with young teenage boys and girls in their white socks, dancing to music like *Venus* by Frankie Avalon, *All I Have to Do Is Dream* by The Everly Brothers, *Mr. Blue* by the Fleetwoods, and, of course, *Patricia* by Perez Prado. Patricia, though, never came to that day's sock hop. I was disappointed and probably would have left right away except Linda Ballard, a cute girl who was in my homeroom, asked me to dance.

Maybe we should have announced on the loud speaker that it was *she* who had asked *me* to dance because we quickly started getting stares. It wasn't just the white guys who were shooting daggers my way.

63

The Hispanic girls were looking at us with disapproval. I was being damned on both sides.

When that dance was over, I tried to hide out with Dick behind a kid no one messed with. He was Jerrell Marshall, an eighth grader and the star running back on the ninth grade football team, as well as the most handsome kid in school. And that's short-changing him. This was Texas, after all, where football was king, and football stars were royalty. But he was also outstanding at any sport he played. In Little League, one season he hit a record number of home runs and became the subject of a long feature story in the Sunday newspaper. In football, his breakaway runs were breathtaking, particularly on a team that was incredibly bad. Jerrell was the kid we all modeled ourselves after. Off the field, his good looks were framed under a hairstyle that looked like that of teen singing heartthrob Ricky Nelson of the popular *The Adventures of Ozzie & Harriet* Nelson family television show. Once, Jerrell happened to mention that he always got his hair cut at Beeman's Barber Shop on Speight Street. That next Saturday afternoon, when I begged my father to let me get my hair cut at Beeman's, I showed up only to find no fewer than half a dozen teenage boys from my school in line to get their hair trimmed by Jerrell's barber. And it wasn't just kids at South Junior who were in awe of Jerrell. His athletic exploits had spread to other junior high schools in the city and to teams that had been stung by Jerrell's heroics in all the sports. Against one team, Jerrell had returned a punt eighty yards for a touchdown. When the score was wiped out by an offsides penalty, he returned the ensuing punt eighty-five yards for a touchdown. When that, too, was brought back by another offsides penalty, Jerrell ran back the following punt ninety yards for a touchdown. It was no wonder that soon boys from other junior high schools were also becoming regulars at Beeman's Barber Shop.

Part of Jerrell's near-legendary status in Waco was also due to the girl with whom he was going steady. As an eighth grader, he was the boyfriend of a beautiful redheaded ninth grader, and a cheerleader: Babs McBride. In its own way, Waco was a small town. The popular kids at one junior high school were often known at other junior highs. At the time, there was University Junior High on the southwest part of Waco, West Junior High that took in part of the western and northwest part of town, North Junior that was traditionally home to the upper class and upper middle class neighborhoods, and the new Lake Air Junior drawing on kids from the far northwest upscale communities toward Lake Waco. Invariably, if you were a student at South Junior and happened to know kids from other junior highs, their questions would inevitably turn to Jerrell Marshall: What kind of guy was he really? Was he swell-headed and stuckup? And his girlfriend Babs: Was she really as gorgeous as people said she was? Sometimes before I could answer, my parents would interject themselves. Jerrell was as cute as Ricky Nelson, no, make that cuter and even cuter than Tony Dow of the *Leave It To Beaver* television series, my mom told a kid we knew from University Junior. My father once compared Jerrell the football player to a young Doak Walker, the legendary running back in the post-World War II years at Southern Methodist University and the 1948 Heisman Trophy winner. And Babs McBride, my dad said, reminded him of Rita Hayworth. My father could be big on the overstatement, but not by much.

The most worrisome days at South Junior my seventh-grade year were after the second game of the season when Jerrell suffered a knee-injury and spent much of the next week on crutches. He still was on them at the first sock hop, where he watched from a chair next to the kids operating the record player. Babs stood beside Jerrell holding his hand and dancing by herself. That said a lot for Babs. She wasn't even supposed to be dancing in the first place. Her family belonged to the Church of Christ, whose members were as conservative as the Baptists. Babs had grown up being told that dancing was a sin, but she later said she never really believed that God could be a party-pooper. So she sneaked around and danced anyway. Jerrell had seen me dancing with Linda Ballard and motioned me over.

"Hey, Castro, I know you dance," he said "So dance with Babs and get her off the sidelines."

He almost pushed me on to the dance floor with his girlfriend, and I could sense the looks again.

"Hey, big shot," said a ninth grade football player on the dance floor. "Who said you could dance with Babs?"

"Babs said he could dance with me," she shot back.

Thanks, Babs. Just what I needed. Infuriate the white furry animals. Later I spoke with Jerrell and asked if he could soothe it over with the jocks.

"Yeah, I wasn't even thinking," he said. "Just watch yourself on the field, though."

That was my introduction to junior high school sock hops and football. In Texas, you didn't mess with its football teams, nor its women, I was quickly learning. It meant that while I was a popular kid at school and had a lot of friends who were girls, they had names like Judy Wammack, Linda Dunwody, Jeanette Cagle, Sandra Barnard, Ginger Faulkner, Peggy Millender, and Darlene Scott. Judy and Linda especially were among my closest friends. We shared almost every class and sometimes helped each other understand homework assignments. But they were white, and I made certain that nothing happened outside the classroom, and that no one suspected that anything ever did.

I ran into Patricia in the hallways occasionally. Sometimes there would be smiles. Sometimes she didn't see me. Sometimes she saw past me. She had no idea how I felt, and there were times when I would work up my courage thinking I would tell her. But I don't think I ever saw her alone in those early weeks of school. Her Gurley friend Linda was often with her. At other times, I would see her surrounded by several girlfriends. It was a good sign that she was popular with girls, who often would target the girls they didn't like with slam books. These were mean-spirited notebooks passed around the school in which a girl would be cruelly harassed with page upon page of negative gossip and rumors.

Then after almost twelve weeks into the fall semester, something completely unexpected happened. My art teacher took an unusual interest in my work. Mrs. McCulley was also the adviser to the school's mimeographed newspaper, the *Panther Post*, and she asked that I join the staff as a writer and artist. I was apprehensive at first, even if there was great incentive for being in the school's Press Club, which was made up of her special homeroom students who published the newspaper. Patricia was on the newspaper staff and in that homeroom, so I would have at least one class each day with her. But I also didn't know what being on the school newspaper staff would require and whether, as a seventh grader, I would be able to measure up. Was I smart enough? Mrs. McCulley assured me that I was. She said she had checked my school record, and presumably my IQ, and felt confident. But if I ever had any doubts, she wanted me to feel comfortable going to her or reaching out to another staff member whom she said was as young as me and, though brilliant, sometimes felt she was over her head as well. That person was Jaquine Hudson, who was actually younger than me but a grade ahead. After Mrs. McCulley had me transferred to her homeroom, I would watch what Jaquine did and tried to emulate it. At the same time, I sometimes sensed that Jaquine was my intellectual guardian angel, much as Miss Taylor, my speech tutor, had once been.

What I often did most during homeroom was to stare at Patricia, discreetly, of course. The Patricia I first met as a twelve-year-old girl had matured to a fourteen-year-old young woman. She was still slender but with a defined figure and curvy. Occasionally, I think she pretended not to notice that I was staring. She would smile for no reason and shake her head back in a way that made her hair flow one way and then whip around. Sometimes I would make excuses to approach her with a question about a piece of handwritten copy that she had turned in. They were usually silly questions, and I felt stupid for asking them. But I was too young and too naïve to have any coy opening lines. She would usually just answer without elaborating. As I would walk away, I thought I could always see the faint trace of a smile on her face. At times, when she was around others, she appeared self-conscious, perhaps because of her height. She seemed to slouch just a little, the way some tall girls do when the try not to stand out because of the difference in height between them and their friends. But the beauty was undeniable. Her flawless skin had the soft texture of smooth silk. I would often hear girls talking with envy and awe about her incredible complexion. In an age when Clearasil emerged as the leading acne medication for pimply-faced teenagers, Patricia may have been one of the few who would never need it.

For the next two years, we worked together on the biweekly newspaper that was mostly filled with news from student clubs, sports, song dedications, and kids' opinions and reactions to world events. As time went on, working on *The Panther Post* opened more opportunities to talk to Patricia, but those conversations were usually about the stories scheduled to appear in the paper, the front cover designs, and the problems involved in the paper's publication and distribution to the school's eight hundred students. When we were in the eighth grade, Dick joined the Press Club. Life was grand. I was helping put out our school paper with my best friend and the young woman who was the love of my life. It also happened that another member of the Press Club was a name that I had been urged by Mrs. Alexander to check out: Lidia Montemayor. When she and Patricia were ninth graders, Lidia became the editor of the newspaper.

Lidia was as Mrs. Alexander said she would be, beautiful and brilliant. She also was even more driven to success than I, and she had the single-mindedness that I only possessed in spurts. We were friends, but I felt that I barely knew her. We also had little in common. We were both on the school's interscholastic league spelling team, but otherwise our academic interests ran in different areas. She was a math whiz. I loved literature. She was passionate about science. I couldn't get enough of the arts. But the most obvious thing missing was the magical spark of any romance that Mrs. Alexander might have envisioned. Lidia also sensed that my real interest lay elsewhere.

"You sure ask a lot of questions about Patty O'Neal," she said to me one time. "What gives?"

I had an easy out, or thought I did. "We're like you and Jerrell

Marshall," I said. "We also went to the same elementary school together."

Meanwhile, the Press Club in 1960 had awakened an interest in national politics. Each week Mrs. McCulley brought new copies of *Time* and *The Nation* magazine to school, and I developed a fascination with John F. Kennedy. Of course, in 1960, I wasn't alone. But it wasn't for the obvious reasons that I found myself devouring any news about him and his candidacy for the presidency: our mutual Catholicism. It was my interest in going to Harvard, his alma mater. Of course, to be a Kennedy supporter in Texas in 1960 was hardly the most popular move. Texas was Lyndon Johnson country, and few Texans could imagine that Johnson, who was the Majority Leader of the Senate and a presidential candidate himself, wouldn't be the one winding up in the White House. Nevertheless, I wore my JFK campaign buttons on my shirt collar to school every day and developed a friendly rivalry with my longtime friend from Gurley, Dwain Moss, who lived and breathed for an LBJ presidency. The sense of LBJ's inevitability, even within me, also seemed to side with Dwain and his own good fortune. Through his newspaper route, he had recently won an all-expenses-paid trip to Brazil, taking two weeks off during the school year, and he was the talk of South Junior.

Or part of South Junior, I should say, because in an incredibly short time it seemed that our school had changed. By my eighth grade year, South Junior had become representative of the dramatic demographic shift that was occurring in Waco. Almost half the school was now Hispanic and the other half white, and I found myself symbolizing that ethnic-racial schism. I was Hispanic ethnically, but I didn't connect with the other Hispanic kids. Still, it wasn't as if I were white, and I often felt trapped as if in some sociological warp. What I had regrettably learned at my young age was that no matter how much I might conform to the expectations of white society, I would never fully be part of it. At the same time, in my rocky immersion into the Hispanic world of my peers at South Junior, I had become aware that my assimilation into the dominant culture made me an outsider to my own. Worse still, I sounded like neither side. All the speech therapy to rid me of a lisp and a stutter in elementary school had also eliminated any Texas drawl or Southern twang. My enunciation and pronunciation were too precise perhaps for a young teenager. My old classmates at Gurley had grown up with me and presumably were accustomed to the way I spoke, but others noticed and were suspicious.

"You sound so fake. You don't even talk like one of us," Rita Mendoza, one of the Hispanic teen-age girls I knew would often say to me. She would say I was "conceited but convinced." I never knew what she meant and neither did my friend Dick, who said I shouldn't bother trying to figure out what stupid people meant by what they said. He was right, but I still felt hurt.

I didn't know what to say in my defense. The truth can only make things worse, I had learned. I had already mentioned to another classmate my early learning disability and my speech impediments, and it had led to ridicule. So I never mentioned it again. Once I had even tape-recorded my voice to see if I could pick up how my speech was different than that of my friends. I listened to my voice over and over, but I was a terrible judge. I could make no discernible distinction between myself and anyone else. I sounded like my classmates, or, at least, I thought I did. But Rita and a few others never let up. To them I was a phony, and they called me that, Tony the Phony, when they weren't calling me Tony Baloney. And if my English was suspect to them, I could only imagine what they would say about my Spanish. I wondered if I now spoke Spanish sounding like a white kid who had learned it in Spanish class at school. If only they knew the truth.

I wondered, too, if Rita Mendoza or her younger sister Dolores thought of me like the Caramillo or Puente kids whose families had been our neighbors when I was a child. Each of those families had several daughters my age or a little older, and they were never allowed to play outside in the sun.

"My mother says we'll get very dark in the sun, and people will think we're Mexican," one of the Caramillo daughters explained to me once.

Duh. Their last name was Caramillo, hardly off the Mayflower. But they resolved that quite creatively. The Caramillos legally changed their name to Miller, and the Puentes became the Bridge family. In the 1950s and perhaps into the 1960s, it was not uncommon for Mexican American families to adopt some loose translation of their Spanish surnames just so that, in their eyes, they improved their chances of upward mobility in the dominant white society. Influenced by the ideal of white beauty, some African Americans straightened their hair and bleached their skin, and many Mexican Americans used some of the same products to lighten their complexions. All of this made sense, I suppose, in the pursuit of belonging. After all, my father's pin-up beauty, Rita Hayworth, had been born Margarita Carmen Cansino.

"You don't know what it's like competing in a white world," said one Hispanic girl who admitted to lightening her skin and her hair. *As if I didn't know what it was like competing in a white world?* Yeah.

But worse things were happening at South Junior. By my ninth grade year, Hispanic-white relations had reached a boiling point. On a daily basis, a clique of Hispanic thugs shook down white students for money. "Loan me a quarter" became a mantra. In the mornings before school and again at lunch, those Hispanic kids would intimidate their white counterparts. The white students were afraid to say no, and they were equally frightened about turning to school officials. Even the teachers were intimidated. They rarely reported kids who misbehaved in class, even when some made threatening remarks. The only adult who regularly stood up to the Hispanic thugs was a math teacher called Arlen Dunham who was also the assistant football coach. At one point, some of the thugs schemed to attack him outside the school, but the Coach Dunham received an anonymous note warning him of the threat. When his station wagon was vandalized, though, the coach confronted a basketball hotshot and challenged him to a game of one-on-one at the Boys Club in the heart of the local barrio, which was home to many of the Hispanic thugs. The coach's ploy worked. After that, they left him alone.

Sadly, the thugs were hardly representative of the Hispanic

community in Waco. In the 1960s, Latinos made up about eight percent of the population in Waco. Many were World War II and Korean War veterans, and most were members of working class families who deplored the *pachuco* culture of the 1940s and 1950s. There were no gangs to speak of, certainly nothing resembling the big city gangs of the years to come. But, as in all groups, there was a juvenile delinquency element. At South Junior, at various times of the year, the new influx of students included Hispanic teenagers who had recently been released from the juvenile lockup facility in Gatesville, some thirty miles outside Waco. Many of them were returning to homes in the heavily Hispanic community that was developing in the neighborhood northwest of the school. That growing barrio was bordered on the south by a public housing project and the north by a Boys Club facility, which became the sanctuary for many of the thugs shaking down students for money at South Junior. Those kids played basketball at the Boys Club, and their reputation for showboating, un-coachable attitudes, and poor sportsmanship was so bad that South Junior's basketball coach had put down a rule against players taking what he called "Boys Club shots."

I had never experienced an atmosphere of this kind of potential violence in my young life, and that included the crazy Resendez brothers who had been the scourges of Gurley Elementary. Gilbert and Mike Resendez were the youngest brothers in a large brood of kids that had gone through Gurley. Mike was a year younger than I, and Gilbert was my age. But Gilbert was as stupid as they come, and he had flunked a year. From about my fourth or fifth grade, when they both were a year behind me, the Resendez brothers, mostly Gilbert, had terrorized their classmates and even the kids in my class. Gilbert was always ready to pick a fight, and his brother was there to back him up. Most of us knew that Mike was, at heart, a good kid who felt compelled to stand by his brother. Gilbert, on the other hand, was a young psychopath with a vocabulary of five words: I'm going to stomp you! He would go up to kids and angrily scowl those words, "I'm going to stomp you!" and then unleash a flurry of fists. The secret was just to stay away from them. But Johnny wouldn't back down. When we were in the fifth grade Gilbert beat him up mercilessly, knocking him down to the ground and then kicking him until Mike pulled him off. After that, when I wasn't day-dreaming about Patricia, I was scheming of how I could kill Gilbert. Yes, kill him. I knew where my father kept his M1911 semi-automatic .45 from his army days, and I was tempted to use it. Kids and guns are a tragic mixture, and I had long ago passed that stage. Every so often, usually when I was bored with baseball and other games, I would get my father's gun from his army footlocker and play with it. I never fired the weapon, but I became quite good at loading the magazine, clicking it into the gun, disengaging the safety, and then aiming. I would quickly reverse the process, removing the magazine and then pulling back the slide to allow the loaded bullet to fall out of the ejector hole. I had learned to do it watching how they did it in the movies. And I was serious about killing Gilbert Resendez. Serious enough that on Saturdays when I went to confession, I would routinely begin by saying:

"Forgive me, Father, for I have sinned. It is a week since my last confession. My sins in that time, Father, are that I have continued thinking that I have to kill Gilbert Resendez."

To which the priest would say: "My son, this is a mortal sin, you have to stop thinking of this. Thinking of this itself places you in a temptation to sin."

"I know, Father," I would say. "But I have prayed to God that he kill him and send him to Hell, and he hasn't answered my prayers."

Once, our parish priest talked to me about this outside the Confessional, and I explained to him the havoc that the Resendez brothers, especially Gilbert, wreaked on the entire school. No merciful God, I told him, could possibly choose the safety of one evil child over that of hundreds. The priest made me vow to let him handle this and promised that he would visit the Resendez family to discuss complaints about Gilbert's behavior. I imagined that all that would come of his visit was a set of flat tires on the priest's car. I continued thinking of killing Gilbert and probably would have had I been able to think of a way of finding him alone. I never could, though, and years later I would consider it one of the great regrets of my life.

By comparison, the thugs at South Junior made the Resendez bothers look like amateurs. To avoid the shakedown for money, my friend Dick and I would regularly leave school for lunch. We ran three blocks south to the edge of the Baylor campus where we ate at a hamburger stand called the Chuck Wagon. Sometimes we would see other South Junior students there, students who were also trying to hold on to their lunch money. We didn't realize that money would also soon become the mother's milk of politics at our school. In the eighth grade, Dick was the student council vice-president, having been overwhelmingly elected to that position at the end of the previous school year. He ran for president of the student council near the end of our eighth grade year, and many people felt he was the most deserving and most experienced person for the position. However, it wasn't until late in his campaign that we would discover what he was up against. The shakedowns had taken on a different approach. Leaders of the toughest Hispanic clique, most of them athletes, warned us that if Dick expected to win, we would have to match or beat the daily payments of quarters and half dollars they were getting from one of the other candidates. We were admittedly political neophytes, having been inspired by the 1960 presidential election and the new presidency of John F. Kennedy. So at our young age, we were shocked at the idea of buying votes, and we refused to pay bribes, which showed how smart we were. Dick lost the election.

Dick and I also didn't realize how unique and isolated our friendship was. It never occurred to us, I don't believe, that we were the only Hispanic and white kids who hung out together every day. We didn't even see the class differences between us, class differences that apparently weighed heavily on the minds of many of the kids at South Junior. With the exception of Dick and a maybe a handful of students who were children of lawyers and other professional people, most of us at South Junior were the sons and daughters of working class parents. I was probably too naïve or idealistic in believing in the notion of equality that I failed to be class conscious. But for some of my classmates, the differences were profound. One longtime friend from Gurley would begin developing a lifelong persecution complex of being "poor white trash from South Waco" that would gnaw away at him even after he became a successful businessman in town.

I didn't understand feeling that I was "poor white trash from South Waco." Maybe because I wasn't white? My surroundings pushed me toward being like the other Hispanic kids and to give up on any dreams or ambitions. But maybe all those books that I had read and the heroes who had sparked my imagination had saved me. Maybe there was a saving grace in pretending in my mind that I was Achilles or Lancelot, maybe even King Arthur or the Black Knight Ivanhoe, possibly *Treasure Island's* Jim Hawkins or Jay Gatsby. Could Gatsby's love for Daisy have been any deeper than mine for Patricia? Yes, they were larger than life and more human than we might have imagined, but didn't they also reflect the best of humanity? Even when we were kids, growing up as we did and in spite of the hurdles put in my way about Patricia, in my heart I always felt that I had been graced as being someone special. Far from being the Atomic Man, a part of me felt like royalty... like a prince: The prince of the kingdom of South Waco.

Dick and I certainly thought of ourselves that way, even in the face of the violence at South Junior. Sometimes we were targeted for shoves and pushes, but we usually watched out for each other. Increasingly, though, the violence at school intensified. A lot of the fighting involved Hispanics against Hispanics, usually boys but sometimes girls who delighted in tearing off each other's clothes. But this began changing in my ninth grade year when more of the violence by the Hispanic boys started being directed against whites.

By then, too, my longtime tight friendship with Johnny Silva had dissolved completely. Johnny had changed. It was not just that he had begun hanging out with the Hispanic thugs at school, but Johnny apparently also thought that meant he had to allow his grades to drop to their levels. In almost no time, he went from the honor rolls to doing the minimum required to get by. Later, looking back, I would recall the low expectations that many in the dominant society seemed to have of Hispanics, and similarly the low self-image many Hispanics appeared to have of themselves. With Johnny, it was almost as if, by siding with the Mexican thugs, he had chosen to live down to the lowest of any expectations. There had been a contingent of a dozen or more of us from our elementary that remained close at South Junior, but Johnny chose not to belong. I tried to talk to him about this and to encourage his involvement, all to no avail. It was his loss, but it was also ours.

In her last few days at South Junior, Patricia and her friend Linda were kind enough to give me their *Evangeline* notebooks, no small matter. These notebooks involved extensive work compiling photographs, excerpts, and commentary on the Henry Wadsworth Longfellow poem of an Acadian girl named Evangeline and her search for her lost love Gabriel. For years it was the traditional ninth grade second semester assignment of an English teacher named Mrs. Spradlin. One of the famous lines from the poem was, "This is the forest primeval, the murmuring pines and the hemlocks..." For Mrs. Spradlin, *Evangeline* was an obsession, and she tried with every ounce of her soul to make a bunch of fifteen-year-olds love it, too. So much so, that many of her students were sure she must have been a childhood friend of Longfellow himself. Still, the notebook accounted for close to half the semester grade, and students went to great lengths to get the work of her previous students as a guide or even a crutch for their own work. These notebooks often were the compilation of years of students adding on to notebooks from years past. Patricia and Linda each received an A on their notebooks and gave them to me trusting I would put any of their work in my own handwriting and my own words. I was floored by their confidence and equally astounded the following year when our eighth grade teacher, Mrs. Ola Mae Mansell, took over the ninth grade English classes and announced that she would not be featuring *Evangeline* in her curriculum that year and would not require notebooks on the poem.

Mrs. Mansell was a testament to all great English teachers. She loved the sound and rhythm of words and the unique meters they could create, especially when strung together in poetry. She also loved her students who shared her appreciation. From the start of my two years with Mrs. Mansell, I had caught her at times looking at me curiously. After a while, I thought it was simply my class work that caught her eye. For additional credit, I had written a short story titled "The Magical Mexican," a fairy tale about a young Latino with exceptional powers that allow him to overcome whatever obstacle was cast in his way as he navigated through a dangerous forest to rescue a blonde-haired princess imprisoned in a castle. Mrs. Mansell loved the story so much she told me she sent it to a friend who worked at the Waco daily newspaper, but nothing ever came of it. I also submitted extra book reports on works that surprised her: Joseph Conrad's *Heart of Darkness*, James Joyce's *Portrait of the Artist as a Young Man*, J.D. Salinger's *The Catcher in the Rye*, and Richard Wright's *Native Son*. I had even submitted a copy of the poem I wrote for Patricia.

"It's lovely," she said. "But how can a ninth grader have written this?"

"I wasn't in the ninth grade when I wrote it, ma'am," I said. "I wrote it just before I started sixth grade."

"You did? Young man, you fell in love with someone when you were twelve?"

"No, ma'am. I was eleven. She was twelve."

Her eyes laughed. "One of those May December romances, oh my!" At that time, I wasn't sure what that meant.

"You know her," I said. "You had her as a student when she was in the eighth grade two years ago."

"Did I? Let me think about it, and I'll try to guess who it might have been."

Then she reached in her purse, got her wallet and pulled out a twenty-dollar bill.

"Mr. Castro, for some time I've been trying to place your face," she said. "I never forget a face. And hearing you talk now, it occurred to me how I know you. You came to my house once. Do you remember?"

I couldn't immediately.

"You were younger, but I know it was you. Here's twenty dollars. Next time you think of it, could you bring me however many tin cans of salve twenty dollars will buy?"

Holy White Cloverine!

I kept Mrs. Mansell stocked for the rest of the year and for a couple of years after. Miss Taylor, as always, had been right: Sweet old ladies swore by the salve.

But tradition, like demographics, was dramatically changing at South Junior. One of the oldest schools in the district, South Junior had been home to city leaders of the past when Waco was smaller in population and more compact. That was the Waco that was sometimes lampooned by some critics. The story even made the rounds that a highway sign heading into the city read, "Welcome to Waco: Home of the Blackest Land and the Whitest People." But they were wrong. That sign, or one similar to it, had actually been posted in the northeast Texas town of Greenville, though perhaps it might have fit Waco just as well. For generations, Waco had been defined by a downtown business and shopping district along Austin Avenue and an old-fashion town square just east of there that backed up to the Brazos River.

My parents had lived just north of the square on Second Street when I was born. My grandfather and his second wife also lived there. My maternal grandmother Catarina died in 1932, just weeks after giving birth to her seventh child who died at three months of age. With a young family to raise, my grandfather married a widow with two sons and a daughter of her own. Her name was Isidra Martinez, and it was a loveless arrangement to their mutual benefit. When they moved to Waco in the late 1940s, it was to an area of the city known as Two Street. It was a name given to an area also known as The Reservation that had been a legal red-light district from 1989 to 1917 when Waco permitted prostitution. For years, up to about one hundred prostitutes worked in the area whose most famous madam, Mollie Adams, operated a bordello in 1910 at 408 North Second Street. My birth certificate listed my parents home address in 1946 as 414 North Second Street. Most of the housing from the area's period of ill-repute

78

remained intact, even as a wave of Mexican American families move in and began calling the neighborhood *Calle Dos*. Among them were my grandfather and Isidra who lived in an apartment building at the corner of Second Street and Jefferson Avenue, two blocks from the Brazos River to the east and a block from St. Francis Church to the west. By then, nearing sixty years of age, his name had been given the Spanish prefix of respect, and he was known as Don Jose Angel.

Calle Dos, teeming with first- and second-generation Mexican American immigrants, was a far cry from North Waco with its stately, older homes that dotted the neighborhoods west and north of downtown. In those days, Waco was actually larger than Dallas, Fort Worth, and El Paso. As time went on, working class neighborhoods rose south of downtown. East Waco had been the heart of the city's black community. Beyond East Waco, newer neighborhoods were created around the General Tire plant and James Connally Air Force Base. Then, after World War II, increasing numbers of Hispanics and blacks abandoning stagnant farming communities in East Texas and southeast Central Texas began an in-migration that in another generation would radically alter the city's ethnic-racial and geographic maps.

By the time we were at South Junior, it bore signs of an urban inner-city school. Graffiti was everywhere, even deeply scrawled into the tops of desks. Usually names and other graffiti were accompanied by the words *con safos*, which was sometimes abbreviated as *c/s*. No one, not even the Hispanic thugs, could explain what the words meant. Even sociologists years later would debate its origin and its meaning. Members of the tough Hispanic clique at South Junior said the term had been used with graffiti for years, ostensibly as an epitaph against anyone who would attempt to remove or cover the writing. Far more serious than the graffiti, however, was the violence and intimidation that now ran rampant. If you were smart, you never went anywhere on campus alone, especially to the bathrooms where white kids, both boys and girls, often found themselves trapped by the Mexican thugs, beaten up, and robbed.

Fortunately for her, Patricia had moved on to Waco High School. Funny, I thought, but for all the "white girls" speeches that I had gotten from adults, I could have also used a "Mexican thug" speech here and there. I had been warned to prepare myself and watch for the white bigot coming after me, but no one had cautioned me about watching my back for the Hispanic hoodlum. Maybe this was my family's legacy.

A wall of my grandmother's house stood as a tribute to her oldest son, Francisco, named after her first husband. He had been killed in his early twenties, and she mourned his death for years, commemorating each birthday and adorning one wall with dozens of photographs of him. As a child, I started asking how he had died, and all I could learn was that he had been shot to death. I couldn't understand why so much secrecy surrounded his death, and it only increased my curiosity. As I grew older, I continued asking each of my relatives what they knew of his death. One day, I heard one of my uncles mention the nickname "La Pantera," the Panther.

"Don't tell him that," my aunt said, punching my uncle in the arm.

"How can I not tell him?" said my uncle. "My Lord, he never stops asking questions. He's like a dog with a bone. He never lets it go. He'll find out one day."

The joy of learning how to stop stuttering and lisping is that you can freely start talking and relentlessly pursuing whatever you want to know or learn. I was in the fifth grade, about the time I first saw Patricia, that I learned that La Pantera in the early 1940s had been a Mexican thug who raised hell in the communities around Rosebud. My father grew up in that area, and my grandmother owned a farm there that Francisco managed for her and to whom this Pantera owed several hundred dollars. One Saturday night, Francisco had gone into Rosebud and, at a dance, he was shot in the back by La Pantera. Friends of my family had long blamed the local police, an all-white law enforcement department, for failing to catch Francisco's killer. But, records from that time later suggested that La Pantera was never prosecuted because the witnesses to the killing, all of them Mexican, refused to come forth to testify.

At South Junior, it seemed as if it was only a matter of time before someone also got killed. Kids were bringing switchblades and knives of all sorts to school; and the administrators, even when told who was carrying weapons, were too frightened to act on those tips. Some of those same kids were on the ninth grade football team, which, for all the violence that a few players could wreak off the field, was historically terrible on the field. Administrators were aware of some of the attacks and the seedy atmosphere surrounding the school, but they naively looked in the wrong direction. A hamburger stand called Dick's Café had opened near the school, and the assistant principal declared it off-limits for students, especially for those on the Student Council. The extent of his crackdown was catching Dolores Mendoza, the council's vice-president eating lunch at Dick's Café and removing her from office. But that assistant principal didn't have the courage to take similar disciplinary action against the thugs.

The only teacher who took a serious interest about our concerns with the thugs was Mr. Purvis, who taught social studies and whose seemingly frail appearance was deceiving. Harold Purvis' slight build was actually the result of being a marathon runner, something few people knew. He also was an urbanite whose sophistication and English suits with vests made him both unique and misunderstood. We became acquainted outside of school one Saturday at the Waco Public Library, which for years had been my refuge. I was in my Carl Sandburg phase, and I was reading his six-volume biography of Abraham Lincoln. It was a collection that the library did not lend and had to be read on the premises. I didn't mind. The library had big old comfortable chairs on which you could curl up and escape into a book. I didn't even notice Mr. Purvis sitting across from me until near closing time.

"There are easier Lincoln biographies to read," he said when he caught my attention.

"I know," I said. "But none are this lyrical and poetic."

"He mythologizes Lincoln a bit too much, though, don't you think?"

He had a point, especially from a Southerner's perspective. There were places where I thought Sandburg made Lincoln appear almost Daniel Booneish. "I suppose," I said. "But I'm young. I like my presidents romanticized."

And my writers, too. I would remember most vividly two things from President Kennedy's inauguration earlier that year: Kennedy's memorable plaintiff line, "Ask not what your country can do for you; ask what you can do for your country"; and the sight of Robert Frost at the podium, his silver hair and breath billowing in the winter air as he struggled in the bright sunlight to read the poem he had written for the occasion. No one would remember Frost's poem, sadly. Instead they would remember that image, captured for posterity on black-and-white television. Perhaps it would be a sign of the new age and new technology, a writer in *Harper's* later put it, that it would not matter so much what you said but how you said it.

Mr. Purvis and I struck up a friendship that afternoon at the library. Over the coming months he listened to my troubles at South Junior and advised me on the reality of my school's unspoken administration policy: turn a blind eye to the thug activity and racial tension. Their reasoning for not involving authorities was that to do so, would mean calling attention to the fact that they had lost control. Instead, Mr. Purvis began quietly recruiting other teachers to stand outside their rooms during class breaks. He would visually scour the cafeteria during lunch, acting as a monitor at times when students were most vulnerable to shakedowns. He also sought me out to help with chores at his aging parents' home in North Waco, paying me well for washing the cars, polishing silver, and occasionally assisting him at weekend teas and dinners that his mother hosted for her friends and bridge club. My parents had recently bought me a three-piece navy blue suit, and Mr. Purvis appeared impressed that I would wear it when I helped at his mother's social functions. I would soon learn that the Purvises were not without connections not only in Waco but also in Texas and beyond.

Mr. Purvis' father descended from the Ewings – not the mythological Ewings who would one day be depicted on the popular television soap opera *Dallas* about a rich Texas family, but the real-life Irish family who in the seventeenth century were among the early colonists on the East Coast. A branch of the family moved to the young Republic of Texas, which existed after the defeat of the Mexican general Santa Anna in 1836 and before statehood in 1845. A privilege for descendants of those who settled the state in that period was membership in two of the oldest, most exclusive organizations: the Sons of the Republic of Texas to which Mr. Purvis belonged and the Daughters of the Republic of Texas, who early in the twentieth century were granted custodianship of the Alamo and its grounds. In turn, the role of the Sons of the Republic of Texas was "to perpetuate the memory and spirit of the men and women who achieved the independence of Texas." Since the battle for Texas independence had been largely white Texans fighting against an army of Mexicans, by definition almost all of the Sons of the Republic of Texas were white as well.

So my two best friends of that period of my life were two people with whom I had so little in common: Dick McCall, the son of the vice-president of Baylor; and Harold Purvis, a man with ties to the country almost as far back at the *Mayflower* and a member of the Sons of the Republic of Texas. In fairness, according to my grandmother, there was her distant uncle who had died in New Jersey during the Revolutionary War and had been mourned by no less than George Washington. It all should have meant something to me. I'm sure it did. It just wasn't anything I made a big deal about. Dick McCall and Harold Purvis were good friends, and it made me wish I had more of them.

By the ninth grade, though, Dick had stopped playing football to focus on basketball. Baseball was still my first love, but I had become smitten with football in the eighth grade, in large part because of Mr. Castillo. He was a former Golden Gloves boxing champion who was new at South Junior and the football coach of the eighth grade team. In those years, junior high teams rarely used a passing game in their offense, but Mr. Castillo changed that. He was a fan of the Baltimore

Colts, the two-time NFL champs in the late 1950s, and their star quarterback, Johnny Unitas. Mr. Castillo believed the pass was the wave of the future in football. That season he issued me No. 19, the number the great Unitas wore, and designed plays in which I threw more than two dozen passes each game, which was a lot for games with short, eight-minute quarters. As a player, I blossomed in Coach Castillo's passing game; but my own football hero was actually Don Meredith, the young quarterback of the Dallas Cowboys. At Southern Methodist University, Dandy Don, as he was known, had made famous the "spread offense" in which he took the snap several yards behind the center, alone in the backfield and with the other three backs and two ends spread out along the line of scrimmage as pass receivers. I once saw Meredith run the spread offense against Baylor in a driving rainstorm at Baylor Stadium and complete pass after pass despite the conditions. After that, any time it rained, I was always outside throwing the football in my back yard. I had set up an old tire on a rope dangling from the top of the crossbar on my younger sister's swing set, and this would be my receiver when no one else would throw the ball with me in the rain. The tire would swing from side to side, and I would drill spirals through its circular opening from ten yards, twenty yards, and thirty yards. I figured throwing a wet ball was as easy as throwing a dry one, and that your receivers should have an advantage against defensive backs making quick cuts on a wet field. On our eighth grade team, I sometimes ad-libbed the spread offense, taking a direct snap several yards back from the center and passing *à la* Meredith. I dreamed of doing it in thunderstorm, but the rain never came.

More important things than football, though, were happening in my life in the eighth grade. I had become close to Mr. Purvis and felt that he was one of the few adults to whom I could turn with a personal issue of which I had been in utter denial. My father often terrorized my mother and me at home. It had been going on as long as I could remember, and my mother had never turned to anyone for help. I suppose that at another time, if a shrink had seen my father, he would have been diagnosed as suffering from some kind of post-traumatic stress disorder. At times he could be the sweetest, most considerate person. This was the man his friends, including our fellow parishioners knew. If you were to describe the other side of him, they would never believe you: abusive, violent, drunken, hateful, angry. He seemed to become most abusive to my mother at family get-togethers. Rarely would we attend a holiday event when he didn't lose his temper at mom over the slightest thing, such as bringing him something he didn't like on a dinner plate. He would then spew his venomous hatred, calling her names. If she said anything back, he would threaten to hit her and order her to shut her mouth, though not those exact words. *Cállate la boca* is shut your mouth in Spanish. My father would use something much ruder: "*Cállate el osico!*" In Spanish, the word *osico* refers to an animal's mouth. That is how he spoke to my mother. The last time he spoke like that to her, at least in my presence, was the summer before my ninth grade. My cousin Gloria and her family were visiting from Houston, and my Uncle Angel and his wife Esther were also at our house for an early dinner when my father didn't like something about the meal. He began yelling at my mother who was trying to explain that something he wanted hadn't been at the grocery store, but he would hear nothing of it. In front of my aunts, cousins, and uncles, he let loose a stream of abusive insults, capping them with "*Cállate el osico!*"

I blew up. I stood up at the table and told my father to stop talking to her that way - that he was humiliating her and embarrassing all of us. I expected my father to take a swing at me, but he was so shocked that he just stood, mouth agape. It was my two uncles who rose from their seats and started toward me.

"You ungrateful snot-nosed kid!" Uncle Lupe said as he took a step.

"You apologize to your father," Uncle Angel demanded. "You're an embarrassment! If we'd spoken that way to our father, he would have killed us."

"Well, that's nice to know where all that vile and violence comes from!" I figured I would get my cheap shots in while I was still standing. "Look, don't be any bigger assholes than you and your brother already are," I said, yelling at them. "You lay one finger on me, and I'll have the cops here so fast, you won't know what embarrassment really is. I've told a teacher, a very well respected teacher, just what kind of hell I live in and what kind of hell my dad puts us through. So if anything happens to me, he'll know."

Lupe sat back down, and Angel looked like he was going to cry. My father disappeared and went outside.

"You've talked about your family to strangers?" Angel demanded. "How can you do that?"

"No, don't turn this around on me being the bad guy," I said. "You allow your brother to talk to his wife this way in front of people? You're the biggest disgrace and hypocrite in the family. You take accolades from the Pope and prance around church in your Knights of Columbus monkey suit, and you don't see anything wrong with how your brother treats your sister-in-law?"

"What goes on between a husband and wife is their business," said Lupe. "You have no business interfering."

"Bullshit! This is practically criminal, and the two of you are equally culpable for allowing it to happen and go on."

By this time, my aunts and my cousins were all crying. My mother was hysterical, but she seemed almost as angry at me as my uncles were.

"You can't talk to you father that way," she said through her tears. "You have to make peace and ask his forgiveness."

"No, never," I said. "He can die for all I care, but I won't ask his forgiveness for defending you and telling the truth about what has gone on too long."

Seeing their opening, Lupe and Angel now got behind my mother's sentiments, telling me they would forgive me and that they were sure my father would, too, if only I apologized."

"No, absolutely not," I said. "The two of you and my father can go rot in hell. I'm not the one who's wrong here. "When my father dies, if mom is still alive, I'll come to his funeral because of her. But the two of you, you're hopeless and pathetic. The moment you die won't be too soon, and, trust me, I won't be there to mourn."

"Now you're being hateful," said Angel.

"You're right," I said. "I'm a regular chip off the old block."

I spent the night awake and curled up with one of my baseball bats. The next morning, no one said anything to me. It was the ultimate in denial of the whole sordid evening. Late that morning I called Mr. Purvis. He came to pick me up late that afternoon, and we drove around Waco while I told him what had happened in detail. He said he wasn't surprised that everyone wanted to act as if the evening hadn't happened.

"All families are a mess," he said. "You shouldn't be so hard on yours. I doubt that things will ever be the same again that your father and uncles will ever look at you the same. All in all, it may have been a good thing that this happened. You'll just have to wait and see."

I decided to focus on my studies and on reading. They killed the Press Club and the publication of the *Panther Post*, so I didn't have that to look forward to. They never gave us a reason, though several of us suspected it was the doing of a kid who hadn't gotten into the Press Club. He had instigated a yearlong campaign attempting to discredit the Press Club as a bunch of spoiled brats who had too many privileges not given other students. It was probably true, but he never knew what he missed. There was also football, though I knew that I likely wouldn't be playing much. In fact, one afternoon, while watching me show receivers how to run crossing routes in the minutes before practice, the head coach took me aside.

"Castro," he said, "we don't throw the ball around here, so don't get your hopes up, son."

The team also had a returning quarterback, Mike Perez, whose specialty the year before had been handing the football off to Jerrell Marshall. Jerrell, in fact, had been the quarterback on the field in all but position. In the huddle, he called all the plays. That team, even as unsuccessful as it was, had been built around its only talented player, Jerrell, who was now in high school. This season promised to be no better and possibly worse. But the coach loved to use his returning players, so there was never any open competition for the quarterback position, even if Mike did throw passes that looked like dying sparrows. Fortunately, he threw those dead birds only two or three times a game. I was relegated to a backup role, playing only a handful of downs in the first game of the season. Actually I was such an after-thought that when it came time to hand out uniforms, the coach didn't bother to give me a jersey with a number usually assigned to quarterbacks. I was given number twenty-two, a numeral usually worn by running backs. The coach even had me running plays as a reserve running back. But a couple of games into the season, fate intervened. I became the team's starting quarterback, thanks to the misfortune that can befall anyone in football. While running a quarterback keeper on the last play of practice one day, Mike went down hard from a clean tackle and didn't get up. From the sidelines all I could see was confusion and panic at the end of the field where Mike lay writhing. Minutes later, they were rushing him to the hospital. The next morning, as Dick and I sat in the cafeteria sipping chocolate milk before school, Agustín Martinez approached us. A little early for a shakedown, I thought. But money wasn't what he wanted. Agustín was one of the halfbacks on the team and a close friend of the quarterback.

"Hey, white boy," Agustín said, looking at *me*. "Are you worth a shit at quarterback?"

I ignored him, but Dick couldn't hold back.

"You'd find out if he ever got a chance," Dick said.

Agustín shot him an angry glance, but Dick didn't back down.

"Well, it looks like you're gonna get your chance to show us," Agustín said. "You're starting tomorrow because Mike's out. He broke his collarbone."

It hadn't occurred to me his injury could be that serious.

"I'm sorry to hear that," I said.

"How long is he out for?" Dick wondered

"Eight weeks," Agustín said. Eight weeks? That was the rest of the season.

"Look, man," Agustín continued, "we can win this game against La Vega tomorrow. But it's up to you not to screw up. So don't fuck it up, sport."

He turned and walked away as Dick muttered under his breadth, "Yeah, man, let's not screw up our losing streak."

The next day Waco was hit by a horrendous rainstorm, leaving the La Vega High School Stadium field in standing rain. La Vega was a school district beyond East Waco, and we were playing its junior high. It was hard to believe that our game wasn't postponed because of what was likely to happen to the sod on the football field, which was used by the La Vega High School team. That day most of our game was played around midfield where the grass became a brown quagmire of mud making the footing treacherous. Early in the second quarter, a La Vega running back broke through the line of scrimmage and past our secondary, scoring what appeared would be the only points of the game. Meanwhile, our offense with the coach calling all the plays from the sidelines amounted to me handing off to the halfbacks and the fullback and then punting the ball on fourth down. I don't think we even made a first down though the first three quarters. Late in the game, La Vega was driving for a clinching touchdown when its quarterback fumbled and lost the ball deep in our territory. During the timeout for the change of possessions, Coach Hepler grabbed my arm as I headed back on the field.

"Castro," he said, "if I open up the game, can I trust you not to throw it away?"

"Coach, I haven't thrown away a game all season," I said. This was my first start, after all.

He gave me a look. "What I'm asking you, son," he said, "is this: Can *you* throw the football in this weather?"

"Sure, I can coach," I said, "and we've got their secondary exactly where we want them..."

But he cut me off. "Castro, we're on *our* 20-yard line, son."

"Coach, what I mean is that their secondary is having to defend our receivers in the muddiest, wettest part of the field. They'll never be able to keep their footing if our receivers make quick cuts, and I know can I hit someone on a crossing pattern or a fly route and score."

He was hoping I was right. "Okay, son," he said. "If you think you can do that, it's your game."

I ran back on the field imagining being Meredith about to fill the air with passes. In the huddle, the first play I called was one in which Agustín would cut quickly down the sideline. I was a pitcher in summer youth baseball, and I had always had a strong arm. I had also won the school softball throwing competition the previous spring. So I knew, that even at my young age, I could easily throw a pass fifty yards and that it would be a matter of whether Agustín could get under the pass and hold on to the football in the rain. We looked at each other just before we broke the huddle.

"Agustín," I said, "I'll get the ball there. Just don't fuck it up."

He grinned and nodded. "Let's see what you've got, sport."

Moments later, I dropped back quickly, drifted away from the blocking pocket to avoid the defensive rush, and threw a long, high spiral down the right side of the field. I saw Agustín racing down the sideline, having beaten his defender by ten yards. Even in the rain, I knew I had led him perfectly. But I didn't see Agustín score because a linebacker crashed into me after I had thrown the pass. All I remember was being picked up on my feet by Tommy Anderson, one of our guards, getting slapped on the back by several of my teammates, and following everyone to the other end of the field. Tommy later told me I had finished the game and completed several more passes, but I couldn't recall much. I had sustained a concussion, and the last thing I remembered was letting go of the pass. I remembered that and seeing my grade school friend Judy Wammack, who was now a cheerleader, with a look of concern on her face as one of the assistant coaches examined me away from the bench as the game neared its end.

The next morning the *Waco Tribune Herald* sports section published a story reporting that I had lofted a long touchdown pass to Agustín that tied the score, then ran the two-point conversion to give South Junior its first win in more than two seasons. Coach Hepler was ecstatic. I did remember jumping into his arms when I returned to the sidelines after we scored the touchdown. At our field house that night, he stayed close to me and insisted on accompanying my dad and me to the hospital where I was to be examined. I had a splitting headache, but I was too happy to let it bother me.

"Coach," I said to Mr. Hepler. "I just wish Jerrell had been a part of this."

"Well, you've done something Jerrell couldn't do last year," he said. "You won us a game."

We won another game that season and, for the first time in a long while, South Junior High was competitive in all the others. By the end of the season, without shelling out a nickel of shakedown money, I had also won the respect of the Mexican thugs on the team, ands they elected me a co-captain. I wasn't a football player. I knew that. I was almost as tall as I would ever grow up to be, and I weighed one hundred and forty pounds, if that. But that fall, I started getting phone calls from players I knew at Waco High School urging me to go to there the next year. At the end of the season, Coach Hepler told me that, while we hadn't seen eye to eye on offensive football, he thought I should continue playing in high school.

"Son, what you don't have in size, you more than make up for in heart," he said. "I don't know what got your dander up and put a chip on your shoulder, but whatever it was, it's set you out to prove the world wrong. And my experience is that those are the kinds of people who get things done."

I took that as a compliment. It wasn't just what had happened with Patricia and the "white girls" speeches that had lit a fire in my belly. It was also what some kids would say. Once, in the fifth grade, when several of my classmates and I were discussing saving money to go to college, a student I greatly admired at the time, made the point of inserting himself into the conversation and saying, "You don't have to worry about saving for college. Your people don't go to college." Another time, another friend whom I respected and would later become the student council president at University High School, interrupted a conversation I was having with someone else about college to say, "You're not going to college. By the time you're eighteen, you'll already have two kids and a girl knocked up with a third." Coach, that's what had gotten my dander up.

There is also nothing more seductive than a coach's words, and the next spring Coach Hepler was again effusive in his praise. Most of my teammates were headed to University High, but I was planning to attend Waco High. In Texas, when anyone talked about high school football in Waco, it was about Waco High School. The Tigers had won several state championships in a row a couple of decades earlier, but the reputation of Waco High as a Texas football powerhouse had stuck. I had no connection to University, especially when you considered that it had started as a technological school. It had been known as Waco Tech High, hardly what you wanted on a transcript to an Ivy League school. I had never even attended a University High football game that I could remember. For years each fall, my dad and I spent Friday nights at Waco High Tigers football games when they played at home. When they were away, we were at the home games of Reicher High School, the small Catholic parochial school in town. But, of course, the real reason I was going to Waco High was Patricia. She had immersed herself in the drama department there, and in her sophomore year, she had been cast as the lead in several plays. My friends Dick McCall and Judy Wammack were headed to Waco High as well. They had been my sense of stability for years, it seemed, especially Judy. I had known her since the second grade when, for some unknown reason, I felt compelled to give her a gift at Christmas that I bought with my piggy bank savings. This was at a time when I could barely string together three words of English, so I had never actually spoken to her. But she was one those few children who seemed to sense that I was struggling and tried to be supportive. Once, while on the playground in the fourth grade, we had accidently run into each other face-to-face, and I didn't know what happened. I wondered if that was what it was like to kiss someone.

Even though University High was practically within walking distance of where I lived, I had already figured out the bus routes from my house to Waco High in the mornings and in the evenings after sports practice, calculating that I would be home by dinnertime. I had gone so far as to have spoken to the journalism adviser at Waco High about joining the school paper. Hearing of my plans, Coach Hepler called me to his office one morning. He had learned that there were least four quarterbacks on the team depth chart at Waco High, he said, and I would likely have a difficult time ever starting there. I didn't tell Coach Hepler, but that didn't bother me. I had read a newspaper story about how Don Meredith, when he showed up as a freshman at Southern Methodist University, was told there were five quarterbacks ahead of him and that he might wind up playing in the defensive secondary. Meredith, of course, had beaten out all those other quarterbacks and become an All-American. So I could at least dream of doing the same thing Meredith did. Coach Hepler also said that the coach from University, who happened to be a friend of his, had expressed strong interest in me. Sure enough, a few days later, University High Head Coach Ira Conner paid a surprise visit to my home. He lived in my neighborhood just a few streets away, he said, and he wanted to meet my family and me.

"They tell me you make straight A's and that you want to go to Harvard," he said. "I like that. I need a smart quarterback."

I felt flattered and thanked him, but I was non-committal.

"Son, I know you're thinking of going to Waco High," he said. "It's a good school, but you belong at University. Your friends will be there, and it's close to your home."

He waited for an answer. I didn't know what to say. I wanted to tell him that I wasn't going to Waco High to play football. I didn't even care that much about football. The only part about football I liked was the passing game, I wanted to say, and I knew I wasn't going to get to do that anywhere. The reason I was going to Waco High, I wanted to tell everyone, was because the girl of my dreams was there.

That's when my father jumped in.

"Don't worry, Coach Conner, he'll be at University," my dad said. "He'll never play football at Waco High."

As it turned out, I never really played football anywhere, but that's getting ahead of the story. The reason we were living so close to University High is that someone had fired gunshots at me at our old house in South Waco. It was in the middle of my ninth grade year, and it was likely connected to the growing violence at South Junior. Police dug out a slug four feet from the front door that they said came from a rifle. They investigated, but never learned the identity of the shooter. But the gunshots were clearly meant as a warning. I had gotten involved in things that weren't my business, though they should have been everyone's concern. I had become friends with a twelve-year-old seventh grade girl who lived in the barrio near the Boys Club, and she had conveyed a frightened account of what was happening to her and other girls who lived in that area. They were all being forced to have sex with some of the Hispanic thugs who roamed the barrio. Some of them attended South Junior. Others were already in high school or had dropped out of school. My friend said she had been forced into having sex when she was eleven years old. The boys had befriended her and then blackmailed her by threatening to harm her family if she did not have intercourse. She was too frightened to report the rape to police and didn't know what she could do. Perhaps foolishly, I had reported this to one of our coaches who said he would tell the school administrators. It was foolish because word soon spread at school that I had ratted out what was happening to these girls. A few days later, the gunshots were fired. My parents, for the first time, shared the depth of my concern for the violence at school. They began house-hunting that weekend, and we moved in a matter of weeks. Sadly, things would never improve for my friend and some of the other girls who lived in the barrio near the school. My friend was pregnant at the age of fourteen and married before she finished South Junior.

At school, I warned Dick to be careful. People were getting crazier. We were seeing more knives. Knives the size made famous by Jim Bowie, the Alamo hero, were being brandished brazenly by guys on the football team. We lived with this terror all year long, and we had started counting down the days until we could move on. Then, with twelve weeks to go, the incident that ended my South Junior days occurred, and it had nothing to do with the Mexican thugs.

For months, a beautiful brunette named Darlene Scott had been passing me letters in class, letters that to an outsider would appear to be love notes. There was nothing to them. Darlene sent notes to everyone, but she and I had developed a special relationship, almost like one of sister and brother. She had been a cheerleader in the eighth grade and probably would have been elected again for the ninth grade. Cheerleaders, though, had to clear faculty approval, and several teachers ganged up against her, citing an attitude problem. Instead of being a cheerleader, Darlene was demoted to dressing up as a Panther mascot in a cute, if silly, costume on the football sidelines. She was devastated, especially when our ninth grade year began and the reality of being a lowly mascot set in. So she reached out to me.

"I'm the laughing stock of the school," she said when we met one day away from school. "How do I make this go away?"

"You're actually quite cute as a panther," I said.

"No, I'm not."

"Yeah, you are," I said. "Besides, it could be worse. You could be Atomic Man."

Then I told her the story, without Patricia's name, of how I wound up wearing an even sillier costume than hers in front of students *and* their parents. She was amused at the thought that there were worse things than being the panther mascot.

This had happened in the fall. But in the spring, Darlene wrote what could have been easily mistaken as a true "love note" to me, saying something about how she missed our intimacy. She meant our heart-to-heart talks, but her words suggested a physical and sexual closeness. The note had "love" and "kisses" written all over it and was signed "Love ya, Darlene." Unfortunately, a teacher intercepted the note. Thinking it was about a real ongoing love affair, she reported us to the principal who seemed almost too happy to call me into his office to deliver another "white girls" speech. I'm not sure what was said to Darlene because I didn't stick around. Just before lunch that day, I made my rounds to all my teachers and had them sign a transfer card documenting my grades. By the end of the day, the gossip was all over school. It wasn't gossip about Darlene and me, but about me having checked out of South Junior and transferring to University *Junior* High, which as just across a major thoroughfare from University High School.

It was my first act of defiance, outside standing up to the men in my family.

I only wish there had been more. That fall, to keep peace with my father and uncles, I enrolled at University High School. They were all insisting that I play football and baseball at University, saying that to not do so would be an insult to the coach who had paid our family a visit, and that my family would lose face. My uncles and my father had been playing these kinds of mind games with me for years. When I was ten, my Uncle Angel had recruited Johnny Silva and me to play on a youth baseball team he had quickly formed at our church, Sacred Heart of Jesus, against a team from another church, St. Francis. It wasn't until Johnny and I showed up at the game that we learned that all the other kids on the St. Francis team were thirteen- and fourteen-year-olds. Johnny and I both sucked that day. I think I struck out every time I came up to bat, and Johnny had managed a ground ball out. We were ten years old in the fourth grade playing against kids who were three and four years older and in junior high school. For as long as I could remember, though, my uncle reminded me of how poorly I had played in that game. That was the same kind of pressure they applied for days about going to University High School as they wore down my resistance. I gave in, but it would be the last time. From then on, I decided, I would no longer be the son through whom my father and my uncles would live their dreams. It seemed as if I had been doing this all my life.

Being that I was the only boy on their side of the family, my father and his brothers had taken it upon themselves to design my future. They all had great expectations of me. In sports my father always stretched the family budget to buy me the best equipment on the market, even when I hadn't asked for it. At the start of the ninth grade, he bought me a pair of the identical football shoes that the Baylor running backs wore – Riddell lightweight kangaroo leather cleats with special lacing and support. I knew from looking at equipment catalogs that those cleats cost sixty dollars. Even with a discount, they were still too expensive, and I asked my father to take them back because I was going to be riding the bench as the backup quarterback. "Just be prepared," he said. "Most people aren't ready when an opportunity comes up, and they blow it." My Uncle Angel, the semi-pro baseball team owner, had even grander dreams for me. He had received a citation of honor from Pope John XXIII for his work and contributions to the church, and he had local political connections to boot. He had spoken to our Congressman, U.S. Representative W. R. "Bob" Poage, a crony of President Johnson, about a possible appointment for me to West Point. Another uncle was pushing me for an appointment to the Naval Academy. If those didn't happen, they said, I should attend Texas A&M University where I could join the military corps there and graduate as a second lieutenant in the army. Like my father, my uncles had fought overseas in World War II and fancied seeing their nephew as an officer serving their country. It was their dream but my life.

"The congressman's people say that with your grades, the way you carry yourself, and the kind of person you are, you would be a strong candidate for any of the academies," Angel told me in front of our entire family at one of our holiday dinners.

"The kind of person I am?" There was a two-ton elephant at dinner that no one wanted to acknowledge. "You mean, that I'm Mexican?"

"That you're Hispanic, yes."

"That's not how I would want to get into any school," I said. "That's not the way anyone should be admitted."

"But they're doing it all the time," said Uncle Lupe.

"That doesn't make it right," I said. "And one day they'll judge those people as being nothing more than a Mexican second lieutenant or a Mexican general or a Mexican admiral."

"Well, we need them," said Angel.

"If you need them so badly, move to Mexico," I said. "They've got plenty of Mexican officers down there. Crooked cops, too. But I won't do it. If I have the talent and qualifications, that should be enough. I shouldn't have to be someone with their hat in their hand, quivering in their shoes, begging for a handout. I won't be their token, and I won't be yours."

Otherwise, that Christmas dinner went well.

Going against my father and his two brothers was no easy matter. Over the years, I had seen the way they ganged up on their two half-brothers whom they treated as children at best and as inferiors at worst. Once, in front of the entire family at a holiday gathering, they brought my Uncle Frank to tears and an emotional breakdown because they didn't like the way he was living his life. The Castro men didn't approve of Frank sometimes staying out all night on weekends partying with his friends. He never got into trouble but was just releasing some pent-up steam. They didn't take into consideration that he worked two jobs and was the sole supporter of his elderly mother, the Castro men's stepmother, who suffered from Parkinson's disease and for whom they did little in helping out. I also had heard stories of how, years earlier when I was about three or four, they had similarly badgered my Uncle Isaac, who was then fifteen years old.

In 1950, several weeks before his 16th birthday, Isaac rebelled by walking into an Army recruiting office and, lying about his age, enlisted for military service. He was sent to Korea as part of the 2nd Infantry Division and there, six weeks after his arrival, Isaac was captured at a place called Kunu-ri. He was a prisoner of war there for almost three years. My memories of Isaac's POW experience were the tearful letters that my parents received and that my mother read to us. I remember little about the letters themselves except the complaints about the food. Mostly I recall the impact those letters had on my family and on his mother, Doña Isidra, who developed Parkinson and almost died. I remember those years as if they were years of mourning. Our home was filled with burning votive candles, and much of our time was spent not only at Mass on Sundays but also at rosaries and other prayer meetings on weekday nights.

Then one night, it was as if the mourning suddenly ended. Someone in an Army uniform visited our house to tell us that Isaac was coming home. Later that day there was a flood of telephone calls and strangers with notebooks and cameras. My father's picture appeared in the newspaper the next day with the biggest grin I've ever seen on his face, beaming at the telegram the soldier had delivered. Isaac's release changed life at our house. His mother had been living with us, and Isaac joined us when he finally arrived home amid fanfare and a hero's welcome. The city and Baylor held a big reception for him at an auditorium named Waco Hall, and pictures of Isaac ran in the newspaper for several days. A local car dealership gave him a beautiful new convertible. Other stores sent him new clothes and shoes. He was introduced at a Baylor home football game, and he was given season tickets to the city's minor league baseball team.

Isaac was a war hero. I would later learn that he had helped keep alive several fellow POWs in a concentration camp known officially as Camp 5 Pyoktong and called "Death Valley" by many who were incarcerated there.

But I also learned there was a price to pay.

There was an Air Force base on the outskirts of Waco, and every time a plane passed overhead or could be heard even at a distance, Isaac would run out of the house to see it and identify it, no matter what time of day or night or what he or anyone else might be doing. Isaac was now home, but a part of him was still a POW. My father complained that Isaac was not good company, and sometimes he and my mother were understandably embarrassed. Once, when our parish priest joined us for Sunday dinner, Isaac reminisced about the food he had been forced to scavenge for in the concentration camp. Worms, ants, weevils, bugs, and even maggots. Those who didn't scavenge, he said, died. As kids, of course, we got a child's delight in hearing these kinds of stories and others that Isaac told. For adults, I imagine they wore thin after a while.

It was almost as if the adults failed to consider the full experience Isaac had endured. Had they forgotten the horrible conditions and the suffering he had endured as a POW, including the battering inflicted on him with clubs, rifle butts, and pistols? Often he had been left unconscious and near death. Somehow we forgot. Eventually, Isaac married a beautiful woman who evidently understood and loved him better than his own family. The first thing she got him to do was to buy a farm near Rosebud and move out to the country.

I should have rebelled myself and gone to Waco High, but football glory can have a seduction all its own, even to a kid who is reluctant to play. It wouldn't have mattered anyway. My University High experience, which began with promise in spring practice, quickly turned into a disaster in the fall. The head coach had said he would bring me along slowly and limited my playing time in the annual spring game to the final series. I played one down and threw a long touchdown pass to Paul Francis, an old Little League teammate. But playing on the junior varsity football team in the fall, I cracked several ribs in practice and broke my left hand midway through the season. The school's team doctor diagnosed the swelling and pain as caused by a ganglion, a lump on the side of the hand, and said I could still play. But I was in constant pain. I couldn't take a snap from under center, nor have any pressure put on my left hand. In the spring, I also discovered that the injury caused excruciating pain when catching a baseball. Even my father and uncles thought I wasn't "gutting it out" and suspected my injuries weren't so serious that I couldn't play. Eventually I went to my family doctor on my own, and his X-rays found a broken bone in my hand. I wore a cast, but it never fully healed. Years later, a surgeon in Houston would repair what he diagnosed as two broken metacarpals that had healed in the wrong way and had to be re-broken to correct. But in high school, the injury put me on the sidelines, athletically and socially. I didn't care.

I had overcome speech impediments and conquered the fear and intimidation of a strange new language, and I hadn't done it to play sports and join social clubs. I also knew I could write as if beyond my years and that, in a three-piece Ivy League suit my father had specially ordered for me from a men's store downtown, I could look older than I was. So one afternoon after school, I walked into the offices of the *Waco Citizen*, a weekly newspaper known for its iconoclastic reporting, and talked my way into my first job in journalism. I was working after school and Saturdays, writing obituaries and local briefs, reporting about the city's high school sports teams, and even occasionally covering Baylor football and athletics. The editors thought I was a high school senior and, later, an undergraduate at Baylor. Their misperception about my age made it easier convincing them to allow me to write about politics and pop culture. In 1964, as Lyndon Johnson rode the wave of national tragedy to a full term in the White House, I covered what there was of the presidential campaign in Texas. I interviewed then Vice Presidential nominee Hubert Humphrey and Texas Governor John Connally, who had survived being wounded when President Kennedy was assassinated. That same year, I also covered the Dallas leg of the Beatles' second tour of America. I had media credentials for the Beatles press conference, and I bought an English-made Edwardian suit that got me noticed by Paul McCartney who commented on it.

"Nice suit, bloke, is it British made?" he asked when he called on me to ask a question.

My suit was likely some anonymous knockoff of Pierre Cardin, but I lied and said Douglas Millings made it. I had read somewhere that Millings was a London tailor who sometimes made suits for the Beatles. McCartney didn't question it. He nodded approval, as I asked if they were aware of the impact the Beatles were having on popular culture in America. The Beatles didn't answer questions so much as turn them into joking banter, which they did with mine. My hilarious account of the Beatles press conference in the *Waco Citizen* was picked up a few days later by The Associated Press, which transmitted the story around the world on its wire service. My reporter friend at the Waco daily, Tommy West, called me wondering why I hadn't tried to get it published in the *Tribune-Herald.*

"I did, Tommy," I said, "and your city editor said he didn't give a damn about a silly story on the Beatles."

A few days later I got a call from the city editor apologizing and saying he had misjudged the interest in that story.

However, for all the highs I experienced at the time, there were also the lows such as the occasional "white girls" speeches and the attitudes that were inescapable, no matter how much I tried to avoid them. As a sophomore, I was involved in the school newspaper, the *Wooden Horse*, as sports editor and feature writer. It was there that I received yet another "white girls" speech from one of the last people I thought could ever share those feelings. My journalism teacher, who had taken an interest because of the promise I was showing as a writer, said she was concerned about the direction of my personal life after learning I had gone on a date with one of the most popular girls in school. The girl was Sallie Baker, the daughter of Paul Baker, who had earned a national reputation as the experimental director of the Baylor Theatre and the Dallas Theater Center, a repertory he used to train graduate students. He and his wife had also founded the Baylor Children's Theatre of which I was a part during my junior high years. Sallie had been my first new friend at University Junior High when I left South Junior in the second semester of the ninth grade. We had speech and drama together, and we sometimes talked about literature and writing. Our friendship continued at University High. When the film *To Kill a Mockingbird* opened in Waco, Sallie told me how much she wanted to see the film adaptation of a book we both loved. She said it while we were walking from one class to another together, and she did it with one of those longing looks that Sallie used when she wanted one of her friends to do something for her. When she did that, no one could resist her. So I asked her out. What could one date hurt?

Of course, all bets were off when you were talking about Sallie. She could be disarming, and I had not been prepared for a tour of the Bakers' remarkable Frank Lloyd Wright-inspired home designed by an associate of the legendary architect. Sallie's father personally knew Wright, who had designed Baker's repertory theater in Dallas. The home featured breathtaking wooden features throughout, including custom-built wood furniture, with part of the house below ground in the style of Wright's designs from that period. Her father happened to be home, and Sallie introduced us, which I hadn't expected. In 1956, when I was in the third grade, my speech therapist from Baylor had taken me to an afternoon performance of *Hamlet* at the Baylor Theater. I hadn't yet read the play, but Miss Taylor had acquainted me with several lines to memorize. She believed, I think, that any kind of exposure to the language would increase my confidence in using it. She said it would be a different *Hamlet* than anything I would later see in my life, and it was. The actor Burgess Meredith played the main speaking role of Hamlet, and three other actors represented three other sides of the melancholy Danish prince. It was experimental and difficult to follow. I told Sally's father I had seen the play.

"You saw my *Hamlet*?" he said, disbelieving. "With Burgess? You couldn't have been more than ten."

"I think I was nine," I said. "A teacher took me."

He smiled. "So what did you think?"

"I liked it, but I especially liked Burgess Meredith," I said, "and I enjoyed the introspective Hamlet that one of the actors played. I'm not sure I got the other two sides of Hamlet."

"I'm not sure too many other people did either," he said, "and they were a heckuva lot older than you!"

My date with Sally, however, was also the most apprehension-filled evening of my life. If you ever wanted to be seen with a gorgeous girl who made you look and feel as if you were going steady with her, it was Sally. She was one of those dream dates who instinctively sits next to you in the front seat of the car, who cuddles up close to you with the popcorn in the theater, and who insists on sitting on the same side of the booth with you at a restaurant. It was the greatest date I had in high school.

But it was a Friday night with a packed theater and a crowded restaurant, and we got looks and stares. Part of it was Sallie. At school, we only saw the tomboyish Sallie, the Sallie who rode horses on the land next to her house, the Sallie who played tennis in the scorching sun, and the Sallie who could trash talk at sporting events with the best of them. Once, at a high school tennis tournament, University's best singles player was getting beaten badly by a teenage phenom from Dallas named Cliff Richey, who later was ranked No. 1 in the U.S. and played Davis Cup. Richey was a growing kid with a big butt, and there were newspaper accounts that his sister Nancy, another Texas tennis sensation, specially made his shorts to fit his posterior. So that afternoon, as Richey struggled to put away the University High player, Sallie led the verbal barrage directed especially at the young star.

"Hey, Richey!" she yelled when he tugged at his sweat-drenched seat after losing a rare but important point, "You better get your sister to make you some bigger shorts!"

Richey, who was known as a hot head, heard her and glared at the stands. Then he proceeded to double-fault and unleash an obscenity-laced temper tantrum. He eventually won the match, though Sallie had captured the moment.

But the Sallie I got on our date to the movies was the young woman we rarely saw. That night she wore a black summer dress and pearls, matching high heels, just enough makeup to cover up some freckles around the nose, red lipstick, and her dark hair styled so that she could have been Natalie Wood in *Splendor in the Grass*. At the restaurant, the Italian Village near downtown, Sallie sat almost in my lap, listening to me talk with her face just inches from mine in a way that made me feel incredible but created the wrong impression for people who were staring at us.

"Oh, let them stare," she said.

"You don't understand, Sallie," I tried to tell her.

"Yes, I do, more than you think, Tony Castro," she said, cuddling even closer. "I want everyone to know that I love being here with you and that I'm having the greatest time of my life."

Ah, if only we had been more, but we were just great friends. My friend Larry Lynch, another speech and drama student whom I had known since the second grade, was the one who was really in love with Sallie the way I was with Patricia. When he learned from Sallie that we were going to the movies, he had begged me to come over to his house after the date, no matter what hour of the night. At almost one in the morning, he wanted to know all about the date. Had she mentioned his name? Did I bring up his name? How many times? What had she worn? And had I kissed her? I'd better not have kissed her, he said. I lied and said we had shaken hands. *Shaken hands!* But he bought it. Sallie and I had kissed goodnight at her doorstep. Then she had called out, run to where I was on her driveway and given me a deep kiss. Wow. It was the first girl I had ever kissed. We held each other for a few moments. Then I asked her to be the sweetheart of my summer league baseball team, a role that was like being a cheerleader, and she agreed. We kissed again, and it looked like it was going to be a great summer.

I think my date with Sallie was as well as anyone in our class did with her. Sallie, I suspect, was beyond all of us. I don't think anyone in our school ever really *went* with Sallie, you know, went steady with her. But thoughts of any romance quickly died. In 1963, Sally's father obtained the rights to stage Eugene O'Neill's *Long Day's Journey Into Night* at Baylor. The contract with O'Neill's widow prohibited editing of the script in any way, and this would eventually doom Baker's relationship with Baylor. There were no four-letter words in the play but what *Time* magazine described as a "drizzle of expletives such as "goddamn whore!" All it took to arouse the conservative Baptist sensitivities was a performance attended by a church-sponsored group that included teen-age girls and their parents who complained to the university. When Baker refused to censor the language at the administration's demand, the school closed down the production. Baker and his eleven faculty members resigned in protest and left Waco for Trinity University. Sallie, of course, moved away with her family. A member of the faculty, playwright Robert Flynn, later wrote a humorous collection titled *Growing Up Sullen Baptist and Other Lies* in which he lampooned Southern Baptists and explained that "much of that sullenness comes from fear of change, fear of the future, fear that God is not the creator and not in control of the universe. We don't have a crisis of courage – we have a crisis of faith." In a scathing editorial when Baylor shut down the O'Neill play, the *Baylor Lariat's* editor Ella Wall Prichard wrote that the decision to close down the play would "serve only to brand Baylor as a narrow-minded, intolerant denominational school concerned with religious indoctrination rather than education." Appropriately, her damning words said as much about Waco as it did Baylor. For me, there was great irony: the Baylor president who effectively ran Sallie Baker's father out of town was Dick's father, Abner V. McCall.

Sallie's last words to me when she left Waco: "Castro, give them hell!"

I tried. In my junior year at University, I was the assistant editor of the school paper, a position that allowed me to virtually run the paper and write a column. I was also still reporting and writing features for the *Waco Citizen*, and I was looking forward to covering the upcoming presidential campaign. With Texas being a critically important state and with Johnson as Kennedy's vice president, it was apparent that both men would soon be campaigning in the state. That fall I had even tentatively made plans to play hooky from school on Friday, November 22, 1963, and to take a Greyhound bus to Dallas to report on Kennedy and Johnson's trip there. The editor of the *Waco Citizen* had secured credentials for me to cover the speech that the president was to deliver at the Dallas Trade Mart that day. School, however, got in the way. I had two major tests scheduled that Friday, examinations that loomed especially large given my dream of applying to Harvard, and there was a deadline as well for putting out the next issue of the *Wooden Horse*. The morning of Kennedy's arrival in Texas, I consoled myself with thoughts that there would be other opportunities to cover JFK.

Of course, by early afternoon that day, University High would be like the rest of the nation, disbelieving the tragedy that had unfolded. I happened to be eating lunch in the special journalism office our school had on the second floor when a student ran into the room hyperventilating. "They've shot President Kennedy!" she screamed.

"Someone shot President Kennedy in Dallas." We were horrified as the two of us ran downstairs to the teachers' lounge where they had a TV. The teachers' lounge was off-limits to students, but no one even noticed us as all eyes were glued to the black-and-white television set where CBS anchor Walter Cronkite announced: "We just have a report from our correspondent Dan Rather in Dallas, that he has confirmed President Kennedy is dead." School let out early, and perhaps I was just typical of many in the country for whom the sadness and the mourning would go on, seemingly interminably. Our varsity football team had a home game scheduled for that night, a game we all assumed would be postponed because of the national tragedy. The game, however, was played as if nothing had happened, though the entire evening was fraught with emotions. I remember seeing a couple of our cheerleaders going through a well-rehearsed routine, screaming near the top of their lungs, all the while tears rolling uncontrollably down their cheeks.

I was "spotting" the game for Ray Bell, a reporter the *Waco Tribune-Herald*, who was covering the game for the next day's paper. I would do this almost every Friday night for one of the paper's writers. We walked up and down sidelines, where it was easier than watching from the press box to check on the yardage gained, who carried the football or caught a pass, and who made the tackle. I would pass on the names and the yardage to Ray who would jot it down between puffs from a Marlboro that seemed to live between his lips. Ray, a middle-aged man with thick glasses and a receding sunburned hairline, wasn't really a sportswriter. He was a news reporter who would help with the extensive high school football every Friday night. Spotters would get twenty dollars a game, and sometimes I would "spot" games on Thursday nights as well. Ray liked working with me, and I wanted to think it was because I was so good at "spotting" that it made his life easier. Much later, when I was on the staff myself, he told me it was actually because I put up with his crazy behavior. Ray loved Jack Daniels, and he would have a small flask of whiskey in his coat pocket that he would hit every ten minutes or so while I kept watch making sure no one was looking. Sometimes Ray had me "spot" out-of-town games to which I would drive his

Studebaker, allowing him to type his game story on a small portable on the way home. There was one trip, however, that was memorable because the game had been played in a rainstorm in Corsicana, and the brakes went out on the car just as we got to the high school field. I drove the fifty-five miles back to Waco without brakes and able to stop only by gearing down and using the engine to slow the car. That itself, though, didn't bring the car to a stop.

"One, or both of us may have to open our door and use a foot to help stop it," Ray said, looking up from his typing and a ring of cigarette smoke.

"Ray, there's gotta be a better way," I said.

"Yeah, well, try to time any lights," he said. "And if you have to run a red light, try to be careful and say a prayer."

Of course, we were all saying prayers the night of the assassination, and around the third quarter Ray handed me his notebook.

"With all that happened in Dallas, I think I should be back at the office lending a hand," he said. "You can handle this. Get back to the office and write the story. They may not give you a byline, but I'll see that you get an extra twenty bucks."

I was disappointed they didn't give me a byline, but that night I didn't care. I stayed at the *Tribune-Herald* that night long after the final edition came out. I hung out with Ray, Tommy West and a couple of other people drinking in the parking lot and listening to Kennedy stories that they were all recalling and getting drunk because you were all dried up from crying.

The following weekend, several of us from our student newspaper attended a high school journalism conference at Texas Woman's University in Denton, and we stopped in Dallas and walked around Dealey Plaza, still not comprehending what had happened and how it had happened. Our eyes kept shifting from the Texas Schoolbook Depository from where Lee Harvey Oswald was said to have fired the deadly shots, down to the sloping street below where Kennedy's open limousine became the target, and then across to the grassy knoll which had been transformed into an unofficial memorial site filled with flowers and mementos. We were not alone. Tourists and visitors were everywhere in the plaza, and it was impossible to get a moment alone to gather your thoughts and grieve in silence.

I consoled myself by immersing fully into my schoolwork at University High School, which had been a welcome relief from South Junior. At University Junior High, where I had transferred in the middle of the ninth grade, all my friends from Little League welcomed me with open arms: Jimmie Carpenter, Ronnie Bradford, Larry Henry, Dana Harmon, Robert Pharr, Paul Francis, Wayne Blackshear, and others. They were the friends who would also be with me at University High. For the first time, too, there was a bit of a newfound freedom in being openly friendly with girls like Sallie Baker. There didn't appear to be a sense of foreboding that any teacher would give me a "white girls" speech just for talking to them. I had a part-time weekend job as a soda jerk at the Williams Drug Store in the Southgate Shopping Center nearby, and sometimes my neighbor Michal Ann Horst, who was my age, would come there to spend hours to talk about homework. I had known Michal Ann since we were eleven. She was in that same junior cotillion class, and we had been partners who learned to waltz together. She was also the only girl who knew about my incurable crush on Patricia. When I was chosen to partner Patricia, I had called Michal Ann and asked her for help.

"How should I act around her?" I had pleaded with Michal Ann. "I'm afraid I'll mess things up."

"Don't be silly," she said.

"I'm not being silly around her," I said.

"No, that's not what I mean," Michal Ann said. "I mean, 'Don't be silly. You're not going to mess things up if you just act with her the way you act with me. Waltz with her like you waltz with me."

I continued partnering with Michal Ann at cotillion a lot longer. She was also one of the few people my age I told about the "white girls speeches" I would get from teachers. It made her angry. She wondered if that attitude wasn't unique to the part of South Waco where I had grown up, in the deepest part of South Waco that surrounded

Baylor. Maybe she had something there. Most of the neighborhoods that surrounded Baylor qualified as Latino barrios and poor white trash communities. The part of South Waco where Michal Ann lived was actually southwest Waco and extended from about South Valley Mills Drive all the way west to the VA Hospital. Nearby, off Memorial Drive that spanned from Valley Mills to the hospital, was an upper middle class incorporated neighborhood called Beverly Hills, a one-light community known for its speed traps but having little in common with the glitzy city of the same name in Southern California. Michal Ann lived just south of Beverly Hills, as did almost all the kids I played Little League with, and they all attended University Junior High School. This was a different South Waco from the one I had known at Gurley and South Junior, and it was to this community in Michal Ann's world that we moved after the gunshots at our former house.

Among Michal Ann's friends were the Holdbook sisters, the twins Jeanie and Barba and their older sister Jackie, who were among the friendliest and most popular girls in school. Jeanie would later marry my Gurley Elementary classmate Dwain Moss. Some of our friends thought that Sylvia Cortez, another of my new neighbors, and I would have clicked as a couple. But she was as vaguely Hispanic as I was, and I couldn't tell them that I really didn't want to go steady with anyone. Perhaps it was also because my heart was at Waco High with Patricia that my social life at University was so restrained. Michal Ann and Larry Lynch were my only friends who knew just how much I pined for Patricia, as well as how much I feared making a premature move to winning her over that would somehow backfire. The last thing I wanted was for Patricia's parents putting their foot down and not allowing her to see me altogether. Michal Ann, though, had been telling me how I would finally have to brave it out and take that chance as our junior year neared its end.

"You have to take Patricia to our Junior-Senior Prom," Michal Ann insisted. "You just have to take the risk and see what happens."

When I told my friend Larry Lynch that I was planning to ask

Patricia to the prom, he looked at me with concern, his gnarled eyebrows suggesting that something wasn't right.

"Stud hoss, you better check with her on the dates," he said. "I know *I* won't be going to the prom, and I bet she can't either. Every speech and drama student worth their salt will be at the state tournament."

As luck would have it, our prom night was on the most important weekend of speech and drama in the state's interscholastic league competition. Larry was perhaps the biggest speech and drama student at our school; and he knew, as I did, that Patricia lived and breathed drama as well. From the moment she stepped on the Waco High campus, Patricia had been involved in the school's drama productions, among them Thornton Wilder's *Our Town* and William Gibson's *Dinny and the Witches*. As a lowly sophomore, she had landed prized lead roles coveted by older students; and, like my friend Larry, she was away many weekends during the school year attending speech and drama competitions that were part of an annual circuit throughout the state. A friend at Waco High checked discreetly and learned that, in fact, Patricia would be away at the speech and drama state competition that weekend.

"Isn't there anyone else you want to take to the prom?" Michal Ann couldn't believe I hadn't dated anyone other than Sallie Baker in my two years in high school.

"Well, there's Barbara," I said, "but I don't know if she would want to go to a prom at University."

I told Michal about Barbara Johnson, who attended Richfield High School, the ritziest school in Waco. She was an editor on her school newspaper, and we had met at a journalism conference and gone out a few times in the past year. I think I must have rambled on interminably talking about Barbara, who had impressed me with her intellect and her wit. Barbara and I were both high school juniors, but she seemed older and more mature than the girls my own age. When Barbara and I were together, I always felt that I was going out with someone in college. Talking to her reminded me of the conversations I would have with some of the student teachers at University who were still undergraduates at Baylor. Barbara, for example, had brilliant ideas about what student newspapers should be covering, far beyond the story assignments made by some of our editors at the *Wooden Horse*. As I spoke to Michal Ann about Barbara, I saw Michal looking at me and shaking her head.

"You say you're in love with Patricia," she said, "but for the past hour, it seems, you've talked non-stop about a girl you've never even said a word about before. Barbara sounds incredible, and I don't know if you realize how much you care about her."

I asked Barbara to the prom, and we had a wonderful time. She was stunningly beautiful and a mystery to many of my friends who had never before seen me out on a date with anyone. Some of the jocks at University, I suspect, were friendlier than usual just so that they could meet her. Most of all, I was pleasantly surprised that no one seemed to think anything about the fact that Barbara was white, making me wonder if maybe people's attitudes might not be changing. One of my friends, though, quickly cautioned that I not read too much into one event, especially as it had taken place in the safe environment of fellow students who had known me for years. My friend Carolyn Neuwirth was also perhaps the one person close to me with an intimate understanding my social dilemma. Carolyn may have been the only Jewish student at University High. I wasn't aware of any others, and we used to joke that we were the school's "social lepers." I felt like an outcast for my ethnicity; Carolyn felt estranged because of her religion. We didn't know whose situation was worse, though possibly those Sullen Baptists, as Robert Flynn called them, could understand and stomach my Catholicism much easier than they could Carolyn's "Jewishness." As one of my Sullen Baptist friends once said of me: "Catholics are Christians who just haven't been saved yet."

As a Catholic, I grew up being taught that you couldn't be saved unless you attended Mass every Sunday, which meant that my family and I were at church regularly. The only time I can remember any disruption to our church-going Sunday ritual happened when I was about four years old, and it was a traumatic event involving my Uncle

Jesse, my mother's younger brother. In the coming years, I would always see him as a mixture of James Dean and Elvis Presley, mostly because of what happened that Sunday. When he returned home to Waco from serving in the Army after World War II, Jesse took to living his life as a free-spirited dandy. In 1950, he cemented that image when he bought a canary yellow Chevrolet convertible, driving it at heart-thumping speeds with the wind blowing his long, duck-tailed hair about. However, there was a price to pay: a horrendous middle-of-the-night wreck.

My mom rushed us out of our house in the wee hours of a Sunday morning to check on Jesse who had just returned from the hospital to my grandmother's house, his broken ribs swathed in bandages and gauze encircling a nasty gash on his forehead. He was wearing a beautiful silk pullover shirt that buttoned from the neck to about mid-sternum, and my grandmother was cutting it off him with scissors.

"Man, I can't believe I ruined this shirt," Jesse kept saying over and over.

"He doesn't know what he's saying," my grandmother would say after each lament of the shirt. "He's delirious."

It would be years before I would learn how Jesse had been hurt and why my grandmother showed so much concern that her son's attention to a shirt might be misunderstood. In the early hours of that Sunday morning, as he drove at a high speed through the streets of Waco after a night of partying, Jesse had lost control of his sports car. The convertible tumbled over several times before coming to rest upside down. Jesse suffered only cuts, abrasions, and a concussion. However, a woman in the car with him died in the crash. The woman was married with young kids, and her death crushed her family. Her husband, who had sworn he would kill Jesse, later died in a traffic accident himself. Jesse was not charged with any crime, but he would be tortured by the memory the rest of his life. Nevertheless, the accident changed him, he later told me. There comes a time, he said, when after you've disappointed your loved ones' great expectations of you, that you can start living for yourself and your own dreams. Over the years as I was growing up, I always looked to Jesse for advice, not because I necessarily thought it would be the best but because I thought it would be unlike any I would receive from my parents or anyone else.

In the summers after my sophomore and junior years in high school, I worked for Jesse who had become the aluminum siding king in the Dallas home improvement business. He had been in Dallas since the mid-1950s, and he had made a small fortune remodeling homes. Aunt Modesta, his wife, and he lived in a lovely suburban home where each summer I had a bedroom of my own. Two days a week he would also let me drive his new Thunderbird through Dallas where I would scour the neighborhoods for older houses that could use new siding. All I had to do was jot down the addresses. I didn't even have to talk to the residents. At the office Uncle Jesse had a man who then got the names of the homeowners from the tax rolls. Those names and addresses became leads that were then turned over to any of the half dozen salesmen who worked for my uncle at any one time. I made $250 each for any leads that led to sales, and there were many. In two summers I saved over $5,000. I think Jesse also liked having me there in the summers because I became his eyes and ears, spying on some of his wayward salesmen. By the end of my second summer, Jesse told me he wanted me to move to Dallas after high school and manage his Dallas office while he tried to expand his business into Fort Worth.

"I know you want to go to college, but this is good money right away," he said. "You would do well in this business. And you could go to college here in Dallas."

I was afraid that I hurt Jesse's feelings in turning him down, so for the first time since elementary school I told someone in my family about Patricia. The odds were long in winning her over, I admitted. I carried a torch for her based on our brief time together when we were kids, but the feelings had not died. If anything, those feelings were now stronger.

"Uncle Jesse, I figure I have one shot," I said to him before my senior year. "If I take that shot too early, in Waco, the whole thing could go poof, up in smoke. I don't even have any idea how her parents would feel about me loving their daughter. And Waco... You know how Waco is."

I told Jesse about all the "white girls" speeches I'd gotten over the years, and he said I was lucky that was all it had been. The racism was real, he warned me, and I needed to be careful.

"So where do you plan to win her over?" Jesse wanted to know.

"Austin," I said. "It's a different atmosphere there, and my friends at her school say she's going to go to college at UT in the fall."

"And what do you plan to do?"

"Go down there," I said. "Even take some time off. And then tell her how I feel. I can't believe that she would just kiss me off. Be put off a bit at first, maybe. But I think she'd want to know why I had pursued her and poured my heart out to her. I'll pull out a stupid *sombrero* and guitar and serenade her if I have to. Does this sound crazy?"

"Tony, when people are in love, I think you have to throw crazy out the window," Jesse said. "Of course, what you're thinking of doing is crazy. Love's crazy. That's what makes it so wonderful when it happens."

"Jesse, I just know that on neutral ground, I can sweep her off her feet."

I didn't tell Jesse that I had a speech all prepared. I had written it just a few weeks earlier in my bedroom in Dallas, my retreat with a turntable and headphones where I hid out from all my young cousins. I came to love my time in Dallas each summer where I could grow my hair long and no one said anything about it. One night, while listening to Beethoven's *Emperor Concerto* and crazily imagining myself with long hair blowing in the wind and a sword in one hand, I wrote the words I would use:

Patricia: This will come as a surprise, maybe even a shock, but it shouldn't. Not when you think back. I have been in love with you since we were kids back at Gurley. You're bound to remember the waltz we almost had, and me taking that picture of you in front of the school at the end of your sixth grade. Maybe you didn't know I was already in love with you, but you had to know I had a tremendous crush. And when we were in the Press Club together at South

115

Junior, you had to have seen how I was such a klutz around you. And you had to sense that I was always looking at you. Could it have been coincidental that every time you looked up, I was staring at you? I know we haven't spent time together, but the last few years, they've been high school. Those, for the most part, are totally meaningless times. The football scores don't matter. The yearbook entries don't matter. All that preening and pretending doesn't matter. What matters is what comes next, what comes now, when we as kids stop building sandcastles that wash away and start building dream homes and dream lives that last with the people who love them. And on that, I promise, no matter who you're with right now or who you've been with in the past, no one can love you as I can, as I have, and as I will. Voltaire once wrote: Never have I loved like this before, because never has there been anyone so worthy of my love. He must have been writing that about someone like you. We are both still so young. What I ask is a chance and an opportunity to get to know one another. I love you. I always have. I always will.

The last week I was there that summer, Jesse took me to a jeweler friend of his off Preston Road in North Dallas. He said he was going to give me something that might help me in winning Patricia. In the jewelry store, Jesse's friend brought out a jeweler's tray with several engagement rings sparkling on it.

"I can't let you do this, Jesse," I said, shaking my head. "These things must cost a fortune."

"You wouldn't let me buy you a car," he said. Jesse wanted to buy me a 1957 Thunderbird, but I told him I didn't think I could drive something like that around Waco without getting it trashed or stolen. "So, let me buy the engagement ring. Take it to the bank and put it in a safe deposit box until you need to use it."

The rings were beautiful, especially two of them: a marquis diamond on silver ring and a heart-shaped diamond on platinum. Jesse's jeweler friend kept pushing the heart-shaped diamond, which was incredible, except that the band seemed too wide. I wondered about that and asked one of the store employees to try it on. She was a young woman with long slender hands and fingers like Patricia's.

"It's the setting," she told her boss. "If we could change the setting

116

so that it's the same kinds of prongs protecting the diamond but on a thinner band. It might even make the diamond stand out more."

"She's trying to help you sell a two-and-a-half carat diamond, Saul," Jesse said. "Can you change the band?"

An hour later, we returned to find the heart-shaped diamond with a new slender band. I had the jeweler engrave the inside of the band: *For Patricia Forever My Love Tony.*

I stored it at my bank and prepared to begin my senior year in high school. But then the last thing I ever expected happened. I had known kids who had been expelled from school, sometimes for an entire year. They almost always were habitual troublemakers who made poor grades and had little promise in their future. What happened to me? Well, I wasn't expelled, but it amounted to the same thing. My journalism teacher, Mrs. Evelyn Orr, had long wanted me to cut back my extracurricular activities and reduce my free-lance work I was doing and to dedicate myself to being editor of our high school paper, the *Wooden Horse.* She was upset that the previous semester I had argued openly, even at a school board meeting, for the desegregation of the city's schools. The Waco school district had elementary schools on the eastside of the city that were earmarked for African American students, as well as a junior high school and high school. I knew some of these students personally. Their neighborhood backed up to the community where I grew up, and sometimes I would walk over to their ball fields to play baseball and football. Being Hispanic and dark-complexioned, I could mingle more easily among the black kids than any of my white friends would ever be able to. I made longstanding friendships with a few of those African-American kids, and in high school they sometimes invited me to music events at a nightclub across the Brazos River in East Waco where they never checked my ID. I think they figured that if I was a brave enough soul to show up at a black nightclub not being black that I was either a fool or old enough so that it didn't matter. But what especially irked Mrs. Orr was my working as a professional journalist. I continued reporting for the *Waco Citizen* in the afternoons and weekends, and on Friday nights I worked at the *Waco Tribune-Herald*, helping on the high school football coverage.

Closer to home, Mrs. Orr also disagreed with me putting my two cents worth into the operation of the school's yearbook. She was the sponsor of the yearbook as well as the school paper, and both were housed in the same room. When the new University High School opened in the fall of 1962, one of its features was a Journalism Department, including a professional photography dark room. Our students had no professional photographer teaching or advising them, but Mrs. Orr was convinced that they were capable of doing most of the photography not only for our biweekly newspaper but also for the yearbook, which would be a keepsake for generations. To insure that the most important photographs in yearbooks are of the best quality, most schools used professional photographers for pictures of the homecoming court, the valedictorians and salutatorians, the prom queen and king, and all the other important memories of the school year. After seeing the poor quality of the photographs and enlargements in the yearbook after my sophomore year, I strongly lobbied with Mrs. Orr to use a professional photographer or possibly even a prize-winning photographer from Baylor whom we knew. Our student amateur photographers shot everything using a 35 mm camera when what was needed for portraiture especially was the use of an expensive Hasselblad camera capable of producing larger negatives and, from them, better quality photographs. She wouldn't hear of it. The result was that the full-page size yearbook photograph of my friend Jeanie Holdbrook, the homecoming queen for what would have been my senior year, does her an injustice. It is of poor quality. Not only is it not sharp but it is also fuzzily focused and grainy; it is hardly what a memory of that event should recall. Our disagreement over photography for the yearbook deepened Mrs. Orr's disapproval of me hanging out at the Baylor journalism department. By then, professors at Baylor and editors of the *Lariat*, the university newspaper, were acquainted with me, and she felt they were having an undue amount of influence on me. I wrote a column called "Castro, *si*" for my high school newspaper, and it had impressed the professors and editors of the *Lariat*, when they judged the annual contests for Baylor Journalism Day, which recognized high school journalism. In two years I won a record number of awards for column writing and features, including a story on Don Trull, a Baylor All-America quarterback who led the nation in passing in 1963 and was a Heisman Trophy finalist. For that story, I spent considerable time with Trull, even with his wife at their home, modeling the feature after the long profiles that often were published in *Sports Illustrated*. A professor at Baylor and the editor of the university paper both called it the best story to be written on Trull in that banner year of his. So, my high school journalism teacher's objections notwithstanding, I knew that I was on the right path career-wise and that I was showing great promise to professionals who mattered. Still, I had to deal with Mrs. Orr's disapproval, though doing so with humor that may have been ill advised and an attitude she considered insubordinate and rebellious. That summer, a week before school began, I was called to University High for a meeting with both Mrs. Orr and the principal, W. O. Griffin, a throwback to an age when men wore their hair parted in the middle. At that meeting, the principal notified me that I was being suspended for a full semester from working on the school paper and would also have to resign being president of the school's National Honor Society chapter. He insisted I sign a document admitting to my insubordination and to having embarrassed Mrs. Orr at a weeklong journalism workshop we attended that summer at Texas A&M University.

I couldn't believe what was happening. Neither Mrs. Orr nor the school had ever before placed the kinds of extracurricular restrictions on other editors of the school paper that they were imposing on me. I also explained that in the two years I had known Mrs. Orr, we had always had light-hearted exchanges that she encouraged. There had not been any disrespect meant in a humorous parody I had written about her at the summer workshop. I pleaded with the principal to check with some of the other adult journalism advisers who attended the workshop. I offered to get the principal the names and phone numbers of several of them, but he had already made up his mind. At some point, I broke down and began crying, finally asking if I could go to the boys' restroom to collect myself. There, as I washed my face, it hit me the hardest: Everything I had worked for all these years was going down the drain, making me wonder why I had bothered. Of course, I knew: Patricia. She had been the motivation when I was an eleven-year-old-boy, and she would continue to be. When I returned to the principal's office, Mr. Griffith once again handed me the document to sign. However, I knew in my heart that I'd done nothing wrong and didn't deserve the kind of punishment that was being imposed.

"You know, this isn't right," I said looking at Mr. Griffith and Mrs. Orr. "Just because you have the power to all but destroy any future I could have doesn't make you right and doesn't make this right.

"This is my future, my life..."

They were unmoved. I knew I could do nothing about it, and I simply became angry at the injustice. I studied the document a while longer and then decided it was time to stand up for myself, regardless of the consequences. I tore the paper in half and dropped it on the principal's desk.

"You know what, Mr. Griffin," I said, looking at him with utter contempt. "Fuck you, and fuck everything you stand for."

As I walked out of the office, I heard Mrs. Orr call to me as if she still had any control.

"Tony Castro, you come back here this moment," she said. "You have no choice in this matter."

Actually, I did. I took a bus to the Baylor campus. I had no real plan except to seek help from the people at the journalism department. David McHam, a professor at Baylor, would play the most influential role in my professional development. I wanted to talk with him as well as with friends on the *Lariat* staff, of my inglorious departure from University High School. Now I might not graduate from any high school in the Waco Independent School District, so could they figure out a way I could get into Baylor? What if I got a GED diploma? Would that work? They all had a good laugh and tried to cheer me up. They took me to lunch at the Chuck Wagon where I used to go when I was in junior high, and they reminded me of the Catholic high school on the other side of town. That afternoon my friend Tommy West, the editor of the *Lariat* who also was a star reporter at the *Waco Tribune Herald,* drove me to the bank and then to Reicher Catholic High School where I plunked down a year's worth of tuition in cash, just under five hundred dollars, and asked the good sister who was the principal to take me in as a student.

"Are you a good Catholic?" she asked.

"Yes, sister, I am," I said. "I serve Mass Sundays at my church and at the VA Hospital chapel. I accompany my mother to rosary every week. I go to confession and communion regularly. And you won't have to worry about me with any of the white girls here at Reicher."

I got her to laugh.

"I don't think that will be an issue here," she said. "We just expect you to respect *all* our young women."

And I kept my word. I was too busy to get into trouble. I knew the football coach, John Vasek, and he wanted me to play football. But I showed him my left hand, which had a bone bulging out of the side that I always managed to hide. He knew immediately that it had been a fracture that the other school's doctors failed to diagnose and hadn't healed correctly. He sent me to his doctor who concluded it would have to be surgically corrected. I couldn't bother with that just then and put it on the back burner of things I needed to do. I was still working at the *Waco Citizen* each day after school and continued hanging around the *Lariat.* By this time, it had become apparent that going to Harvard was out of the picture. My grades were still great, and I thought I could get accepted. But for several months I had been come to the realization that I had a big choice to make: Harvard or Patricia. I couldn't be in Cambridge, Massachusetts, and expect to have a chance with her while separated by half of America. That senior year, I visited friends in Austin several times and tried to track her down at the University of Texas, secretly carrying the engagement ring to propose the moment I found her. On the first visit I was overwhelmed. The university had forty thousand students, almost ten times the size of Baylor. The phone directory was useless, as was the university's admissions office. Secretaries sent me from one office to another. A friend at the *Daily Texan*, the university newspaper, tried to track her down and wondered if she was, in fact, enrolled there. Back in Waco, I checked back with my friend who had known her at Waco High. He was as sure as he could be of anything, he said, that she was at Texas.

What about my friend Dick McCall? I thought about calling him, but I felt guilty that I hadn't talked to him in such a long time and that it had been me, for the most part, that had put our friendship aside. When I decided not to attend Waco High, I also had felt that I betrayed that friendship. He had his circle of friends there, and I had my own at University. I also knew that my social life had its limitations. I rarely dated. I wasn't a member of RAs, the Royal Ambassadors young Masons-to-be group to which he belonged; and, as a Catholic and being Mexican, I never could be. I also didn't think I could fit in with his friends, likely to be those "snotty" guys from North Waco he once had told me about. So I let our friendship gather dust.

Meanwhile, I felt increasingly isolated. I didn't know anyone at Reicher, and almost everyone in my senior class of thirty-eight students had been together since grade school. I was the odd-man out literally. My classmates were friendly, but they didn't know me. Worse, a rumor began spreading at Reicher that the reason I had transferred there was because I had gotten a girl pregnant at University High. I went out with one girl at Reicher who told me that was the reason she could no longer see me.

"I'm the only one brave enough to go out with you," a senior named Judy Mayr said one day. "And that's because, like you, I'm also new at Reicher. We're like the two of the *Outcasts of Poker Flatts*."

If these kinds of stories were being rumored about me at Reicher, I could just imagine the gossip running rampant at University. I didn't know who was still talking to me and whom I should call. Fortunately, my friend and neighbor Michal Ann Horst sensed I desperately needed someone to talk to. She checked in on me regularly and championed my reputation among my old friends at University. She telephoned Judy Mayr's mother and assured her that the stories circulating about me among Reicher students and their parents weren't true. Michal Ann's assurance was good enough for Mrs. Herbert Mayr, who personally visited with the administrators at Reicher who were all nuns and threatened legal action if something wasn't done to discourage all the gossip mongering. Soon the rumors began to die down. On my birthday that December, Mrs. Mayr begged off on having dinner with Judy and me and encouraged us to spend that Saturday night alone. Judy, in turn, said she wanted to visit my parents to get a recipe from my mother. We drove to my home and there I got the biggest shock of my life to that point. The first face I saw as I opened our front door was Michal Ann, who yelled "Surprise!" together with classmates from Reicher and University.

As my senior year moved along, I became increasingly involved in theater and drama. I played Scrooge, the central role in the school Christmas program, and performed scenes from Paddy Chayevsky's *Gideon* and a series of *Hamlet* soliloquies in several interscholastic league competitions. In the spring, I played on our tennis team that went all the way to the state tournament. My only social life involved occasionally dating Judy who had just moved to Waco from Alaska and who made it clear she was looking for a nice Catholic boy to marry, the sooner the better.

A popular sophomore brunette, Cathie Flahive, became my best friend at Reicher. She was a free spirit who liked that sometimes I wore to school the Edwardian suit I had bought for the Beatles press conference. I would wear that suit when I had a reporting assignment for the *Citizen* weekly newspaper, and Cathie would usually come up to me in the hall and make sure the Windsor knot on my tie was straight. Cathie herself was a young *fashionista* who seemed to enjoy the English style and fashion of the day. She had jet-black hair cut into a short, layered bob hairstyle, and she wore black eyeliner that made her look like a pretty bohemian eccentric you might see photographed in a magazine with Andy Warhol. I was fortunate to have friendships with the Baylor students who worked on the *Lariat*, and occasionally they would give me tickets to performances at the Baylor Theatre and to Waco Hall, a concert auditorium on campus – to performances of *Antigone*, to Handel's *Messiah*, to Ferrante & Teicher, to The Lettermen. Cathie became my regular date to those Baylor events, and I felt as if I were already a student at the university. We saw Herman's Hermits when that popular pop group came to Waco, and she went with me to interview them back stage. How that ever even happened would amaze me for years.

In the spring of 1965, I was part of the Reicher tennis team that travelled with the school's track team to Dallas for the state tennis championships and track meet. They were held the same weekend that Herman's Hermits were appearing. The finals of our state tennis tournament were Saturday morning, and I anticipated being home no later than late afternoon, giving me enough time to make it to the evening concert with Cathie. However, I had not anticipated that our coach would be called back home because of an emergency, leaving those of us on the tennis team to come back with the track team on their school bus. When I realized around mid-afternoon that the track meet was nowhere near its end, I started trying to find a way to get from Irving, a suburb, into downtown Dallas, thinking I could take a Greyhound bus back to Waco. It seemed impossible until I called Uncle Jesse and happened to catch him at his office. Once I explained my situation, he hurried to Irving, but we never made it to the bus station. Instead he drove us to his home where he got out of the new Cadillac El Dorado he had recently bought and handed me the keys.

"Why don't you take the bus home tomorrow after you bring back the car?" he said.

He saw that I couldn't believe what he was saying.

"Look, I trust you," he said. "Drive home safely and have a good time at that concert, and drive back here tomorrow."

My parents couldn't believe Jesse had given me his car to drive back to Waco and use for a date. I don't think they would have trusted me that much. Cathie and I had a magnificent time, just as we did again when I used Jesse's El Dorado to escort her to my senior prom.

Cathie also celebrated with me the night after I won a journalism scholarship at Baylor. I had known the journalism department people at Baylor liked me and liked my work. Every spring the university held Baylor Journalism Day where it hosted high school journalism students from throughout the region. The event included seminars, workshops, and contests in which schools submitted the best work in their student newspapers. The students were involved in running the day under a group called the Central Texas High School Press Association, which during my junior year had elected me its president to serve in my senior year. The highlight of Baylor Journalism Day, though, was the awarding of a journalism scholarship. I had applied, but I wasn't sure how much the flap at University would affect my chances. I knew that Mrs. Orr had written two letters highly critical of me over what had happened at University High to the two organizations that could most seriously impact my immediate career: To Baylor, where she believed I would seek admittance; and to the *Waco Tribune-Herald*, where she knew I had hoped to work during the summers and on weekends. There was nothing I could do except hope that, in Lincoln's words, "the better angels of our nature" would lead people to see things differently.

I counted my blessings that through the grace of God the people at Baylor and at the *Waco Tribune-Herald* had seen more in me than the teacher I had angered. In mid-May I was awarded a scholarship to Baylor, and the following Monday I had more good fortune. While in the middle of religion class one morning at Reicher, I was called to the office of our principal, Sister Walter Marie, who said I had an important telephone call. I panicked briefly, thinking something had happened to one of my parents. But I saw that she had a knowing smile on her face and figured it wasn't bad news. She said that Dave Campbell, the sports editor of the *Waco Tribune-Herald* was on the telephone.

"I think he wants to interview you," she said.

"Sister, there must be some mistake," I said. "The scholarship I won wasn't an athletic scholarship."

I figured this had to be someone playing a practical joke. It was probably one of my friends from University High calling to invite me to a party, or to remind me of a crazy dream I had once expressed when we were kids: That when I graduated from high school, I wanted to play shortstop, which had been Mantle's original position, for the New York Yankees. I decided to play along with the joke.

"Hello, Mr. Campbell," I said to the caller, "I just wanted to let you know that I've decided not to sign that bonus baby contract. I won't be playing shortstop for the Yankees."

The caller didn't say anything until I heard a deep, serious voice.

"I'm sorry, this is Dave Campbell, sports editor of the..."

I almost dropped the phone. It turned out that Campbell was calling to offer me a highly coveted position as a full-time writer on his staff. I would be covering high school sports at a starting salary of $80 a week. It was a job graduating college journalism seniors would kill for, and I was getting it coming right out of high school. Admittedly, it was a low-ball offer, but I didn't care. I had some money in the bank. The catch was that I had to start immediately.

But I was still concerned about the letters from my former high school journalism teacher coming back to haunt me. Dave Campbell didn't know anything about it, so I decided I needed to speak to Harry Provence, the respected longtime editor of the *Tribune-Herald*. It turned out to be not only an informative meeting but also one that I was glad I had arranged. Provence confirmed that his managing editor had received such a letter but that Mrs. Orr's complaint about me had been dismissed as a disgruntled teacher's sour grapes in light of recommendations from other people. I assumed he meant possibly Tommy West, David McHam, or someone from Baylor.

"Abner McCall and Bob Poage speak highly of you," Provence said. I wanted to fall out of my chair. I couldn't recall ever having met McCall, though possibly I had when I was in junior high and his son Dick and I were best friends. Or perhaps Dick had spoken so positively about me at home that his father had developed some fond memory. Poage was the local congressman I knew from an interview for an appointment to one of the service academies that I had turned down.

"Abner says his son once told him you could be governor or U.S. senator one day," he said.

"Dick and I are friends," I said. "I think *he* could be president one day."

"Speaking of presidents, I want you to have this." Provence reached into a shipping box behind his desk and pulled out a book that he then inscribed to me on the title page. It was a new biography of Lyndon Johnson he had written. I had read something about the book in news magazine, but I had no idea he was the author.

"And Bob said he all but nominated you for West Point, but you begged off, something about becoming a Jesuit priest," Provence said. "Is that true?"

"I didn't want to make the military my career," I said. "As for becoming a Jesuit priest, I think that's a story that's been floating around, but I don't think I ever said that to him. I transferred from University to Reicher, and maybe someone on his staff thought I wanted to be like St. Augustine, but he wasn't a Jesuit, was he?"

"Bob also said you'd studied Greek and Latin?"

"Yes sir."

"That's unusual today," Provence said. "But that speaks well for your parents, and Bob says you come from a very good family."

"I like to think we're the Tyrones," I said.

Provence didn't now what I meant.

"The Tyrones from *Long Day's Journey Into Night*," I said.

The reference caught Provence off-guard, and he began coughing and stood up to get a tissue from a nearby table. He was wearing golf attire, including the new small rubber spikes that allowed you wear golf shoes almost anywhere, so I asked him how he played.

"I have a ten handicap," he said.

I gave him a skeptical look. I had no idea what his handicap was, but I knew golfers usually fibbed about it.

"Okay, fifteen," he said. "Do you play?"

"I'm lucky to break ninety," I said.

That little exchange led to Provence inviting me to dinner at his home and later to some rounds of golf at the Ridgewood Country Club. Provence was a smart man, and I got a sense that he was trying to reach out to a new generation of the age that was presently creating waves at some of the country's university campuses. But I also was aware of my uniqueness in his company. At his country club, I was the only Hispanic to play golf or eat at the clubhouse on any given day and possibly ever. At his newspaper, I would become the first and only Hispanic on the editorial staff. This was Waco, after all, representative of Texas at a time of history that would soon change. I would get to know a lot of editors and publishers in the coming years, but they would pale in comparison to Provence. Perhaps it was my romantic notion of my first job, and an important man in town making me feel extremely comfortable and a part of things when he didn't have to. The perks didn't hurt either. Every so often I would get a note from Provence reminding me I could play at Ridgewood any time I wanted to and to not worry about the green fees or the restaurant charges.

Little did I realize until later that I was giving Provence a better understanding of an unknown part of his community at a time when he was part of the process orchestrating a dramatic sociological and cultural change that was taking place in the city. Provence, who had been at the *Waco Tribune Herald* since graduating from Baylor in the 1930s, was a leading member of a group known as the Committee of Fifty. They called themselves "senior civic leaders" and they included the president of Baylor, the heads of the major department stores and auto dealerships, presidents of banks, and top law firm partners among others. In the mid-1960s, about the time I met Provence and was playing golf with him, this Committee of Fifty was meeting regularly with the president of Paul Quinn College, the all-black school in East Waco, over the integration of restaurants, hotels, movie theaters, and other public facilities as directed by the Civil Rights Acts of 1964. Black leaders in the city, including the NAACP, had complained to the Paul Quinn College official about "the lack of progress being made in integrating Waco, Waco being (according to them) the largest city in Texas not having been integrated," according to a document prepared thirty years later by a leader of the Committee of Fifty. That document detailed how the Committee of Fifty planned for and arranged what were virtually rehearsed events with merchants and black customers in which restaurants and other facilities in the city were slowly and quietly integrated in those years. There was little public outcry in a city with a long history of racial antagonism and segregation because people never read about them in the Waco paper. The reason: Harry Provence, who went against every newsman's inclination by making sure all those historic events of black diners breaking the local color barriers were effectively covered up. In a 1996 paper for the Waco History Project housed at Baylor, former City Councilman Joe L. Ward Jr., a member of the Committee of Fifty, wrote:

"We were very fortunate in having the complete cooperation of the Waco News Tribune in not reporting anything in connection with this, although a great deal of "news" could have been created by so doing. Unfortunately, this would not have been the case under the present ownership of the paper. One incident occurred that could have completely blown the whole project and created a great deal of turmoil by a "crusading" reporter working for an editor with no regard for the consequences as to how a news story was treated. Word having gotten around among the blacks as to what was taking place, a group of Paul Quinn students took issue with something involving the Williams Drug Store across Elm Street from the campus in East Waco and created a potentially dangerous incident. That sort of thing is to a great extent done for and thrives on publicity, but the paper completely ignored it. As soon as we heard about it while it was taking place, the Council was notified and, also realizing the possible danger to our program, they managed to calm the troubled waters and things returned to normal."

Provence, I believe, meant well. He was surprisingly candid with me. During one conversation, he raised the topic of Hispanics in Waco and conceded that, sadly, he did not know any except a few in service and maintenance jobs.

"You are my window into your world," he said.

"I'd hate to disappoint you, Mr. Provence," I said. "But I don't think I'm very representative of Mexican Americans, in Waco or any place else. My parents and most Mexican Americans haven't been blessed with some of the opportunities that I've been given. The fact I'm here having lunch with you at a country club where there are no Hispanic members is a testament to that. Do I think that's changing? Yes. Do I think it's changing fast enough? No. Can I do anything to help bring about a better understanding – can I help change the world as it is here? Yes. But so can you. If the history of mankind shows us anything, it's that change can come as a violent upheaval of the status quo, which I don't think any of us wants to see happen. Or it can come from two sides agreeing that the way their world exists right then doesn't work the way it should fairly for both sides and then to agree on the changes that need to take place. I hope that's what happens not in my lifetime but in our lifetime."

I'm not sure if that conversation did any good. I'm not even sure how much power Provence had on his own to be able to dictate any changes in his city. I don't know if any single leader ever has that kind of influence. But I hoped that it gave him a better understanding toward making those decisions in the future.

As for me, over time I unexpectedly came to know more about my family through Provence. His knowledge of my family appeared to be through Bob Poage and Abner McCall, who really never knew my folks that I know of, at least. But there was another source who did know my family well: My family doctor, R. J. Franklin. I suppose I should not have been surprised. Despite its size, with a population of about 100,000 in the 1960s, Waco had the feel and sense of a small town. Everyone didn't know each other necessarily, but enough people did.

"Did you know your father had been in OSS during the war?" Provence asked me one afternoon while we were playing at Ridgewood.

"OSS? My father?" I shook my head. I had always had a strong interest in my father's war. How could I not with my mother so often pulling out that photograph of him with a nun in a European hospital? So I knew of the Office of Strategic Services, the wartime intelligence agency that had been the predecessor of the CIA. But my father had never said anything about being a spy or working for OSS, and I told Provence I could not believe he wouldn't have told me.

"Why would he? I wouldn't have told my children," Provence said.

"Yes, but my dad had something like an eighth grade education," I said. "I've seen his military record. There's nothing in it that says OSS or anything like it."

Provence gave me a long look. "I'm surprised," he said. "You're smarter than that."

"Look, my dad was in infantry," I said. "He got shot up pretty bad at Bastogne, and he was in a hospital recuperating for a long time."

"A pretty long recovery from what I understand," Provence said. "Doesn't that make you wonder what he might have really been doing? He could have easily convalesced back here closer to home."

After the round of golf, Provence gave me a lesson on World War II that I had never read about in my high school or college history books. Owing Germany hundreds of millions of dollars for assistance during the Spanish Civil War, the Francisco Franco government had supported the Nazis and Axis Powers, though it was disputed just how much. At the same time, Spain had a heavy reliance on U.S. oil supplies, which was something the Americans sought to leverage in dealings with Franco. Intelligence, both military and diplomatic, became even more valuable as the war wound down and the U.S and other Allied nations prepared for post-war isolation and trade embargoes of Spain and others who had aided Germany.

"I don't think we'll ever know the true role of many of these countries," Provence said. "But at the time there was a worried flurry of activity trying to figure out what theses hundreds of thousands of cables going back and forth between Spain and the Nazis meant. They were in Spanish and German, and I imagine our people were using anyone they thought could help with translating those languages in a wartime environment. And you yourself said your father knew Spanish better than he knew English. Could he read and write Spanish?"

I had to chew on that a while. My father was extremely literate in Spanish. He might not be able to put the accents marks in all the right places, but I couldn't either and I'd taken several years of Spanish in high school.

"I see what you're saying," I said. "But where did you hear of his OSS involvement?"

I assumed it was from Poage, whose Congressional connections certainly should have qualified to know. And it may well have been that Provence had learned some of this from Poage, but that's where my good family doctor came in.

"One day you should have a long talk with Bob Franklin, your family doctor," Provence said. "It may interest you to know that he didn't become your doctor by accident. He knew your father at the hospital in Europe where your father was convalescing. Coincidentally, I understand it was a hospital where the OSS was working out of as it was ferreting out and deciphering all the mumbo jumbo that it was intercepting between Spain and Germany. Covertly, of course. Has your father ever told you specifically where or what hospital he convalesced?"

"I don't recall, but I don't think so," I said.

"I'm not surprised," he said. "And I don't think you'll get the name or exact location from either him or Bob Franklin."

Harry Provence would turn out to be one of the most influential men in my life. We would have many more rounds of golf, lunches, and talks. Later, he would check on me from time to time, always offering advice and letters of recommendation. Needless to say, when I graduated from Reicher, I had a great friend, a good job, especially for an eighteen-year-old, a college scholarship, several thousand dollars stashed away, and a heart-shaped diamond engagement ring in the bank. But I had no wheels. I thought about the 1957 T-Bird that a friend of my Uncle Jesse said he would sell him at any time. But I had my eyes on something else. So my high school graduation gift to myself was a new Mustang convertible in a hazel color to match Patricia's eyes.

Life, however, throws all kinds of unexpected curves. In the coming months, my mother became ill and it was only after long weeks of testing that it was determined her condition wasn't terminal. A new friend of mine at Baylor was killed in a freak sand buggy accident, and his single mom asked that I go to Padre Island to help plan a memorial. I was also smoothing matters over at home. My younger sister was now at University High School, and she was receiving a backlash from administrators for my memorable sendoff to the principal. But she could handle herself. As a sophomore she became a member of the high school pep squad, and the teachers and students accepted her as her own person, independent of her trouble-making older brother.

And where was Patricia? Maybe it wasn't the University of Texas but Texas Woman's University in Denton where Patricia had enrolled, my friend from Waco High was now telling me. Two other people who knew her said the same thing, and one friend thought she had seen Patricia in the Baylor Student Union. I thought of possibly calling Patricia's younger brother Michael. I had known him slightly at South Junior. He was a grade behind me, and we knew each other when our basketball teams scrimmaged against each other. A couple of times I asked him about his sister and how she was doing in high school. But I'd only gotten one-word answers. Good. Fine. You know how little brothers can be about their older sisters at that age. But I also knew how protective little brothers can be about their sisters as they get older. I hadn't spoken to Michael in years, and I thought this might not be the time to start. It may seem like an easy thing to have just called Patricia's parents. But I didn't know them, and I didn't know how they would react to an old classmate of their daughter calling out of the blue for information about her.

"Just lie and say you're someone else," one of my friends said.

"No, I'm not going to lie," I said. "That's how bad foundations are laid. I mean, she's only a sophomore now. What's she going to do? Get married this young?"

So my freshman year moved on with me working as a sportswriter, taking occasional assignments from the *Lariat*, and continuing to make money with Uncle Jesse. I would call him with leads of Waco houses in dire need of new siding, and his salesmen were closing those deals.

I was living the American Dream. Then in mid-April, my life's dream shattered.

I shared a class at Baylor with a night-shift phone operator at the *Tribune-Herald* who I recently learned had been in Patricia's Waco High graduating class. He said he knew who she was, but that a friend of his had known her quite well. By then, I had determined she wasn't at Texas Woman's University and wondered if he could ask his friend if she knew where Patricia was. The next day, as I was walking upstairs past the phone alcove, the switchboard operator called me over.

"Hey I've got news about Patricia," he said. "My friend said someone told her she just got married in Dallas a few weeks ago."

Married? Married! Patricia? She had just turned twenty. This couldn't be possible, could it? I became visibly nervous and tried to keep from shaking. My head felt like it was going to explode, and I started to get sick. I walked into the newsroom and, feeling nauseous, walked over to Tommy West.

"Tony, you look like you've just seen a ghost," he said.

"Tommy, help me," I said, almost pleading. "How would I check on whether someone got married?"

"The county clerk," he said. "A license would be registered. Call the county clerk."

"But if the marriage took place in Dallas?"

"Then call the county clerk in Dallas County. They'll have it, if a license was issued."

Minutes later Tommy saw that I was having trouble dialing the phone.

"Hey, you don't look right," he said. "What's going on?"

In measured breaths and stuttering, I told him of what had frightened me and brought on a panic attack. I half expected Tommy to laugh, but instead there was genuine concern on his face. Tommy had been among the first people at Baylor to recognize that I might have talent as a journalist, and he had always been there to offer support and advice.

"Do you want me to check on it for you?" Tommy asked.

I nodded and slumped in a chair. When Tommy got off the phone, his long serious face told me the news he dreaded giving me. Dallas County confirmed that a Patricia Lynn O'Neal, born April 3, 1946, which was Patricia's birthday, had married April 2, 1966, exactly two weeks earlier.

As the newsroom began to spin, I saw people looking at me. They were talking about calling a doctor, but Tommy convinced everyone that I just had a touch of the flu. He led me to the bathroom and kept everyone else away. I don't remember how long I was in there before Tommy came to help me to my car. He was going to drive me home, but I convinced him that I had just needed fresh air. For a few minutes, I actually felt better with the spring breeze hitting my face. I started the car and began driving home with plans to crash in my bed for the rest of my life. But at The Circle, a Waco landmark adjoining two highways, I decided that home was the last place I now wanted to be. The interstate heading to Austin was nearby, and I got on it. I didn't know where I was going, so I just drove. I drove in shock and silence for hours, past Austin and through San Antonio.

Had I ever really known where I was heading, I wondered. I was numb emotionally and mentally. My thoughts lumbered like a movie of my life snagged in a projector and the words dragging out, sounding slurred and drunken. Whhhhyyyy haaaaaddddn't ahhhhhh moooooved ahhhhnn Pahhhtreeeesia maaaahhcch maaaahhcch soooooooner?

135

Over-thinking. I had over intellectualized the situation. I was always doing this. The "white girls" speeches had done more than warn to the dangers ahead. They had paralyzed me. They had frightened me beyond the impact I thought they had had. And then I had read too much and lived in all those books. Had I memorized Hamlet's soliloquies and acted them on stage without realizing, not even once, that his failure and his inability to act in avenging his father had mirrored my own paralysis of passion in pursuing Patricia? I was so afraid that I had feared to risk. Why hadn't I ventured? Why hadn't I gambled that she herself might have accepted or rejected me? Why hadn't I given her a chance to take this leap along with me?

Some time that night I found myself in Laredo. I ended up in a cantina in some back street that made you wonder which side of the border you were on. If there was such a thing as a Mexican cowboy bar, I thought, this had to be it. A couple of sets of longhorns on the walls. Pictures of armadillos. Silver spurs in a glass box. Stetsons all around, along with jeans and work shirts. All the men wore boots and years of windblown summer sunburns on their faces.

I wanted to drink myself to oblivion as quickly as possible, which I figured should not take long. I was not a drinker. I had two beers the night before registration at Baylor. I was also underage, though Tommy West would occasionally invite me to have a beer with him in his car after work. At that time, the *Tribune-Herald* city side staff also included Thomas Harris, who would go on to write a series of suspense novels including *Red Dragon* and *Silence of the Lambs*. Even then, Harris had a knack for crime stories of the bizarre that he would regale us with after hours at a local bar to which I'd be invited. But at most, I would have two beers.

Here in Laredo, I ordered tequila and went through four setups when it hit me that I felt as sober as ever. But the fifth tequila, yes, the fifth tequila gave me a warm glow. I was getting certifiably drunk. I ordered another tequila and a beer. Even in my drunken stupor, I could see that the only men who didn't seem to fit in here were myself and two guys with flattops who looked like they might be jocks from the

University of fucking Texas. Within a couple of hours, the three of us were downing tequilas and beer at a table that soon grew covered with salt and leftover lime juice. They were from Texas A&M. Big frigging difference from where I stood. They were in the corps and away from campus for the long weekend. They only person I knew foolish enough to go to Aggie land to study was my friend Doug Calmelet, who had been smart enough to get out of the corps within weeks of getting in.

"We came to get laid," the first Aggie boasted. "You wanna join us?

"You a virgin or what," the second Aggie demanded when I was slow to speak up.

"I just got way-laid, that's all," I said. "But I'll go along."

Along the ride, one of the Aggies pulled out a joint and lit it.

"Colombian Gold, man," he said, offering me a toke. There was a first time for everything.

We drove in my Mustang to a whorehouse a guy at the bar gave us directions to. It looked like another bar, only with mariachis in a corner stage and girls lining a wall, cigarettes dangling from their mouths and blowing smoke our way. They wore slinky dresses, a lot of makeup, and perfumes so cheap and bold that they smelled like they had just walked away from a five-and-dime cologne counter. Some also wore gold jewelry in their teeth that made them appear even more menacing and intimidating to someone who had never been with a woman in this way. A few reached out to us as we walked past them to the bar, and they uttered broken English offers of what they could do to satisfy us sexually.

After a few minutes, the two Aggies picked out women and left me with the fifth of Cuervo. I drifted to a small table to finish it off, but a posse of women quickly joined me. They were as old as my aunts and did as much for me sexually as any of my middle age *tias*. The only woman I found even remotely attractive looked to be no more than a teenager with a frown standing against a wall. She ignored me for a while. But business was slow, and she moved my way when she saw that I was staring.

"Would you like to go with me?" she wanted to know.

"Could you sit and talk for a while?" I felt alone and just wanted any kind of conversation.

"We can talk back there." She motioned the darkened hallway where the Aggies had disappeared.

I nodded that I was interested.

"It's twenty dollars," she said

"How about forty if we can just talk."

"Sure. It's your money."

More than small talk, I needed to just rest my head.

"This isn't what I usually do," she said as she took my hand.

"It's not what any of us do."

"No, I'm serious. I'm a student."

"Well," I said, "don't look to me to be the teacher."

Her name, she said, was Lourdes. She didn't appreciate my attempt at humor when I asked if I should pray. She was a junior college student hoping to transfer to Texas A&I University. But she had run out of money, and she had to get out of the house where she was living.

"I'm thinking of leaving Laredo," she said.

Then she got angry and thought I was being patronizing when I complimented her on her perfect English. "You speak in complete sentences," I said. Complete sentences? What an imbecile!

"Look, just because you're going to fuck me doesn't mean you can judge me," she snapped.

"Please, don't be offended," I said. "And I'm not going to fuck you."

"Are you queer?"

"No, I'm not queer. I'm just going to be very sick."

The tequila came up from my gut, and I puked into a large pot with a mop in it that guarded the hallway.

Then the hallucinating began.

Bright lights flooded the hallway, and ahead I could hear a woman moaning in pain. I looked over at Lourdes, but she wasn't there. She had been transformed into an angel with large feathery wings.

I felt like I was trying to make my way through cobwebs that had engulfed my mind, and I could hear the woman moan even louder. Her crying erupted into wails as we walked closer to her room where a white partition, the kind separating hospital beds, guarded the door. Inside several nuns in all white robes and habits hovered around a pallet, caring for the woman. A nun saw us.

"She's been in labor for two weeks," she said.

On the bed, I could make out a woman laying on her back with her long, white creamy legs propped up in the position for childbirth. The nun motioned for me to come closer. The woman moaned again. Was I the father, I asked. The nun smiled but didn't answer. Her head turned to the woman on the bed, and my eyes followed. The woman's young face was pale from exhaustion, and her blonde hair wet from perspiration, but I immediately recognized the hazel eyes.

"Why is she here?" I demanded of the angel. "Why is she here giving birth? She's not supposed to be here."

A nun changed the compresses on Patricia's forehead. Another nun with a stethoscope checked her swollen abdomen and shivered.

"Maybe we can save the baby," she said.

"Is she dying?" I screamed. "She can't be dying. She's twenty years old. Can't somebody help her? Goddammit, somebody tell me!"

I made a sign of the cross and fell to my knees. "Please, please, God," I begged. "Not her. Please, not her. Take me. Take me, and let her live."

At that moment the nuns heightened their feverish activity around her, and I heard one last, horrifying wail that silenced the room before the hush was broken by a baby's cry. Two nuns carried the baby to a nearby table while two other nuns ministered to Patricia. One of them pulled a sheet over her face.

"No!" I tried to go near her, but the angel's grip froze me.

"Why? Why did she have to die?" I pleaded with the angel. "Why did she have to die?"

The angel touched my forehead and helped me to my feet. "She had to die," she said.

"No, no she didn't! She's young. She's full of life."

"She had to die," she said, "to give life to you."

Those words were still ringing in my mind when I awoke to find myself sitting with Lourdes in the Mustang. She offered me a Coca Cola to sip. It was the next day. The midday sun was ablaze, and I was wet with sweat. I had only partial vision in my left eye. My left eyelid was swollen, and I felt a Band-Aid on the eyebrow.

"You hit your head when you fell," she said. "It's just a bruise and a small cut, but you'll have a shiner."

"How did we get here?"

"Your keys. They were for a Mustang, and this was parked out front."

"Why didn't you just steal it?" I asked rudely.

"Fuck you," she said. "I'm a whore, so you think I'm a thief, too?"

"I didn't call you a whore." She was crying, and I could see that I had hurt her. "Look, I'm sorry," I said. "I'm pretty much wasted. I don't know what I'm saying or what I'm doing. I didn't mean to treat you badly. Thank you for helping me out. I know I've got a great way of showing my appreciation."

Then big tears started welling in my eyes, and I broke down crying. She tried to comfort me and held me for the longest time. Lourdes didn't seem like someone who would be working where I met her. Maybe if my head hadn't been hurting so much I might have asked why. Instead she was the inquisitive one.

"So, who's Patricia?" she asked.

I was tongue-tied that she would know the name.

"You kept saying her name when you were out," she said. "Is she why you're down here?"

I didn't answer, and the moment grew awkward.

"Look, guy, I hope you find what you're looking for," she said. She got out of the car and walked away, disappearing into a side street. She had left the forty dollars on the passenger's seat. I wanted to go after her and insist she take it, but I didn't. There would be a scene, I knew, and she didn't need me complicating her life.

I tried sitting up straight, but my head wouldn't stop throbbing. Part of me wished my head would just explode and leave me in peace. It didn't, and I found myself driving around Laredo without knowing where I was. I thought about crossing the border into Nuevo Laredo and continuing into Mexico. For being the Mexican in so many other people's eyes, I had never so much as set foot in that country. For me, Mexico was only a place on the map, a place my grandfather used to tell me about when I was little.

He used to tell me there were two Mexicos. There was the Mexico that he dreamed about, isolated as he was in America from his homeland. Then there was the Mexico about which he had nightmares. Mexico was like the gifted child who had foolishly squandered all his talent, he said.

"Mexico," my grandfather used to say, "will always break your heart."

But then, my grandfather, like most Mexicans, was a romantic. Besides being a miner, he had been a revolutionary, and he had fought with Pancho Villa. One of his prized possessions was a faded sepia photograph of himself with Villa. At least, he claimed it was himself when he was young standing with Villa, each with bandoleers crossing their chests. When my grandfather died, his sons and daughters wound up in a royal row over that photograph and a Bible on which he said Villa had sworn to fight until the revolution had been won.

I remember once asking my grandfather why, if he dreamed about his homeland so much, he had never once bothered to return to Mexico or even set foot back there.

"Because," he told me, "the revolution isn't over."

It wasn't my revolution, however, and it wasn't my country. My country was the most magnificent land in the world, God's chosen kingdom on earth in which we were taught from our childhood to defend the defenseless, protect women and children, welcome the poor, help the sick, champion right, condemn wrong, love your neighbor as yourself, and earn your rewards through merit, talent, and good works.

But right now, all that seemed illusory, images sold to romantics.

Near the main border crossing, I veered on to a side road that ran west along the Rio Grande. This hardly seemed the place where one world ended and another began. I expected something more dramatic, an ocean or the Berlin Wall instead of a riverbank of sagebrush, broken bottles and shattered dreams. I could see pieces of the river and walked toward it. I wanted to scream. I wanted to be a brooder no longer. Brooders never win. Couldn't I be a man of action for a change? At last, I came to a clearing with an unobstructed view of the choppy waters rushing eastward.

"April is the cruelest month!" I yelled at the top of my lungs as I plowed through the soft ground. "Breeding lilacs out of the dead land, mixing memory and desire."

Oh, God, couldn't I at least be original in ending all this. And I didn't mean it anyway. April wasn't the cruelest month. Patricia had been born in April.

I trudged forward.

"I have not loved the world, nor the world me," I shouted as I came to the river's edge, ripping off Byron. "So let us part fair foes."

I was done. I stood, uneasily, on the southernmost edge of America, my America, looking southward to the land where I was supposed to belong, the land of my kind. A teenage couple made their way past, meandering through stretches of hardened mud where the river had run dry. I couldn't tell if they were coming or going. They stared at me suspiciously even as I offered the bottle of Cuervo that they didn't want.

So I had come to the Rio Grande, symbolic of the border of my existence and the two sides of who I was. And right now I wanted to be neither. This is where you came to when you were me, after the sun, the Colombian Gold, the Cuervo Tequila, and thoughts of the golden blondes kept you up until five in the morning, with thoughts surfing on the suicidal and you'd indulged in enough black coffee to need something to reduce agitation. Then you came here to drown your sorrows.

I splashed down into the Rio Grande, looking for the deepest part and finding only large calf-deep puddles. It would have to do. I sat down and, as I sank, I took one final look at both sides. I belonged on neither, so I belonged nowhere.

One last thought of Patricia flickered through my mind.

Then I took another hard swig of the Cuervo, dropped my head backward into the river and surrendered to the tears and the water that quickly obliterated my face.

*My maternal grandmother and grandfather, Concepción
and Francisco Segovia, Rosebud, Texas, 1920*

*My fraternal grandfather and grandmother, Jose Angel
and Catarina Guevara Castro, Houston, 1917*

*My father and mother, Antonio and Maria Emma
Castro, Waco, Texas, May 9, 1944*

*My father and mother, Antonio and Maria
Emma Castro, Waco, Texas, 1944*

*My father and mother, Antonio and Maria
Emma Castro, Waco, Texas, 1945*

*My dad suited up to play
for his Civil Conservation
Camp baseball team, 1937*

*The Castro clan -- Front: Isaac Martinez, Frank Castro; back:
Connie Castro, Angel Castro, Josephine Castro, patriarch Jose
Angel Castro, Doña Isidra Martinez Castro, Lupe Castro,
Pauline Castro, Manuela Martinez, circa 1944*

My uncle, Jesse Segovia, Waco, Texas, 1948

My great aunt and curandera Doña Juana, circa 1970

Tony Castro

*Don Juan de Miralles Trailhon, identified by my grandmother
Concepción Rivera de Segovia Veracruz as a distant Spanish uncle
who was King Carlos III's envoy to General George Washington and
the interim colonial government during the American Revolution*

My parents with me at my baptismal, Waco, Texas, 1946

My uncle, Francisco Segovia, with me, Waco, Texas, 1947

Me at six months, 1947

Me in a rare heavy snowfall
in Waco, 1949

*My mom and me on Austin
Avenue in Waco, 1950*

*My dad and me at home
in Waco, 1950*

My second grade class photo at Gurley Elementary, Waco, 1954, when they were about to put me into Special Education, fearing I was mentally slow. The problem was I couldn't speak or read English and was only saved from Special Ed because of the intervention of two classmates in the photo: Ronnie Barber, second row, fourth from the left; and Donna Oliver, front row in the polka dotted white dress next to the only kid in dress pants that my parents forced me to wear.

MAY 1958

My fifth grade class at Gurley Elementary School, Waco, Texas, 1958
Front row: Butch Davis, Ardie Meeker, James Roy Roberts, Dwayne Moss,
Donald Barrett; second row: Frank Simon, Tony Castro, Terry Woodard,
Randy Sullivan, Gene Liggett, Gary Edelman, Johnny Silva; Back Row:
Kay Roberts, Shirley Franks, Brenda McCurdy, Mary Alice Veracruz,
Judy Wammack, Name forgotten, Name forgotten, Rhoda Dellinger.

*My friend and boyhood crush
Patricia O'Neal, age 12, sixth
grader at Gurley Elementary
School, Waco, Texas, 1958*

Southern Little League All-Star team, 1959, Waco, Texas Front row: Joey Foster, George Caddell, Dana Harmon, Jimmy Spence, Mike Richards, Joe Tighe; Second Row: Earl Naylor, Jimmie Carpenter, Tom Henson, Paul Francis, Tony Castro, Wayne Blackshear, Roger Butler, Larry Henry, Donald Hale; Back row: Paul Francis Sr, manager, and Jack Hale, coach.

The South Junior High School Press Club Waco, Texas, 1959-1960
Front row: Linda McMahan, Patricia O'Neal, Bonnie Curry, Lidia
Montemayor; Middle row: Nancy Lord, Mary Dunwody, Duana
Gwynne, Jaquine Hudson; Back row: Mrs. McCulley, sponsor,
Charles Christian, James Lamb, Tony Castro, Charles Patterson.

The South Junior High School Press Club Waco, Texas, 1960-1961
Front Row (from left): Lidia Montemayor, Linda Jordan, Roylyn
Johnson, Ruby Bradbury, Sue Sides; middle row: Dick McCall, Randy
Stewart, Bonnie Curry, Patricia O'Neal, Linda Dunwody, Judy
Wammack; Back row: Leonard Kramer, Mrs. McCulley, Tony Castro

My South Junior High friend, cheerleader Barbara "Babs" McBride, 1959, (photo used with permission of Barbara McBride-Smith)

My South Junior High friends, star athlete Jerrell Marshall and Barbara "Babs" McBride, 1959, (photo used with permission of Barbara McBride-Smith)

My South Junior High friend, Barbara "Babs" McBride, 1960, with her fellow cheerleaders, from left, Charlene Henderson, Sharon Peebles, Sue Nix, Barbara McBride-Smith, Judy Taylor and Jeannie Lillard. (photo used with permission of Barbara McBride-Smith)

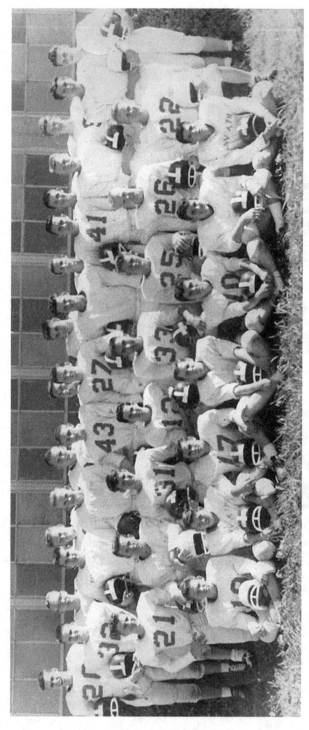

University High School JV football team, 1962. Team includes: Larry Grantham, John Robert Pharr, Tony Martin , Dana Harmon, Jimmy Messec, Tony Castro, Gray, Wayne Blackshear, Larry Henry, Jimmy Kroll, Russell Martin, Tommy Anderson, Donald Hale, Eddie Dennard, Roger Butler, Paul Francis, Joe Woodard.

*When I landed an interview
with 1963 Baylor All-America
quarterback Don Trull at his home
for my high school newspaper, my
friend Mary Lee Wright who was
a firebrand football fan insisted she
had to go along to meet him. Trull
and his wife entertained us until
near midnight when we had to leave
because of Mary Lee's curfew!*

*In 1964, as a 17-year-old high school senior working for the Waco
Tribune-Herald and the twice weekly Waco Citizen, I interviewed
President Lyndon Johnson's running mate while covering my first
presidential campaign. Here I'm walking out (skinny tie, white
shirt) of the LBJ local headquarters with Humphrey and a county
campaign official. (Photo with permission of Tommy Thompson)*

In May 1965, Baylor University awarded me the first Charles
Johnson Journalism Scholarship named after the founding chairman
of the school's Journalism Department. David Cheavens (right), then
chair of the Baylor Journalism Department, is shown here me and
Curtis Clogston, recipient of another scholarship to the university.

My freshman photo at Baylor
University, 1965-66

Baylor Journalism Professor David McHam has been a mentor and friend since my sophomore year in high school. I dedicated my first book, Chicano Power: The Emergence of Mexican America, *to him.*

When I met David McHam, I also met Tommy West, then the Baylor Lariat *editor and a* Waco Tribune Herald *reporter, who took me under his wing as a journalist and a friend while I was still in high school.*

The Baylor Lariat editors of the early 1960s who recognized my work, befriended and inspired me: From left: Bill Hartman, Ella Wall Prichard, Ray Hubener, Tommy West, and Ed DeLong.

The dust jacket author photo for Chicano Power: The Emergence of Mexican America *(E. P. Dutton, 1974), hailed by Publishers Weekly as "brilliant... a valuable contribution to the understanding of our time."*

PART THREE:
Camelot and Curanderas

My grandfather's last Christmas gifts to me came early sometime in mid-summer of the year when I was four. They were simple gifts. A stuffed lion and a bear, but they were expensive gifts for him to give for no apparent reason other than I was his grandson and that he loved me. It was neither Christmas nor my birthday. And he was a poor, broken down old miner with bum legs but a proud heart that shared a chest with a pair of polluted lungs, the miner's hazard. I had been in the hospital a long time that summer, and he stayed with me after the first bad night when I had been alone and frightened.

The nuns, with tall white habits that looked like sailboat spinnakers on a sea of black, came that night to feed me intravenously. I'd resisted

167

and I cried. They had finally used a wooden pallet to which they bound my legs and arms and then stuck me with those needles.

My grandfather came the next day, bringing me the two stuffed animals. One of them would have done. The lion. The old man had long told me stories about the lions. Something about them fascinated him, maybe their masculinity, their machismo. I was afraid of the nights and afraid of the needles I had to have each day, but he would be there telling me about the lions.

"Think of the lions, son," he would tell me. "Remember the lions. The lions in your dreams will protect you."

I would think about the lions and about my grandfather, and I was safe.

My grandfather was a fine old man, his walk a shuffle. He limped on bad legs braced in black ankle-high shoes that never laced to the top. He always dressed in pin-stripe navy pants, supported by suspenders, a starched white shirt, a vest, and a white gold pocket watch.

"*Este reloj cuenta la vida de nuestra familia*," he would tell his friends. "This watch tells our family's story."

Many years ago, when he was barely more than a boy himself, his father had given him the watch, he said, and he, in turn, one day would give that watch to me.

That day, unfortunately, would never be. One day, while we walked the streets of the small barrio near the Brazos River where the old man lived, a gang of *pachucos*, Mexican thugs, surrounded us. He tried beating them away with his cane, which they stole along with the pocket watch.

"They took your watch!" I cried as we watched the *pachucos* flee up the street. "They took your watch!"

"The watch is worthless to them," he said, checking to make sure that I was okay

"But it was your watch," I said. "Your grandfather's watch. You were going to give that watch to me."

"Sometimes," he said, "we can't have what is ours. You have to learn to be a man then."

I looked up at him. He, too, was crying.

The watch was never mentioned after that. It would not pass from him to me, nor would a lot of other things. The chain was broken. And that summer in the hospital, he almost seemed apologetic, as if he wished that he had more to give.

My two stuffed animals had been enough.

"Think of them as this year's Christmas," he said.

"But it's not Christmas yet, grandfather," I said. "That's still a long way away."

He knew, of course, and I kissed his stubbly face, smelling rosewater and talc, hearing the heavy breathing struggling in his chest.

The last time I saw my grandfather was two months later. Not December, but early autumn of that year. He was in the hospital where he lay sedated and unconscious. A clear plastic oxygen mask covered his nose and mouth, and two needles with long thin tubes stuck out from an arm.

I wanted to stay, as he had with me, but my dad said I could not. My stuffed lion, however could, and I left it at his bedside. To protect him.

A few days later he was dead. I cried much of that afternoon and again that Sunday when they buried him. I had the stuffed lion with me and, as I strutted past him at the cemetery for the final time, I stopped and looked at him once more.

A gift. I wished I had a Christmas gift to give him as he had given me.

I saw his face and hoped that he was dreaming. Then I realized that I had an answer for my wish.

I placed my lion near his hands across the vest at the place where the white gold pocket watch once had been. I walked on past, thinking of the lions and of a Christmas that would never come again.

My grandfather's grave was in a cemetery in Rosebud, not far from where his sister Doña Juana lived. She was a *curandera*, a healer bearing witness to the centuries-old folk beliefs still alive in a separate society. Her reddish round face with its deep wrinkles and the twinkling blue gray eyes had been etched for years, people said, and even her silver hair had long looked as if it was pulled back and wrapped in a bun for eternity's sake. Some people called her Doña Juana, using the term of respect before her Christian name, and others like my father called her Tía Juana. She was my grandfather's sister, and my great aunt. In my younger years, Doña Juana told me that her mother's side of our family were Yaqui, descendants of a native American tribe that lived in the Northern Mexican state of Sonora. Her people practiced old Yaqui beliefs that were a mixture of Catholicism learned from Jesuit and Franciscan missionaries and sorcery stemming from Mexican shaman and healers relying on native desert plants.

Through my bleary eyes, one of them swollen and half shut, I was trying to understand why I was now seeing Doña Juana, her wide thin lips smiling, as she spoon-fed me sips of a tea that smelled of spearmint. Some of it dribbled down my chin, and she dabbed it with a napkin. I knew her house. The scent of burning candles and old tobacco smoke was embedded comfortably throughout. My throat was also swollen, and I felt beaten up all over. I pulled the sheet and blanket up and realized that I was fully naked under the covers. Doña Juana tried to assure me in the formal Spanish she always spoke.

"Lourdes cleaned and washed you," she said. "You needed it."

"I don't understand, Doña Juana," I said. "How did I get here?"

"Lourdes," she said. "She drove you here. She saved you life..." She made the sign of the cross. "And then she drove you here."

I tried to sit up but couldn't.

"Don't worry," she said. "Your car is here. It's safe."

"And Lourdes?"

"She was so tired. Let her sleep and rest awhile."

Then she said the oddest, most unexpected thing.

"You must protect her," Doña Juana said. "You cannot take advantage of her. You cannot have her the way you want. You must promise me this."

"Of course, Doña Juana, but I don't know what you're talking about. I just met her."

"And you will want her."

I was too tired to protest or to understand more.

In the coming days, I would feel embarrassed and confused trying to understand why I had tried to kill myself. I knew why, of course. I had lost Patricia. I had failed in the most important thing in my life. Nothing else really mattered now. My life and everything surrounding it now seemed empty, meaningless, and without purpose. For all I had put in motion in my life for myself, it had all rested on her pedestal, which had been swept away in the tide of her own dreams. How do you reclaim your destiny when it has been so connected with a love that has been lost? How do you extricate one part of yourself from the past to go forward? How do you rebuild your own dreams? For any brilliance I may have shown in the past, these were questions I couldn't answer at the present. Maybe there wouldn't be any answer, only more questions.

Physically I was exhausted as well. I felt feverish and spent the nights shivering in a cold sweat and hallucinating. All the while, there was a warm presence, helping me change damp clothing and making me sip broth and tea. Lourdes slept next to me and didn't leave my side. A few times I overheard her on the phone talking to my editors at the newspaper and to my professors at Baylor. Food poisoning in Nuevo Laredo, she told them, and evidently elicited enough sympathy for sick days at work and understanding at school. She also spoke with my parents and used a different story.

"Mrs. Castro, Tony wanted me to tell you that he's with Jesse," she said. "You know how that is, they lose track of time. They're working on something, but he'll call you tonight."

When she got off the phone, she could see the quizzical look on my face.

"Only Jesse knows that you're here," she said.

"How? How did you get hold of him?"

"Your notebooks in the trunk of your car," she said. "You are organized beyond belief. Phone numbers, next of kin, who to call in an emergency, thank God. But you know, you should be in a hospital."

"No, no hospital," I said, begging.

"Of course. I wasn't going to put you through that."

A hospital would have called the police who would have learned that I had been discovered trying to end it all in the Rio Grande. There would have been a police report, calls to my parents, probably a psych evaluation. No telling what else. Thankfully, Lourdes was smart enough to know and to protect me. But Jesse? How did she know to call him?

"Guy, you shouldn't go around with your bank records in your trunk," she said. "You have a receipt for a safe deposit box, and he's an authorized signer. I didn't think you wanted your folks to know what was going on, but this guy you obviously trust."

"He's my uncle."

"I'll say. He keeps calling to check on you every two hours."

"Jesse told you to bring me here?"

She nodded. "Directions and what to tell your great aunt."

How Lourdes had found me wasn't something I particularly wanted to know. In Laredo, she said she had been staying with friends in a *colonia* of dilapidated houses near the Rio Grande. She hitch-hiked after leaving my car, she said, and was walking along a street near her home when she spotted the Mustang and some teenagers milling around it. She had been drawn closer, she said, by a couple's cries for help from the river. There she saw a young man and a woman dragging a seemingly lifeless body out of the water.

"We did CPR and, man, there was river water, booze, and vomit coming out of you," she said. "You owe me for the CPR."

"You did it?"

"That couple sure as heck wasn't going to do it," she said. "They'd done enough anyway. They said they had seen you walking down there and you'd offered them some tequila."

"Yeah, I remember them," I said.

"Man, I thought you might try to do something like that. Why? Why did you do that?"

"It's complicated," I said.

"Yeah, but don't complicate it more for those who care about you."
She barely knew me, but her concern was genuine.

Lourdes Magadalena Montenegro would turn out to become one
of my dearest friends. Meeting her as I did, I had not looked much past
the façade, and maybe I had not even looked at that too closely, at least
while drunk. She was the most exotic-looking woman I had ever seen:
thick long black hair, smooth tan skin, full lips, and light brown eyes.
Her family was from Coatzacoalcos, a port city in the Mexican state of
Veracruz. At the age of seventeen, she left home with a young American
officer from a prominent family in South Texas that didn't approve
of its son's choice for a wife. Too proud to return home, Lourdes had
worked as a nanny for an oilman and his wife in Corpus Christi. She
taught herself English, earned a high school diploma equivalency,
and enrolled in a junior college in Brownsville. Lourdes, though,
didn't have luck with men. She fell in love with a young lawyer from
Laredo who helped her move there, and only then informed her he
was married and that all she could aspire to was being the kept woman.
Hers had not been an easy life, and it got harder when the lawyer was
indicted for embezzlement. She had no money, no home, and no real
skills. When I met her, she said, she was only in her second month
working where she did.

"You do believe me, don't you?" she asked.

"It doesn't matter," I told her. "It doesn't matter what I think
or anyone else thinks. Know that. It's what's here..." I tapped her
forehead. "And here..." I touched the left side of her chest. "That
determines whether you're a good person or not, and you're the only
person who can know that."

We spent a week with Doña Juana in which time Lourdes managed
to wrangle out of her my life, as the old woman knew it. She told Lourdes
that I had suffered from mysterious fevers, incredible headaches, and
stomach problems from early in my childhood, and how she would
come to my home and cure me of "ojo" and "susto." As she told the
story, I recalled those visits vividly. I would lie on the bed with arms
outstretched, my body forming a cross. Then, holding a small white

handkerchief and a Mason jar of water, she would say, *"Es agua santa."* It was holy water. She would cover my face with the handkerchief, then dip her fingertips in the water jar and in short quick motions would sprinkle the white cloth. She would place the Mason jar on the night table and pick up two short palm leaves, yellowing and brown in the shadows of the candle light in the room. She would make a small slit near the center of one leaf and insert the other through it forming a cross. She would form three more crosses the same way, placing one just above each of my hands and the third below my feet. The fourth palm cross Doña Juana kissed, then used in making the sign of the cross: to the temple, near the heart, the left shoulder, then the right and to the lips again. She would ask me to uncross my legs. She would lean over me and begin sweeping the cross made of palms over my body, praying as she swept: "Our Father, who art in heaven..." Still sweeping the cross of palms, Doña Juana would finish the series of prayers and would call out: *"Tony, vente. Tony, vente. No te quedes."* "Tony, come. Tony, come. Don't stay behind." And I would answer: *"Hay voy."* "I'm coming." *"Hay voy."*

At other times, Lourdes sat by and listened as Doña Juana spoke to me about the source of my most recent malady. She listened patiently as I recounted the story of Patricia and my longing for her, from the grade school years to even now. The more current I brought the story, the more I could see her brow furrow and her face take on an ominous look.

"You have to stop, *mijo,* you have to put an end to this," she said with a mixture of exasperation and concern.

"I don't know if I can, Doña Juana," I said. "I still love her."

"That's not what I'm talking about," she said. "Love her through eternity, but you cannot pursue her. You cannot come between her and her husband. What exists between a wife and her husband is one of God's most sacred trusts. It is inviolable. *Mijo,* you must respect this. You must promise me. You must promise God. Or I cannot help you."

Lourdes came and sat at my side, holding my hand and stroking it. Every time she did I felt my heart beating faster. I felt terrible, but surprisingly I was also sexually excited.

"You must listen to what she's saying, Tony," Loudes said. "The story I just heard you tell about how you've loved her all these years is so tender and beautiful. It makes me wish *I* was Patricia. Don't destroy all that by threatening the happiness she's found. Cherish her. Cherish your love for her. But be happy for her."

Doña Juana returned from the kitchen with another cup of *estafiate* tea.

"Lourdes understands, *mijo*," the old woman said. "Your love for Patricia now must change. She is no longer one person. She is part of a union. And if she was holy, as you saw her, then her union is holy. And so is the man she married. You now have to take a vow, as they did, that you will love, respect, and protect not only her but her husband as well. If your love for her is so great that you would lay down your life for her, then it must also be great enough to lay down your life for him."

That afternoon, as I knelt in an altar in one of her rooms filled with candles and incense and religious icons, Doña Juana offered a ritual in which I made my vow of eternal faith and commitment to the woman I had long loved and her new husband. "Our Father, in a holy act of faith, Tony vows his everlasting fidelity to his friend Patricia and the man she has chosen as her partner for life. In the name of Jesus Christ, please show your grace, mercy, and love on this man and woman and give your faithful servant Tony the power and the path to serving and protecting them in their happiness."

Doña Juana, however, had even more instructions for me. That evening, Lourdes and I sat on her comfortable old duck feathered couch, holding hands again as it seemed we were becoming inseparable, and wanting to be together to make love, even as Doña Juana said she had something important to tell us. She sat down across from us and looked disapprovingly at our increasing intimacy.

"*Mijo*, you are not going to like this either," she began, "but it is just as important as the vows you have taken. *Mijo*, you cannot have Lourdes. Not in the way that you want her. And Lourdes, you, too."

"I don't understand, *Tia*," I protested, and I sensed that Lourdes also couldn't see why we couldn't be together. It was the first time I had called Doña Juana Tía, the name most others used. And I did it raising my voice. "I can't have Patricia because she's married," I said, "and now you tell me I can't have Lourdes who isn't married. Why?"

"*Mijo*, I love you as if you were my own son," she said. "But your heart is like the tornados we get here. I am so afraid that now that your heart's been unleashed and that you've not gotten what you desired most, that it will do nothing but leave a path of destruction for anyone who comes close to you."

She warned Lourdes that I had an "outlaw's heart." Her exact words to me were "*tu corazon es un desperado.*" "Your heart is a desperado." And there was more.

"Lourdes, do not fall in love with him," she told her. "He has been ruined. He will hold every woman who comes into his life to the unrealistic ideals that he saw in Patricia, and it will be impossible for any woman to meet up to them. I don't think that even she could have, but he would not have realized it because she was his goddess whose image could be whatever it chose to be. But he will not be as forgiving with others. And you, *mijo*..." She turned to me. "You will drive this poor child mad. You will want to know every man she's ever been with, and even that won't be enough. It will kill Lourdes, and it will destroy you."

She made the sign of the cross and left the room shaking. We didn't know what to say, either to her or to each other. We stopped holding hands, and I now felt embarrassed about what I was feeling toward Lourdes. Moments later Doña Juana returned, looking as if nothing had happened. She took Lourdes' hands and put them in mine.

"I'm an old woman," she said. "Sometimes I forget what it was like to be your age. Life is all our mistakes that we call experience, and we must all make our own."

That night Lourdes and I cuddled in bed. We stayed up all night talking. We kissed tenderly, and I shivered. I still wasn't feeling well, but Lourdes mistook my chills for fear. She also whispered words of endearment in Spanish like "*mi querido,*" and I didn't know what to make of it. I couldn't recall ever having spoken to a girl close to my age in Spanish, much less as I snuggled up to one in bed.

The next day Lourdes and I drove home to Waco. Jesse arrived before we left to check on me. He said this was another reason I should join the Rosicrucians. For two summers, Jesse had tried to recruit me for the Rosicrucians, a secret society of mystics that he never fully explained to me. Someone had said they were like the Masons for Catholics, though I grew up thinking those were the Knights of Columbus. Besides, I didn't like the name. It sounded like they were crucified Rastafarians and too ethnocentric for my taste. I didn't join, and now I knew I would hear this from Jesse for a while. He handed Lourdes a wad of twenty-dollar bills and asked her to take care of me. I didn't know what to make of that, just as I didn't know what she and I would make of each other separately or together. But I wanted to see. She did, too. That next week we moved into an apartment just off the Baylor campus. I returned to work and also managed through the finals to end my freshman year, a year when I had learned so much and gained so little.

One of the things I had learned was a line from the novelist and playwright William Somerset Maugham, who once wrote "the love that lasts the longest is the love that is never returned." I had come to wonder if that was why I continued to long for Patricia. A day didn't go by when I didn't think of her, wondering where she was, what she was doing, what she was thinking. Did I ever cross her mind? I doubted it. Doubts were now my new companions, making themselves comfortably at home. I had come to doubt myself and to question much of what I had believed as well as what I was. They were like emotional piranha, small doubts eating away at me, and that summer became longer and hotter than it should have been.

Lourdes and I went to the movies often, and we took long walks through the Baylor campus, which was almost deserted in the summer. We had the bear pits to ourselves, and I taught her to play tennis on the clay courts behind Marrs McLean Gymnasium. But it quickly became obvious that she didn't like Waco nor fancied the idea of staying there while I finished college. I encouraged her to go back to school and enroll at Baylor for that fall semester, but I suspect she wasn't comfortable at the university and around the students. She thought the girls were stuck up and that the guys couldn't take their eyes off her ass. Well, she *was* beautiful, and she did wonderful things for shorts and a pair of jeans.

Baylor and surrounding Waco could also be an acquired taste for someone who had not grown up with the distinct Bible-belt, conservative, white society values that had been ingrained in the locals over generations. A perfect example of that mindset took place September 10, 1966, at Baylor Stadium in a nationally televised football game in which Baylor upset nationally ranked Syracuse and its two future NFL All-Pros, running back Floyd Little and fullback Larry Csonka. The game marked the first time that an African-American played for a team in the previously all-white Southwest Conference made up of schools that included the University of Texas, Texas A&M, Southern Methodist University, and Baylor among others. SMU had recruited a highly prized black running back named Jerry LeVias, who happened to be African American and who was expected to break the conference's color-barrier that fall. But when ABC moved up the Baylor-Syracuse game to kick off the entire season, that distinction fell to John Westbrook, an African American running back who walked on at Baylor without a scholarship. Westbrook entered the game in the second half with no announcement of the historic break of the color-barrier. But in the press box, in an unfortunate attempt at humor after Westbrook rushed for short gain, the public address announcer alerted the members of the news media with this: "And that's Baylor's contribution to color television."

Having grown up in Waco and spent so many years around Baylor, I was accustomed and perhaps immune to some of the subtle racism that could sometimes be found. In high school, one of the few blatant racist comments directed at me had come from a waitress at the Elite Café, a Waco landmark on The Circle not far from University High.

Several friends and I went there for a midnight meal, and the middle-age waitress brought me a carton of chocolate milk when I had ordered hot chocolate.

"Ma'm," I said. "I ordered a cup of hot cocoa, not chocolate milk."

"Well, I didn't understand you," she said. "You and your people should learn to speak better English."

I didn't know what to say, but my friends did. They got up, and we all walked out.

The waitress was old and set in her ways, not that she should have been excused. But there was no excuse for someone who was educated making the overt racist remarks I got at the *Waco Tribune-Herald* that spring from another Baylor student who ran the photo engraving operation at night. In those days, preparing a photograph for reproduction in a newspaper involved the time-consuming task of having the picture engraved into a sheet of plastic that was then forwarded to the printing department. One early evening, I ordered a photo engraving for a late arriving photograph that was to appear in the sports section. Later that night, half an hour before the paper's deadline, the photo engraver had still not prepared the picture. I reminded him of the late hour and the need to get the engraving done when he snapped at me.

"I swear I never thought I'd live to see the day when I'd be taking orders from a spick!" he yelled, loud enough for everyone in the office to hear.

He had followed me into the sports office as if to intimidate me. He was six-foot-four inches tall and weighed about two hundred and twenty pounds. "You can tell me what to do," he said. "But you're still a spick, and that's all you'll ever be. You wanna make something of that?"

"No, Keith," I said. "I'll just remind you of some history. My ancestors were building pyramids and a civilization when yours were building log cabins and slaughtering the natives. So I guess you shouldn't be expected to act in a civilized manner. Now would you kindly engrave the picture?"

But Lourdes wasn't as amused at some of the Waco town folk's lack of civility. It would have been too long and difficult to explain to her, and perhaps it was my fault in failing to try. Maybe she would have tried harder at holding on if things were right between us. We slept together and regularly made out long into the night before falling asleep in each other's arms. There was an undeniable physical attraction, but we had yet to have sex. We wondered if it might have been what Doña Juana said to us. Maybe she had hexed our relationship. The problem we were having in bed was me. I just couldn't perform. For that matter, I had never performed. I was a virgin, and maybe that was an issue. Lourdes couldn't believe I had never been with anyone.

"This Patricia? The two of you never?" she asked.

"No."

"You're sure?"

I think that's one thing I would have remembered.

"And none of your other girlfriends?"

"There would have had to be one," I said. "There weren't any."

"My God, priests aren't this celibate, Tony. Did you ever want to be a priest?"

"My mother wanted me to."

"That doesn't count," she said. "All Catholic mothers want their sons to be priests."

I started taking high potency vitamins. They didn't help. I began calling myself Lourdes' Jake Barnes, the Hemingway character in *The Sun Also Rises* whose "war wound" left him impotent and came between him and the love of his life. I called Lourdes Lady Bret Ashley, the woman Jake Barnes loved, and she wasn't happy.

"This isn't funny, Tony," she said. "This is something very important in your life. If you haven't had sex before because you were saving yourself for this Patricia, and now you can't have sex... Don't you see, something isn't right."

I saw my family doctor and underwent a series of tests. I was fine, the tests showed, and the doctor suggested it was something psychological. I was referred to a shrink. I made an appointment, but before I could go, Lourdes made a dramatic announcement. She had decided it was time for her to leave.

"Doña Juana was right," she said. "We'll destroy each other, just not the way she thought we would."

That night we called Uncle Jesse to ask if he could find Lourdes something to do in Dallas. In a day, he arranged a job with a Realtor friend who promised to show her the ropes of the business and fast-track her into getting a real estate license. In a couple of days, we were in the Mustang driving to Dallas to spend the weekend with Jesse and Modesta. Jesse insisted that we take a couple of his department store credit cards so that Lourdes could buy some clothes to get her through her first few weeks on the job. Jesse was the most magnanimous man I knew, and I hoped that one day I could repay him.

"What's she going to do about a car?" he asked me.

"That's what I wanted to talk to you about, Jesse," I said, taking him aside. "The guy who has that T-Bird. Will he still give you a deal?"

The next day, alone, I drove to the jeweler in North Dallas that I had visited the previous summer and asked if he would buy back the heart-shaped engagement ring he had sold me. He looked stunned.

"I'm surprised," he said. "May I ask what..."

He saw that I had been crying and that, even then, was holding back tears, and he kindly didn't finish asking.

"I know I shouldn't because these heart-shaped diamonds are hard to move," he said. "Beats me why people aren't attracted to them."

"It's a magnificent stone," I said.

"But you know, Jesse's a friend, and he says you're a good kid who just caught a bad break. I'm so sorry."

I took the money and, after another good cry, went to buy someone a car.

Two hours later, Jesse and I drove back to his home with a two-seat baby blue 1957 T-Bird that we presented Lourdes. She didn't want to take it, but how could she not. She told Jesse that if he weren't married, she would want him for herself. And she promised to pay him back. With what I had left over from selling the ring, we put a deposit down and rented her a luxury apartment in the Oak Lawn/Turtle Creek area of Dallas. Lourdes fell in love with Dallas and got off to a great start on her job. Before I finished my sophomore year at Baylor, she had earned a real estate license. She had also started seeing a young banker who was crazy about her. I went up to Dallas and stayed with them on a weekend when he confided in me that he was going to ask her to marry him and asked my permission, being that she told him we were like brother and sister. I was flattered. I don't know why, because I didn't live there, but he then asked me a curious question: Did I know a reliable jeweler in Dallas. My jaw dropped. I directed him to Jesse's friend, Saul, in North Dallas.

"He has great things," I told him. "Ask him to show you a heart-shaped diamond, if he has one."

When they married in the spring of 1967, I gave Lourdes away. She was the most beautiful bride I had seen. She wore a jewel beaded wedding gown and a diamond ring on her hand that looked familiar and brought back thoughts of what might have been but never was.

Then my life went back into the limbo it had been in since I learned that Patricia had married. My grades had become mediocre, as did my work at the paper. I missed more classes than I attended, and I often shrugged off work. Mostly, I slept. I had moved back home, and I would sleep in regularly. I stopped contributing to the *Lariat*, and I no longer hung around the journalism school as I once did. I was also losing money gambling. I had met a bookie through work, and I was regularly betting college games and baseball. For the first time in my life, I also stopped serving as an altar boy at Mass and was no longer even going to church. The only constructive thing I did was play golf. Years earlier, Jesse attended a pro-am golf tournament where he played in a foursome with the pro Julius Boros, a former two-time U.S. Open champion. Jesse was given a complimentary set of top-of-the-line Ben Hogan golf woods and irons. He had three sets already, he said, so he gave me the new clubs.

Then in my junior year, the enthusiasm for life that had gone out of me when Patricia married returned in the most unexpected way. In Texas, high school football reigns supreme in the fall. Friday night football games are as much a celebration of that culture as they are a competition. Daily newspapers in small towns and big cities alike fawn over high school football, and Waco was no different. Covering those games sometimes became a challenge, particularly in those high school stadiums where the construction of the press boxes took in little account for sight lines to the playing field. In those instances, sportswriters covered the games from the sidelines, often getting the help of "spotters" to identify the players.

On the first week of the season that year, I was assigned a game at La Vega High School, site of my own football success when I was at South Junior and a place with a terrible press box. As I was walking the sidelines in the first half that night, my eyes locked for a flicker of a second with those of a La Vega cheerleader. I took it as just one of those moments when you see someone you wish you knew, and then the moment is gone. That was all it was until halftime when I recognized Tommy Anderson, a friend from junior high and high school, who was just outside the sideline talking to two cheerleaders. One happened to be his longtime girlfriend. The other was the cheerleader I had seen just minutes earlier.

Carrie Leigh Stanton was the prototypical high school cheerleader, a tousle-haired blonde with a dazzling smile. She was athletic, tall, coltishly leggy, confident, friendly, luminous, smoky-eyed, and gorgeous. She caught me off-guard when she extended a handshake and then spoke what seemed like a language of her own that I immediately understood. It was as if she were a cross section of haiku and a sonnet with a vulnerability that was surprisingly disarming. In 1967, this was also the age when society started seeing a blurring of the looks between many high school girls in their teens and college coeds in their early twenties. In hairstyle and appearance, both Carrie Leigh and Tommy's girlfriend looked like they just as easily could be students at Baylor.

That night, in the few minutes left before the start of the second half, I met the young woman who I would marry.

By the end of our first date: a lazy Sunday afternoon at a Hayley Mills movie, a long drive around the lake where we talked for hours, and an evening watching television with her folks... by the end of the day, we had begun falling in love. On Monday, we pledged our love to one another on the phone. On Tuesday I sent her roses. On Wednesday, our romance was over. Or should have been over, if Carrie Leigh had followed her parents' orders.

"They don't want me to see you," she said as we talked on the phone.

"Why? Because I'm in college and you're in high school?" I asked. I couldn't understand. They seemed to have liked me Sunday night, offering homemade ice cream and asking me all kinds of questions about my work as a sportswriter. We watched *The High Chaparral*, a popular western TV series, late into the evening with Carrie Leigh sitting practically on my lap as we shared a love seat.

Carrie Leigh didn't answer me at first and she was hesitant even when she did. "No, I'm embarrassed to tell you," she said.

"Is it the age difference?" I asked. "That I'm twenty and you're sixteen?"

"No, it's not even that," she said. "Oh, I'm so embarrassed because I didn't think my parents were like this. But they don't want me seeing you because you're Mexican."

Ah, enter Banquo's ghost. Carrie Leigh, if you didn't already guess, was white, blonde, blue-eyed, and protestant.

I wasn't upset or sad. I wasn't angry or hurt. I was experiencing profound disbelief. I knew this was Waco, but her folks had seen the best of me. I was well-spoken, respectful, courteous, and deferential. They had seemed genuinely kind and impressed with the fact that I was working full-time and going to school full-time. Her father and I were both golfers. Her younger sister couldn't stop talking with me. In an ideal world, this would have been the way I would have hoped any meeting with the O'Neals would have gone had that opportunity ever happened. And now I was discovering that nothing I could do or could have done would have mattered. Carrie Leigh's parents were judging me based on some neurotic fear of who I was, based on my skin and my heritage.

I wanted to just hang up, but I wasn't that rude, even to these kinds of people. I also could hear Carrie Leigh crying on the other end of the phone.

"Look, maybe we can still be friends," I said. "I'll be covering a few more of your team's games. We'll grab a Coke during halftime or afterward."

"Wait, don't you want to see me and go out with me?" she asked.

"Carrie Leigh," I said, "your parents don't want us going out together." I wanted to tell her about all those "white girls" speeches from the past and to make her feel a little better in knowing that her parents weren't the only people who felt that way.

"But you said you loved me, that you'd fallen in love with me?

"I did fall in love with you," I said.

"And I with you?"

"Yeah, Carrie Leigh," I said, "but how would we see each other and wouldn't your parents find out?"

I would learn later that on the night she was forbidden by her parents to see me, their household had been the scene of an emotionally charged confrontation.

"If you were to have his children," her mother had tearfully demanded to know, "what would they look like?"

"Oh, mom, how can you ask something like that?" Carrie Leigh answered. "I don't know. Maybe they'll be polka dotted. Is that what you want to hear?"

When Carrie Leigh told me about this, I asked her how the subject of children had come up.

"She asked what I could possibly see in you," Carrie Leigh said. "And I told her I wanted to fuck you."

It was the first of countless times that she left me in drop-jawed wonder and amazement.

185

One of those times was definitely the first time we made love. We were both virgins, and I certainly didn't expect our first time to come as it did. It was after a Thursday night pep rally when we had planned to have burgers, shakes, and scheme how to drop her off at home without me being seen by her parents from the den. We ate the burgers in my car at a park near her home with Carrie Leigh sitting on the console between the Mustang bucket seats with her legs draped over my right leg. Actually, I don't think we ever ate the burgers. As we made out, I found the large Pirate emblem on her cheerleader uniform top getting in the middle of things. She said she had a solution and in one motion pulled her uniform over her head. I don't even recall how we got into the small back seat. I think I lost all thought focusing on her surprisingly incredible breasts. After my performance problems with Lourdes, I hadn't even thought much about the actual act of making love to Carrie Leigh. Perhaps that was best because this happened so unexpectedly and without warning that there had been no time for self-doubt. Maybe that's what it took, along with the love and tenderness of two people wanting each other so recklessly that nothing else could get in the way. Our love-making was the most magnificent experience of my life. I had never thought that loving someone could be like this. I thought it, but Carrie Leigh said it. We wanted to hold on to that fulfillment for eternity, but it could be only a long moment under a full moon. The clock on the dashboard read 10:00 p.m., and reality set in. We had indulged in the moment without thinking. Carrie Leigh wasn't on the pill. I hadn't used a condom. I asked Carrie Leigh when she'd had her last period. She looked at me wide-eyed as she realized why I was asking.

"My God, I'm in the middle of my cycle," she said. As he did she must have noticed my anxiety jump-start. "But it's okay."

"Not if you get pregnant," I said.

"It's okay – I want to have your baby." I thought she was intoxicated with our passion instead of realizing the enormity of if she were pregnant. "You do love me? You said you did."

"Yes, that's not what's worrying me if you're pregnant," I said. "I love you. I want to marry you. And if ..."

Before I could finish, Carrie Leigh was in my arms kissing me. "And I want to marry you. If I'm pregnant, we'll just get married. Can't we?"

"Of course, Carrie Leigh," I said. "That's not the problem. The problem is that you're under-age.

"Oh, God, I'm jail bait, aren't I?" It hadn't occurred to her before.

"Yeah, and the way your parents feel about me, even if we get married, they're likely to try to bring statutory rape charges against me."

"They won't – they can't," she said. "Well, then, I'm not pregnant. I can't be. I won't be."

Carrie Leigh wasn't pregnant, but there was trouble just the same. A few days later she wanted to know how I would feel about spending the night with her. She had been invited to an after-game slumber party from which she felt she could leave and then arrange a ride home in the morning. It sounded iffy, I told her, because there were too many people to trust, the girls at the party especially. But she insisted they were all her friends. Besides, she knew even more secrets about their indiscretions, including one girlfriend who had been having an affair with a music teacher. However, trouble began the morning after our night together when the girlfriend who had promised to drive her home had car trouble. Panic set in, even though Carrie Leigh rejected the most obvious plan: Using a taxi and, if her parents saw the cab, concocting some story about how her ride's car had broken down. Instead she called the girlfriend who had been carrying on with the teacher. Over the coming two weeks, Carrie Leigh behaved strangely. She said there were some school meetings she was having to attend but wouldn't talk about what was happening. I saw her only once during this time, and she let on nothing. It was not until that weekend when I saw her that I learned that someone had tipped off the cheerleading squad adviser that Carrie Leigh had left a slumber party to crash all night with her boyfriend. The person ratting her out had all the details about how a girlfriend had picked up Carrie Leigh from her boyfriend's car early on a Saturday morning to drive her home. By the time I learned any of this, Carrie Leigh had resigned as a cheerleader. I couldn't believe she hadn't fought allegations that, though true, could have been easily fended off. The charges were all based on second-hand hearsay without her confessing to them or turning the tables on her likely accuser, the girl screwing around with the teacher. Carrie Leigh didn't believe she was the snitch. Even if she was, Carrie Leigh said she refused to stoop so low as to rat on a girlfriend. It wasn't the time to be noble, though it was part of what I loved about her. She was also noble in another way: Trying to hide our relationship from her parents, she had refused to involve either me or her mother and father in challenging the allegations.

"I never wanted to be a cheerleader," she said. "It was just something that I kind of fell into."

I didn't believe her. I also felt horrible and guilty. I had screwed up a lot in my life, but I had never hurt anyone this way or caused someone to lose something they had earned and treasured. I didn't know what to do. The truth of the matter was that I now couldn't do anything.

What Carrie Leigh and I learned from that debacle was that we needed to be more careful. For starters, she had learned that she couldn't completely trust her friends. That meant that I had to confide in some of my friends, explaining our situation and hoping that, when we had plans to see each other, they were free and willing to pick her up in their car and drive her to where I would be waiting. Dropping her off at home around midnight was easier. He parents usually spent their time watching television in their den, which had a limited view of the driveway.

This is how we "dated." At first, I thought this would only be a temporary arrangement until Carrie Leigh's parents could be convinced to allow her to see me, but they were unbending. I gently pressed Carrie Leigh to ask her parents for the source of their anti-Mexican or anti-Mexican American sentiments. Was it a general dislike or was there something specific that had happened to them or a loved one in the past? Several weeks later, she had an answer. Years earlier, Carrie Leigh's grandmother or aunt had been sexually attacked, physically abused or maybe just accosted by a Mexican worker. She couldn't get a clear story on the details. It didn't seem to matter. Some of the men in the family had tried tracking down the offender, she said, but she didn't know if they caught him or what may have happened. It brought back old stories and old warnings, and I let it go. So whenever we went out, Carrie Leigh would be picked up by some of my friends from Baylor who were white and who would be willing to meet her parents on the pretense that they were her date. Sometimes my friends' dates would stay out of sight by waiting with me in my car for the exchange of "dates." After a while, though, this became embarrassing and humiliating. I was having to explain to friends' girlfriends the ethnic-racial sociological reality of my life, and it was deepening my own hurt each time I retold the story.

But there was no denying we were in love. My parents, who knew nothing of how Carrie Leigh's parents felt toward me, fell equally in love with her. My mother started calling her "*mija.*" If a weekend went by when I didn't see Carrie Leigh, which sometimes happened when we couldn't get someone we trusted to pick her up, my mother would become concerned that we had quarreled.

"If you hurt that girl, I will never forgive you," she would tell me. "You're my son, but she's just as dear."

It was amazing how much my parents loved Carrie Leigh, considering how they met her. My parents often spent weekends, especially the evenings, away. When they weren't visiting relatives in Fort Worth or Houston, they would attend banquets and dances at their lodge. Other times they were often at weddings, rosaries, or funerals. Many times my parents would be gone for hours, and that meant that Carrie Leigh and I had the house to ourselves. Whoever said forbidden love breeds desire knew what they were talking about because, as we continued to see one another, our dates often consisted of nothing more than a lot of sex. In motels. In my Mustang. In empty offices at night at the *Tribune-Herald.*

In the accounting office where she worked part-time after school. In the Baylor journalism rooms. At drive-in movie theaters. In the balcony at downtown theaters. On the manicured lawns at Cameron Park. During her school lunch period. During my work dinner break. At halftime of football games I was covering. In the 1960s, young women still wore a lot of undergarments: slips, sometimes petticoats, corsets, and always pantyhose. Carrie Leigh was one of the first girls in her crowd to discard the pantyhose. They made quick dressing and undressing so much harder and longer, especially in the back seat of a Mustang. She sometimes wore garter belts with thigh high hosiery in a look out of *Playboy* magazine. She always struck me as being naked even when she wasn't. We were obsessed and consumed with one another, and we always figured that my home was the safest place of all when my parents weren't there. My bedroom was in the back of the house, past a long hallway. It was a room where the only thing that looked in place was the bed. My mom insisted on making it up each morning in a meticulous manner that was difficult to duplicate. Carrie Leigh, though, had memorized the way it was made up and could duplicate it. Otherwise, my bedroom was a maze of book stacks, newspapers, notebooks and journals. I had an old black Smith-Corona typewriter on my desk and a small, lightweight Hermes Baby Rocket portable I had picked up in Dallas on a TV tray.

Early on a Sunday night, after we had gone to the movies, Carrie Leigh and I returned to my home feeling certain we had several hours there alone. My parents were at church for a rosary and had plans to later visit a sick friend at the hospital. On the nights they went to the hospital, which was on the other side of town, they would usually stay until the end of visiting hours and did not return home until well past ten. That night, though, it could not have been much past seven o'clock when we heard the distant sound of the garage door opening. Locked in a passionate embrace, we were startled. I jumped out of bed, stumbling over a stack of books as I turned on the lights. The bed was a mess with its covers strewn about.

"Is that your parents?" Carrie Leigh asked as panic attacks set in.

"It can't be anyone else opening the garage," I said, looking for my clothes. "Get dressed."

But she froze and started crying. The obvious hadn't even occurred to me. "I can't believe this how I'm going to meet them," she said. "What are they going to think?"

I knew what they were going to think. I also knew that my mother would be the first one into the house. The Mustang was parked on one side of the driveway, and she would know I was home. She likely would be walking down the hallway at any moment.

"Get dressed," I said. "I'll head them off."

Famous last words, I know.

My shirt was still unbuttoned, and I was pulling my jeans just above my knees midway down the hallway when my mother spotted me at the other end of the hall. She knew what was going on and immediately broke into tears, disappearing into the kitchen. My father was right behind her and couldn't understand what was happening.

"He's got a girl in his bedroom," she told him. "And look at him. You know what they've been doing."

My father didn't seem upset. In fact, he appeared unusually proud.

"Look, dad," I said, joining them in the kitchen. "It's not exactly as it seems. The girl in my room is special..."

I detected a smile on his face.

"No, dad, she's a great girl," I said. She's smart, and she's beautiful, and she's a cheerleader, and, dad, she loves the Dallas Cowboys."

Don't say I didn't know the way into my father's heart. The Cowboys had replaced the Yankees as the love of his life. Sundays in our house revolved around the Cowboys. If they were playing an East Coast game with an early starting time, he would insist that he and mom attend a very early Mass so that he wouldn't miss the kick off.

"And look, dad, we're in love," I said. "We really are, and we're going to get married. So this isn't just any girl."

My dad's eyes lit up even more. "Did you hear that, Emma?" he said to my mom. Her first name was Maria, but he always called her by her middle name. "Tony is going to marry the girl in his room. She's going to be his wife. She's going to be our daughter-in-law."

Minutes later, having assured her that my parents would love her unconditionally, no matter how they had found us that night, I convinced Carrie Leigh to come out of the room. She had collected herself quickly and looked incredible despite the circumstances.

My father already had a Coors in a hand, and his first words to her were memorable:

"How do you think the Cowboys will do against the Giants Sunday?"

Incredibly, the depth of my parents' love for Carrie Leigh became such that my mom one day told me she would not object if I converted and became Lutheran and if we raised our children as Lutherans, which was Carrie Leigh's religion. That was true motherly love indeed for a woman who was a devout Roman Catholic.

Carrie Leigh engendered that kind of love and devotion. Everyone at the *Tribune-Herald* adored her, though they assumed she was a student at Baylor. She read voraciously and could talk to fellow reporters about any subject or issue, from foreign policy and the war in Vietnam to hunger in America and the war on poverty. She had just finished reading a major new biography of Eleanor Roosevelt and debated her role in influencing New Deal policies with a reporter who had been a Franklin Roosevelt scholar.

"You should marry that young woman," the reporter later advised me. "She's going to help change the world."

We made plans to marry as soon as she graduated from high school. Hard as it is to believe, she was a high school junior and would not graduate until the spring of 1969 which was when I would graduate from Baylor. I gave her a solitaire diamond engagement ring that she hid in a secret compartment of her purse, and she wore it only when we were together. I know, I know. *She was sixteen.* But she didn't look sixteen, and she didn't dress like a sixteen-year-old. Little by little she had added designer pieces to her wardrobe from upscale local retail stores, pieces she told her mother she bought on sale, with the result being that she usually dressed better than her high school teachers. She had a part-time bookkeeping job, she told the curious teachers who noticed and asked how she could afford to look like she had stepped out of a Neiman Marcus catalog. Of course, she was buying on the charge cards that I rarely used, but I still had my nest egg from Dallas, and I loved her. I never would have imagined that a sixteen-year-old could look as mature as Carrie Leigh did, nor have the depth of her feelings. It gave me new understanding and appreciation about Patricia's own maturity at nineteen years old, almost twenty, when she married.

Carrie Leigh and I weren't going to tell anyone about our plans to marry, but our happiness sometimes spilled over. A couple of my friends knew that we were secretly seeing each other and secretly engaged, as did a couple of her closest girlfriends. We were the consummate romantics of our time. We saw *Camelot* no fewer than fifteen times, identifying with the forbidden love of Lancelot and Guinevere. We recited love poems to one another. We talked about the future we imagined together. And, for the first time since the fifth grade, my life and dreams didn't revolve around Patricia. She had been the girl of my dreams and perhaps always would be in a special way. But Carrie Leigh was the woman I loved and expected to live my entire life with.

It soon became apparent that Carrie Leigh's rebellion against her parents was just typical for whom she was. On her own, she became a local champion of the civil rights movement, attempting to raise social consciousness among her classmates. She had read all of Martin Luther King Jr.'s speeches and many of Robert F. Kennedy's. She took an interest in the anti-hunger and Poor People's Campaign of the Rev. Ralph Abernathy, in Cesar Chavez's farm workers fight in California, and in the crusade on behalf of the Chicago Seven after the 1968 Democratic Convention. She was upset by the increasing American presence in Vietnam and grew adamantly opposed to the war. From her part-time job after school, she gave more money than she could afford to a relief effort in Bangladesh. I was both impressed and proud.

She had broadened my own awareness of the world beyond baseball and literature.

"Do you love me?" she would ask.

"Yes, I love you," I would tell her. "Beyond words. Forever."

"But I love you more," she would tell me.

"How's that possible?"

"Because I will love you forever and a day."

She was perfect. And I rarely used that word. There had been Don Larsen's perfect game in Game Six of the 1956 World Series, but I couldn't think of anything else I would have called perfect until I met Carrie Leigh. She wouldn't hear of it, though.

"Look at my knee," she said, as if to prove she wasn't flawless. "This looks dreadful."

She pointed to a spot about the size of a dime, if that big. It was a scar.

"I fell down, sand got it in and, it was never properly cleaned out," she said. "Feel it."

I actually enjoyed feeling it. If it made her feel less perfect than I thought she was, so be it. We had just seen *Barefoot in the Park* with a handsome young actor everyone was talking about: Robert Redford.

"This little scar of yours is like the moles on the side of Redford's face," I said. "If he didn't have those moles, you'd think he wasn't human. He'd be too perfect."

She wasn't convinced.

"Well, look at my ankles," she said. "They're not perfect. They're not well-defined. It's difficult for me to wear slingbacks. My ankles won't hold them up."

I studied Carrie Leigh's ankles a lot. I didn't see what she was talking about.

"You're silly, Carrie Leigh." And she was. "I wouldn't trade your ankles for anyone else's in the world.

And we felt on top of the world. It was easy feeling that way when I was with her, especially if something funny came up and she let out her infectious, giddy laugh that boomed so loudly that it needed its own warning, especially if we were in a movie theater where people would turn to figure out where the sound effects were coming from. But, when alone, I could sense the pressure of the secrecy mounting. I was becoming increasingly depressed at feeling like I was unworthy, certainly in her parents' eyes. Without intending to hurt me, some of my friends made jokes about my predicament. Once, while I waited for Carrie Leigh to return with one of my Baylor friends who was picking her up, his girlfriend said she felt sorry for me.

"Her parents really object to you?"

I nodded.

"Because you're Hispanic?" She held my hand, kissing it, and I didn't know what to make of this. Tears welled in her eyes, and I barely knew her. "I don't believe it. Why do you put up with it? Any girl in my sorority would love to go out with you, if only you would ask us out."

I hadn't known that, and now it seemed too late and didn't matter anyway.

I was still haunted by Atomic Man, masked and anonymous. Carrie Leigh and I never talked about this, even though we should have. I don't know why we didn't. Perhaps it was because sometimes our moments together were so limited that we didn't want to dwell on the negative.

Then there were the threats. I started receiving phone calls at the newspaper warning that some dreadful thing would happen to me if I didn't stop seeing Carrie Leigh. The callers had teenagers' voices: young, angry, hateful, and vile. They were young rednecks from Carrie Leigh's school who didn't approve of one of their own dating a Mexican. I don't think they suspected that her parents felt the same way or they would have certainly made them aware of seeing Carrie Leigh and me together. We were also increasingly worried that our luck would give out and that her parents would discover we were seeing each other. Deception, of course, always raises paranoia among the deceivers. Carrie Leigh, for instance, swore that her mother was now regularly checking on what cars dropped her off at home. Her mother, Carrie Leigh said, remembered that I drove a Mustang. So friends started loaning me their cars, but hooking up with pals to borrow their wheels at midnight gets old quickly.

Grudgingly, I agreed to trade in the Mustang. It hurt. Slowly, the things that I had associated with Patricia and my dream of being with her one day were falling by the wayside. I knew I would never forget her, but the Mustang had been so symbolic of all my hopes with her. The spring of 1968, half a year into dating Carrie Leigh behind her parents' backs, I traded in the Mustang for a new Pontiac Firebird 400, a muscle car if there was ever one, with four hundred cubic inches of horsepower. Her parents didn't know it was mine, but the wrong people did. One Saturday night after dropping off Carrie Leigh at her home, two guys in a GTO pulled up alongside. They threw a full beer can at my car, barely missing the windshield and yelled ethnic epithets about what they were going to do to me. I tore off on a connecting road to Texas Highway 6 barely ahead of the GTO. For the next hour, sometimes hitting speeds in excess of 100 miles an hour, I outran the GTO until we reached the outskirts of Bryan and College Station some ninety miles outside Waco. I lost the GTO and after a while turned around. Returning home, just outside of Bryan, I saw the GTO pulled over on the side of the highway with the hood up and the radiator spewing steam.

This was also the age in the South, depicted in the film *Easy Rider*, in which redneck hunters became associated with driving pickup trucks whose back windows were adorned with rifles dangling from a weapons hanger. Many of the working class, middle-age men in Waco like Carrie Leigh's father drove those kinds of pickups and were hunters with rifles that could bring down any prey. Understandably, Carrie Leigh worried that her father, though a church-going man, might react violently at learning that his oldest daughter was seeing someone she was forbidden to date and a Mexican, at that.

"I'm just afraid he would try to kill you," she said.

"That's just now occurring to you?" But then I had never told her about all those "white girls" speeches warning me that this could happen.

We began brainstorming about how we would handle that situation, were it to happen, and whether we could reason with her mother and father. It became a real concern after Larry Lynch's younger brother Rodney Lynch showed up at my house late one night with the back window of his Mustang shot out. The shooter was the father of a young woman in Carrie Leigh's neighborhood. When that father discovered that his daughter was seeing a someone of whom he disapproved, because Rodney had long hair and an attitude modeled after James Dean, he pulled out his shotgun and did a remarkable job of scaring him off.

"I couldn't bear to see you killed," Carrie Leigh said as we made our plans one day.

"*You* couldn't bear seeing me killed?" This wasn't funny. "How do you think I'd feel?"

We came up with the only solution we could think of. That summer of 1968, on a weekday morning, we drove to Waxahachie, a southern suburb of Dallas, and at the Ellis County Clerk's Office we took out our marriage license. Carrie Leigh and I were married in a civil ceremony that afternoon by a Justice of the Peace. But there was a small hitch: We needed a witness. Thankfully, a sheriff's deputy happened to be escorting a prisoner in handcuffs into the courtroom for his arraignment.

"Deputy," the old judge asked the lawman, "could you do us the honor of witnessing the marriage of these two young people?

"Judge," the prisoner said, surprising all of us, "if the deputy can't, I'd be obliged to do it."

We later wondered whether we shouldn't have let the poor guy do it.

We dated secretly for ten months, and we were secretly married for just as long. We planned to announce that we were married and take our chances in early June, just after her graduation. But in May of 1969, two weeks before her high school graduation, it all became public in a way we never anticipated. An outstanding student, Carrie Leigh was named valedictorian of her senior class. It came as news that did that not sit well with one of her friends who knew she was married and was aware of the school district's policy forbidding married students from receiving any honors. The next day, Carrie Leigh was yanked out of class by the school principal who confronted her with documentation that we had been married the previous summer. That afternoon she prepared to deliver two blows to her parents. She didn't know which would anger them most: The news that the school district had removed her as valedictorian or that the reason was that she had been secretly married to a Mexican they detested. She called me as she was about to break the news to her parents just to warn me that something crazy might happen. At the very least, I thought, her parents would attempt to have the marriage annulled. That afternoon, I waited by the phone for a couple of hours before Carrie Leigh called. What she told me came as an utter surprise. She asked me to come to her home to meet my new in-laws.

"It's a trick, Carrie Leigh," I said. "Your father is going to shoot me."

"That's what I thought, too," she said. "But they've calmed down. Now they want to meet their new son-in-law."

I suppose I probably really needed an emotional decompression chamber because I wasn't prepared to go from being the dreaded Mexican to the beloved son-in-law. I hadn't seen Carrie Leigh's parents since the first time we met, not even in chance meetings. There had almost been one accidental crossing of our paths when Carrie Leigh competed in the Miss Junior Waco Pageant. She made the finals, and on the night of the pageant I stayed out of sight in the back of the hotel ballroom where I watched as she finished as a runner-up. Now, though, it was time for the real thing, meeting the two people who had made my life hell for the past two years. A few months earlier I had told Tommy West about the secret marriage, knowing this day would come and wanting someone I trusted to know what might happen, should the worst come about. Just before heading to the Stanton's home that evening, I called Tommy again to let him know this was D-Day. I didn't know what to expect of the Stantons, who were surprisingly low-keyed and dry-eyed when I finally met them again. I figured they weren't about to allow me to see just how much their oldest daughter had disappointed them. Fortunately, by the time I got to their home, the Stantons had also redirected their anger at the school district for taking away Carrie Leigh's honor of being valedictorian and the scholarship that went with it. From me, they mostly wanted to know what I had in mind for our future. For so long Carrie Leigh and I had been so concerned with scheming how to see each other under our circumstances that we hadn't really thought much beyond where we were that night. I could see in their eyes that the Stantons were truly worried about what was in store for their daughter. The only time I had ever thought that far ahead was when I dreamed of how Patricia and I would start out. It still seemed like a plan for a future with Carrie Leigh.

"I don't think we can live in Waco," I said to the Stantons. "I know I can't, and I would hope Carrie Leigh would follow me."

"Where are you thinking of living?" Mrs. Stanton wanted to know, though she said it kindly and not in a demanding way.

"Dallas to start off with," I said. "I'm confident I can get a newspaper job there after I graduate. And then in Washington or New York."

"Oh, my, that's so far away," Mrs. Stanton said with some sadness. "You would take our daughter that far away? Does she want to go there with you?"

"Mom, I want to be wherever Tony is," Carrie Leigh said, tightening her hold on my hand. "We never want to be apart. Never."

What she said and the way she said it brought a sense of relief to me and seemed to bring her folks into full acceptance. The rest of the evening was about where we would live while I finished school, what church services we would attend, about the Stantons meeting my parents, what I did besides work and school, and kids. They wouldn't be polka dotted, but we assured the Stantons that Carrie Leigh wasn't pregnant and that we planned to wait a while before we had children. What wound up finally unifying us that night was agreeing that the school district was wrong in removing Carrie Leigh as valedictorian and deciding we had to do something to correct that.

A week later Carrie Leigh and I were on the front page of the *Waco Tribune-Herald* and on the local television news. An attorney hired by the Stantons threatened to sue the school district on a civil rights violation by challenging the policy forbidding married students from receiving honors. Our lawyer notified school district officials that he would seek a court injunction stopping La Vega High School's graduation ceremony scheduled in the coming days unless Carrie Leigh was reinstated as valedictorian. We were fortunate that it was the ideal age to put the fear of God and the courts into Southern schools over civil rights and equal opportunity matters. In the preceding years, Congress had passed the civil rights legislation that ultimately changed America. Waco, like many other cities, became the targets of successful lawsuits challenging the equal but separate nature of those districts' policies. Not surprisingly perhaps, two days after our lawyer threatened to stop graduation, the La Vega school board caved in to our demands. Carrie Leigh was officially renamed valedictorian of her graduating class again.

We never found out who ratted us out to school officials, though we had a good suspect in mind. It also became apparent on graduation night in the speech of the salutatorian, a former friend of Carrie Leigh's who would have been valedictorian in the event Carrie Leigh was removed. This young woman delivered a speech preaching the virtue of honesty to your school and your community, which everyone suspected was a transparent dig at us. Carrie Leigh, though, stole the thunder that night with a speech challenging her classmates to go out into the world committed to fighting hunger and poverty, discrimination and injustice, inequality and man's inhumanity to man. She urged them to trade in childish games and pettiness for pursuing a path to changing their community and their world. Ever the social conscious rebel to the end, Carrie Leigh had called on her classmates and her community to do what those Sunday sermons throughout this Bible Belt city had long preached.

It never occurred to us that we hadn't had a honeymoon nor the church wedding that Carrie Leigh's parents had hoped to host one day for their oldest daughter. Everyone had had to change their dreams. But the strangest thing was happening. Among the people from whom we were receiving congratulatory cards and gifts were longtime friends of my family who knew both my father-in-law and me equally well. Among them were some of the Mexican American men who had played on my uncle's semi-pro baseball team and who had for years worked alongside Carrie Leigh's father at the local General Tire & Rubber Co. Some of these men with Spanish surnames like Duron, Gonzalez, and Hurtado even played golf with Carrie Leigh's father and also served with him on the company's credit union board. I was getting messages from these men telling me what a wonderful man my father-in-law was, and they apparently were telling him the same thing about me. Hardly a week went by when I didn't hear from either of my in-laws that they had gotten congratulatory phone calls from one of their friends who also knew me. Of course, none of these people knew of the hell my in-laws had put me through for two years simply because of my being Mexican background, which, ironically, was also that of these well-wishers. They didn't know that these ordinarily good people happened to be blatant racists who now were confronting their own prejudices.

"It's a small world, isn't it, Tony," my father-in-law said to me one Sunday as we spoke of yet another Mexican American co-worker, who had recently congratulated him on the new addition to his family.

"It sure is, Roger," I said. "You just never know who knows what about you."

When I graduated in January 1970, I had a reporting position waiting at the *Dallas Times Herald*, which had been only one of several job offers I'd gotten. Carrie Leigh and I moved into this great townhouse with a fireplace and a pool on the edge of a golf course off North Preston Road in far North Dallas. One of my great illusions, though, had been that when we left Waco, I would be leaving all the negativity that it had represented in my mind such as my marginalization based on the color of my skin, my heritage, and my Spanish surname. I was young and naïve, of course, but I didn't know that at the time. Had I, maybe I would have immediately looked to move to one of the big cities in the northeast. It might have brought different issues, but anything would have been more welcomed than one where I felt so stuck in the past.

The illusion was shattered as quickly as it took to get my first big story at my new job, all of a week. My civil rights story on a student takeover at the chapel of a local black college was scheduled to be the lead story at the top of Sunday's newspaper, and Carrie Leigh and I were excited at the prospect of my first big city newspaper by-line. In those days, big city newspapers published what was known as "bulldog" Sunday editions that came off the presses early Saturday night. That Saturday, as we headed out to dinner, Carrie Leigh and I rushed downtown to get a copy of the bulldog. I parked the car in front of a corner newsstand where Carrie Leigh jumped out and bought a paper. I could see a proud smile on her face as she grabbed a copy of the *Times Herald* off a rack, but she quickly returned to the car with a quizzical look.

She handed me the paper, and I immediately understood what had troubled her. "By ANTONIO CASTRO," the byline read.

My heart sank and then raced. I called a night editor who told me he didn't have the authority to change my byline. I got the same answer from another editor on Sunday. When Monday morning came, I hadn't slept well, nor eaten much. I had another story due to be published on Tuesday, and I was desperate to make sure the same mistake wasn't repeated on my byline. My city editor checked and said the order to use the "Antonio Castro" byline had come down from the editor of the paper, and that only he could change it. Late that afternoon, I met with the editor and co-publisher, a legendary Texas newspaperman named Felix R. McKnight, who had personally welcomed me to the staff just a week earlier.

"That byline stays, son," McKnight told me.

Perhaps on another issue I might have accepted McKnight's word as gospel. For six decades, he was synonymous with Dallas journalism, and his judgment was rarely questioned. When he was twenty-six and working in the Dallas bureau of The Associated Press, McKnight had answered an urgent call from a correspondent about a horrific gas explosion at a school in East Texas that had killed almost three hundred students. He was soon among the first reporters at the scene along with his young competitor from United Press, Walter Cronkite. Among McKnight's first visits was to a roller rink serving as a morgue. "The force of that explosion was so great that hardly a child was identifiable except for clothing," he later said. While there, McKnight was drafted to help sponge down remains of the children with formaldehyde to help preserve them, and the horror kept him awake for five straight days. This was one of the first stories I heard when I joined the staff of the paper, but it would not sway me on the issue of my byline.

"That's not my name," I insisted. "My father is Antonio. They gave me that name at birth to honor him. I'm junior, but I've never used it."

"It's your legal name," he said.

I pointed out that using legal names on the bylines couldn't possibly be the policy. I showed him that day's front page with bylines of first names like Bill instead of William, Bob instead of Robert and Jerry instead of Gerald.

"Son, what's the real issue here?" he wanted to know.

"The issue, sir, should be the byline any reporter feels most comfortable with, and in my case it's Tony," I said. "If you're asking me if I feel that Antonio makes me uncomfortable, that I think it's too ethnocentric, well, yes, it does and it is. If I were a *maitre'd* at a restaurant or a bullfighter, maybe it would be perfect. But I think I know why you want me to go by Antonio, and, with all due respect, I can't do it, and I won't do it. If you still want me on the paper and if that requires me to legally change my name, then that's what I'll do. If that's not enough, then I guess I can resign and go work for one of the other newspapers that offered me a job. I think they would be understanding and amenable to how I would like my byline to read."

McKnight gave in and allowed me to change the byline, but he also was so pissed off at me that he must have repeated the story and my threat to resign to other editors. Word filtered down to the newsroom where I quickly became known as the "Uppity Chicano" and the "Hilltop Chicano." Chicano was the term that Mexican American activists in South Texas, California, and Colorado had begun using to identify themselves since founding their movement in the mid-1960s. I didn't use it to identify or define myself, but then I had never liked labels on myself or on anyone else.

I also didn't realize until my first weeks at the *Times Herald* why so many newspapers had offered me jobs in the last semester of my senior year at Baylor. Being so full of myself, I suppose I thought it was because those editors had been told of my talents by my journalism professors or had been impressed by the reporting clippings that they may have seen. But most of those potential employers, I came to strongly suspect, saw something in me that had nothing to do with skill or talent. In 1970, there were no other Hispanic newspaper reporters in Dallas, Houston, and Fort Worth. In the entire Southwest, including Southern California, there may have been all of a handful. I also wasn't the only one aware of this journalistic demographic phenomenon. I heard it often from fellow reporters at the *Times Herald*, as well as at the *Dallas Morning News* across town. A few months into my tenure at the *Times Herald*, I reported a series of stories on the troubles at a public housing complex in west Dallas. The stories caused an immediate sensation. The local Public Broadcasting Service affiliate had recently started an innovative show called *Newsroom* hosted by Jim Lehrer, a former newspaper city editor who would go on to originate and anchor the *MacNeil-Lehrer Report* and later the *PBS Newshour* on national public television. Lehrer invited me on to the *Newsroom* show to talk about the series and immediately after the show offered me a job on the program, making almost twice my newspaper salary. I should have taken the job, but I loved newspaper work too much.

What I didn't love about the work was the "token" comments I soon began getting from other journalists. I had been prepared for the backstabbing among ambitious journalists that historically has gone on at all newspapers. But I had no inkling until I got to Dallas that I would feel like an outsider among what I thought would be my own kind, journalists. My anger and frustration would build up, and the only person I could talk to about them was Carrie Leigh. The "token" and "hilltop Chicano" digs from fellow reporters only intensified when Carrie Leigh and I attended the first staff party one Saturday night. She was tall, runway model svelte, and looked like she had just stepped out of a Neiman Marcus fashion catalog – and my co-workers hadn't been ready to learn that the uppity Chicano was married to a young, beautiful *white* woman.

Neither had I been prepared for the way some news sources would look at me. To my surprise, I would discover that I received the best treatment, professionally, from political conservatives and Republicans. The 1970 U. S. Senate campaigns of George Bush and Lloyd M. Bentsen provided me unusual access to the candidates who both treated me the same as they did our longtime political reporter. But I would learn a life lesson from white liberals, who historically had always beaten their chests as champions of Latinos and the downtrodden. Ralph Yarborough had been the patron saints of Texas liberals since 1957 when he was first elected to the U.S. Senate. But in 1970, Bentsen, a wealthy South Texas businessman and former Congressman, challenged Yarborough in the Democratic Party primary. This also happened to be the year when a new Chicano political party, La Raza Unida, began its attempt to get on the state's general election ballot for 1972.

It was the goal of La Raza Unida organizers to run a statewide candidate for governor, but the road for getting on the ballot was long and arduous. The Chicano activists would have to gather tens of thousands of petition signatures, and they began their campaign in 1970 by asking Mexican Americans, who traditionally voted for liberal Democrats, to stay away from the polls that year. It was necessary for La Raza Unida to develop that loyalty of Mexican American voters to effectively boycott the electoral process because the voters who would sign Raza Unida petitions to get the party on the 1972 ballot could not legally vote in the primaries. That meant that in the 1970 Democratic primary, in which Bentsen was challenging Yarborough, La Raza Unida organizers were urging Mexican American to not vote at all. Liberals and Yarborough supporters were furious and felt betrayed. They launched a campaign of their own for the Hispanic vote, but the turnout among Mexican American was significantly down nonetheless. On primary election night, Bentsen scored a resounding victory, with some analysts immediately concluding what seemed obvious: La Raza Unida's campaign of keeping large numbers of Mexican American voters from the polls had cost Yarborough the election. Late that night, when my newspaper still had not gotten a comment from Yarborough, an editor asked me to call his hotel room to see if I could get any kind of statement to add to the next day's story.

Understandably, the man who answered the phone in Yarborough's suite sounded upset. He may have also been drunk. He identified himself by a name that was familiar to anyone in Texas journalism. He was associated with a liberal political journal that often had some of the best reporting and commentary around – nothing you could ever read in the editorial pages of the state's dailies, most of which were moderate to conservative in their political views. He was also close to Yarborough. I didn't know what role, if any, he had in the senator's campaign. All I was trying to do was to get a comment or statement that we could attribute to Yarborough, who had just lost a close and bitter election. I identified myself and asked if I could speak to someone from the campaign. However, he must not have heard much past my Spanish surname. Or, if he did, he was too upset to care. In his mind, I was one of *them*.

"You people!" he blurted out. "You goddamn people have just lost the only man who gave a shit about you! I hope you're proud of yourselves..."

People may have mistreated me in the past for being Hispanic, as my in-laws had, and they may have contemplated the most awful thoughts, but this was the vilest thing I'd ever personally heard directed at me. I didn't even know if this man was even who he had identified himself as being or if he was with the campaign or talking on its behalf. I didn't know what to think. So I immediately reported the conversation to the city editor, who said that nothing of what he had said was fit to be used in the paper.

"Don't let stuff like that get you down," the city editor said to me after deadline. "You may not know it, but you're going to hear worse."

"Yeah?" I said. "Well, I wouldn't mind if every other reporter also had to take that kind of crap."

"I know, kid, I'm sorry," he said. "You're just going to have to get thicker skin. You've heard of Jackie Robinson, haven't you? Well, you'll just have to be our Jackie Robinson."

Not what you want to hear, though, when your hero is Mickey Mantle.

But there was one incredible personal payoff that first year in Dallas. Mickey Mantle had retired to Dallas in 1969, and I found his telephone number one day in the newspaper's city desk Rolodex. My editors, though, weren't interested in a story about the hero in retirement. I couldn't understand why until I realized that Dallas wasn't a baseball town. For Mantle, Dallas at this period was like a man-made baseball purgatory. It was a big city in America without a Major League Baseball team. As the country finally exited the troubled Sixties and entered the Seventies, Dallas was also a city still in mourning for the most defining event of the recently completed decade, or of the century for that matter. The Kennedy assassination had left Dallas not only with a civic black eye but also at a loss for a national identity beyond the Dallas Cowboys. That alone said volumes. Dallas was a big enough city to have its own professional football franchise, two of them, in fact, when the Dallas Texans of the old American Football League had been around before the move to Kansas City. However, it wasn't a big enough city to have its own Major League Baseball franchise. When big league baseball did come to the area in 1972 with the move of the Washington Senators, Dallas would share the franchise with Fort Worth and Arlington. Mantle, though, was hardly a newcomer to Dallas. He had lived there since the 1950s and in that time had irked local sportswriters more than any other sports figure in town. His drinking and carousing, which still were rarely reported in the news media, were already legendary in Dallas, where he had also gained a bad reputation for his boorish behavior, especially toward members of the news media.

Of course, you don't just telephone your childhood hero as if it's any other call. I had butterflies each time I dialed the number but never could get an answer. When I finally was able to get Mickey on the phone, I quickly explained that I was a reporter, but not a sportswriter, and that I wanted to explore writing a free-lance story on him as a golfer for one of the country's golf magazines. An avid golfer, Mantle played almost every day. He was known to hit drives off the tee well past three hundred yards, even in the days of old-styled wooden drivers. His game from tees to greens was another matter. It took a while, but Mickey agreed to meet me at a restaurant in the Turtle Creek area of Dallas. I showed up twenty minutes early to meet my childhood hero, but Mantle was more than half an hour late, arriving already drunk and making silly jokes to the waitresses about, "Honey, did ya drop the peanuts?" It was a restaurant whose floor was littered with peanut shells, something popular in its day.

It took all my willpower to stop staring at him. I imagined this would be the way I would look at Patricia if she were finally sitting in front of me. I was as nervous as if it had been Patricia until Mantle gave me a handshake worthy of a lumberjack. I was surprised, though, to find that he was only a couple of inches taller than I, maybe five-feet-ten-inches tall. But he was massive, as if chiseled from flesh and muscle. He had the shoulders of a linebacker and the arms of a bodybuilder. He was also sloshed and slurring his words.

Fortunately for me, I had the experience of having grown up in an extended family of alcoholics. They would never admit it, of course, but my father and his two closest brothers had drinking problems of which their friends were also in denial. When my mother finally acknowledged the issue, it dramatically changed her life for the better. It had happened on a Sunday afternoon when I was nine years old and my dad got so drunk at a baseball game that he passed out in the back seat of our 1949 Chevy. The problem was that the game had been played in Austin, well over an hour and a half from home, and everyone we knew who was at the game had already taken off to return home to Waco. My mom and I each tried waking my dad, but he was fast asleep, as was my little sister. My mother didn't know what to do. She had never driven a car in her life, and the Chevy had manual transmission with a stick shift on the steering wheel column. I had seen my father drive the car so many times that I thought I could drive it myself except that my legs were too short to reach the pedals. But I knew my mother's legs could reach them, and I convinced her that we could drive it together. So that afternoon my mother drove a car for the first time, hugging the shoulder of the asphalt road that ran parallel to the highway, doing all of maybe thirty miles an hour on a trip of almost one hundred miles For the entire drive home, I sat next to my mother, almost cuddling her, as I shifted gears awkwardly while she gripped the steering wheel tightly with both hands, hit the clutch when she needed to, and said the rosary praying for divine intervention yet one more time. That next week, my mother did two other things she had never done in her life. She got a driver's license, and she started looking for a job.

If I had learned anything from my father and his two brothers, Angel and Lupe, it was that you never cross an alcoholic. Instead you roll with them, as if riding a wave, surfing on whatever booze has created the storm. The reason I had arrived early for the meeting with Mantle was that I sensed what kind of shape Mickey would be in, and I wanted to do what I often did with my father. I asked the waiter and bartender to heavily water whatever drinks we ordered and to add a mixture of tea and sugar to them. It sounds awful unless you've tried it, and anyone who was already drunk wouldn't have noticed. We ordered cheeseburgers and beers. Mickey had three cheeseburgers and several beers, and he proclaimed himself sober enough to drive home. But, of course, he wasn't. I ended up driving him home, and had a difficult time finding his house. I finally had to pull into a service station, near a phone booth, to call the *Times Herald* city desk to ask for Mickey Mantle's home address.

It was a strange experience driving your childhood hero home in a drunken state, something that would happen often in the coming months. Mickey was never passed out, at least not by the time we reached his house. I'm not sure what I would have done then. He would have been too heavy to carry, and from my experience it was best to leave a sleeping drunken man alone, lest you get an inadvertent but damaging wild swing thrown your way. My mom used to leave my dad passed out in the car, allowing him to sleep it off and to later come into the house on his own strength. With Mickey, I got the impression that part of him was always awake through the drunken stupor. It led me to believe those baseball stories of how Mantle, hung over and possibly still drunk, came off the bench to slug a pinch-hit home run. This apparently happened more than once. In one story, Mantle complained that he was seeing three baseballs coming out of the pitcher's hand, leading a teammate to ask how he had known which ball to hit.

"I just hit the one in the middle," Mantle is reported to have said.

In another instance, a hung-over Mantle had been pretending to watch the game on the bench, not realizing he was no longer on the disabled list and was being called upon to pinch-hit. Told by his manager that he had been placed on the active list that day, Mantle struggled to the plate unable to see straight. Former teammate Hank Bauer was then a coach for the opposing team, the Baltimore Orioles, and knew Mickey was both rusty and hung-over. Calling a timeout, Bauer went to the mound to tell the pitcher that Mantle would never be able to get his bat around on a fastball. Mantle swung at the first pitch, a fastball, and hit it out of the park. He circled the bases with Bauer looking on from the Orioles' dugout in stunned silence. Once back in the Yankee dugout, Mickey slumped down on the bench next to teammate Whitey Ford.

"Kid, great hit," said Whitey. "I dunno how you hit that."

"Hell, hitting the ball was easy," Mickey shot back. "Running around the bases was the tough part."

I could imagine Mickey doing all that. Even when drunk, there was a part of him that appeared completely normal unless you knew him. I learned that the first time I drove him home. I made sure he got inside his house where his wife Merlyn took one look at him and turned up her eyes in disgust. She had a drill for whoever brought Mickey home. She wanted to know where Mickey had left his car, where his car keys were, and did he have his wallet with him. She didn't seem to care about any of the money in the wallet. It was Mickey's identification.

"It is just so much trouble for Mickey to get his drivers license replaced," Merlyn told me once. "He has to do it himself and once they know it's Mickey Mantle, there's a long line of people that builds up wanting his autograph. He winds up staying there for hours."

This, of course, was before the memorabilia boom that hit a decade later. There were no baseball card shows, to speak of, in 1970. Few people knew the value that would later be attached to Mantle's cards, especially those of his rookie season that would eventually sell as high as $100,000, which equaled his salary with the Yankees at the height of his career. I had a couple of those rookie cards myself, not to mention dozens of duplicates for each season up through the mid-1960s when I stopped collecting. It never occurred to me to ask Mantle to sign any of the memorabilia, nor to mug for photos with my boyhood hero. This was just something I never did as a writer. The only time I'd ever had a photo shot with a subject of a story had been when I was in high school and interviewed Don Trull, the Baylor All-American quarterback. I recall the lectures from David McHam, even then, when he had seen that picture of me with Trull. Professional reporters never did that, he said. In fact, I don't think I ever saw photographs of any reporters with the people they interviewed, even famous subjects, until years later when I visited the home of a feature writer in Los Angeles whose entire hallway was decorated with framed pictures of herself with probably everyone she had ever interviewed.

Merlyn never worried if Mickey left his El Dorado at the Preston

Trails Golf Club in far North Dallas. It was the exclusive new course designed by golf legend Byron Nelson where Mickey played two or three times a week. At other times, Merlyn insisted on personally retrieving Mickey's car, usually having a girlfriend drive her there. On a few occasions, I drove her myself and was surprised to learn how much she loved country music. Once in your car, Merlyn took control of the stereo and would pull out of her purse eight-track tapes with Willie Nelson and Waylon Jennings music that she would accompany as you drove. She had a nice voice, and she was a beautiful woman who had built her entire life around Mickey. In her late thirties, Merlyn was at a period when her life had begun changing from what she had known it to be for almost two decades. The children were in their teens or pre-teens. Mickey Jr. was in high school; David and Billy were fourteen and twelve years of age, respectively; Danny, the baby of the family, had just turned ten. They had their own sets of friends and their own lives.

"The only child I have to take care of now is Mickey," Merlyn said to me on one of those drives to pick up his car when he had been too intoxicated to drive home. She didn't say that sadly, so much as matter-of-fact, almost the way I would imagine my mother talking about my father when he came home drunk.

I asked her once what it was like having Mickey home during the summer, which had never happened until he retired the previous year.

"Well, we're still getting to know each other again!" she said. "We've never had this much time to ourselves."

Merlyn would later write in her own book about life with Mickey that these had been among the most difficult years of her life. She would develop a drinking problem herself, she wrote, in part from trying to be close to her husband. In 1970, Merlyn showed no sign, to me at least, of having a drinking problem yet. She appeared sober but concerned whenever I brought Mickey home. Sometimes she would be angry, especially if he had forgotten that they had plans for that evening. In our time together, Mickey rarely spoke of her, not that he necessarily should have. When he did, it was usually something about "Merlyn and the boys." I suspected this is how he had come to think of her, as the mother of his children. For all his reputation as a womanizer, I also never saw Mickey attempt to pick up any women; and there were numerous opportunities in the clubhouses at the golf courses where we played or at restaurants where we ate. There was some expected flirting with waitresses and women who brought their sons to our table seeking autographs. There were also numerous instances of women, either alone or with friends, catching Mickey's eye and possibly expecting him to get up from the table and to walk over to meet them. But he didn't. The only affection I ever saw from him toward a woman, both while sober and drunk, was toward Merlyn who still had a shock of blonde hair and beauty of a cheerleader, which she had been at Picher High School in Oklahoma in the late 1940s. She met Mickey in 1949 when he was a star athlete at archrival Commerce High School. "I developed an instant crush on Mickey Mantle," she wrote in her 1996 memoir *A Hero All His Life*, "and by our second or third date, I was in love with him and always would be." They married two days before Christmas in 1951, after Mickey's rookie season with the Yankees.

Merlyn was not unlike the women of her time, especially the wives of successful men. Her existence was so closely interwoven with that of her husband that she had never developed a life of her own. She was Mrs. Mickey Mantle. Her life, as she had more or less put it, was taking care of Mickey and his legacy. When she finally got around one day to ask me what I did for a living, she was stunned and mortified to learn that I was a journalist.

"A reporter?" she asked, astonished. "Does Mickey know that?"

I told her the story of how I had called him and how we met.

"Are you going to write about us?" I'm sure she was wondering why she has been so open with me.

"No, ma'm," I said. "My editor didn't have any interest."

She looked disappointed when I said that. She couldn't understand either why there would be no immediate interest at a Dallas newspaper about Mickey.

"Well, if you ever do," she said. "I would just ask that you be kind and wait until we're dead and buried."

In the weeks ahead, I came to understand a little of what Merlyn was dealing with in living with Mickey Mantle in retirement. I learned that it was advisable to get Mickey talking about golf and as little about baseball as possible. He had just recovered from his most embarrassing injury as a Yankee, and it upset him to dwell on it. While trying to get into his suite that spring, he had put his hand through a glass door at the St. Moritz Hotel in New York and needed stitches. The injury also put an end to the idea that he could coach first base for the Yankees that season, which had been a public relations disaster from the start. "I wasn't naïve. I put extra people in the stands, that's all," Mantle said of his days as a Yankee coach. "There I was, pacing back and forth in the [first base coaching] box, and saying, 'Let's get it going now!' and feeling like a fool when Bobby Murcer drew a leadoff walk in the fourth inning, called time and asked me what the signs were. I said, 'Mine looks good. I'm a Libra.' I was nothing more than a public relations gimmick."

In Dallas, Mantle now lived in virtual anonymity.

"It was like Mickey Mantle had died," he said about life after retirement. "It was weird. I'm thinking, 'Geeze, what did I do?' It seemed nobody cared what I was doing."

Well, some of the people at the Preston Trail Golf Club with its exclusive membership of Dallas's elite cared. They knew Mickey as a fun-loving guy who sometimes gave them some unexpected awkward moments. Mickey, for instance, had a tendency to walk into the club's restaurant to order a drink completely naked. Mantle had also on occasion shocked members of a nearby country club by going skinny-dipping in the club's pool. At Preston Trail, Mickey's naked antics led the membership committee to finally institute what became known as "The Mickey Mantle Rule," prohibiting anyone nude from entering or lounging in the club's restaurant.

"The problem with people in Texas," Mickey said, "is that they're so busy trying to be taken seriously they've forgotten how to have fun."

I suppose that made me the perfect choir member. Finding a wide-eyed young reporter who wanted to talk to him about golf was just what Mickey needed at the moment. It was a bonus that I could also play a decent game of golf and could take off early a lot of afternoons to get in nine or eighteen holes. More importantly, I had the moxie to play for money without folding under the pressure. But then it also wasn't my money. Mickey loved to gamble – on the round, on holes, on putts, regardless of whether they were his or mine. If a putt was six feet or shorter, he was betting.

"Hey, Waco." He called me Waco, and I would answer to it. "You wanna keep playin' with me, ya be sure to make those putts."

I blew a four-footer once, and he didn't talk to me for two holes.

"Waco, I was thinkin'. Blow another put like that," he said. "Then be damn sure you make the next one."

"Mick, I won't miss another one," I assured him.

"Nah, miss the next one."

I didn't understand, but I intentionally missed the next short putt, and he lost a bet. Then on the next short putt I faced, it all made sense. Mickey upped the stakes, tripling the bet, and cleaned up when I sank a seven-footer.

We played a round or two a week until that fall when Mickey tore an abdominal muscle hitting drives on a practice range. It was also time for me to resume being more serious about my own career. I had slacked off several weeks, and drinking with Mickey had taken its toll, no matter how much I tried to monitor my intake. I was waking up grumpy and needing several cups of strong black coffee just to drive to work at six in the morning. Several reporting friends and editors had also begun gently pressing me to consider the opportunities they said were uniquely opened to me. Of course, they meant the opportunities ahead in journalism because I was Hispanic and one of the few Latinos working as a reporter in the country.

All that had come falling upon me after the tragic shooting death late that summer of Ruben Salazar. I had never heard of Salazar, nor had much of America outside Southern California, until *Time* magazine that year published a story about him in its "Media" section. Salazar, who had moved from the *Los Angeles Times* to the city's Spanish TV station, had become the "rage of the people," as Jean Paul Marat had said of himself during the French Revolution, in reporting abuses and injustices suffered by Mexican Americans, particularly at the hands of law enforcement agencies. Cops and authorities were beside themselves and had complained to the station and to the *Times*, which was publishing his columns about the discrimination and inequality of life experienced by the city's Hispanics. Several of my fellow reporters at the *Times Herald* brought the article to my attention, but it was a veteran former war correspondent who took a more active interest in me meeting Salazar. Warren Bosworth, one of the paper's assistant city editors, knew Salazar personally. They had been reporters together covering the Vietnam War in the mid-1960s, and one day Bosworth called me over to his desk and handed me his telephone. Ruben Salazar was on the other end.

"You need to be in L.A.," Ruben said after dispensing of the niceties. "Come to L.A. I'll get you on at the *Times*, and you can help me kick butt here."

I was flattered, but I was barely out of college, and I had goals of going to the East Coast, not the West Coast. Still, moved by Ruben's encouragement, I made tentative plans to visit him in Los Angeles. That visit, though, never materialized. A few weeks later, Salazar's time as a cause celeb was cut short. On August 29, 1970, Salazar was killed – assassinated, some activists believed – at the height of his fame as the most controversial Chicano journalist of all time. Ruben and his TV crew had been covering an anti-Vietnam War demonstration in East Los Angeles where an estimated 25,000 Mexican Americans from across the Southwest were protesting the disproportionately high number of U.S. Hispanic troops killed in Southeast Asia. Taking a break, Ruben and his crew went into a bar called the Silver Dollar Café where deputies were soon responding to a report of an armed man inside. Those deputies later maintained they were trying to empty the bar when one of them fired a ten-inch tear gas canister into the darkened premises that struck Ruben in the head, killing him instantly. Salazar's friends and others insisted he was targeted by law enforcement because his aggressive coverage of Mexican-American issues had created a growing voice for Latinos caught up in the turbulence of the civil rights and anti-Vietnam War movements. At the time of his death, Salazar was also investigating allegations of misconduct by sheriff's deputies and Los Angeles police. He had told friends that he thought he was being followed by authorities and feared they might do something to discredit his reporting. Investigations found mistakes committed by the deputies, but no arrests were made in a controversy that would continue for decades.

"They killed Ruben, but they haven't silenced correcting the injustices," a teary-eyed Bosworth said to me on the Saturday night that Salazar was killed. We were both working Saturday night shifts, and I was surprised by Bosworth's emotional reaction. He was a no-nonsense former Marine who had covered the Kennedy Assassination and rarely gave any hint of what he was thinking about stories he assigned. Even when discussing Salazar, he told me that he personally had not liked the man.

"We didn't see eye to eye in Vietnam, and I didn't like the son-of-a-bitch," he said, without elaborating. "But that doesn't mean I didn't respect him. And I thought you should meet him."

Salazar's death also opened up Bosworth in talking about the Kennedy Assassination, which was a sensitive subject not only for many residents of Dallas but also for journalists there. A story of that magnitude happening in a newspaper's backyard was tailor-made Pulitzer Prize-winning fodder, but the *Dallas Times Herald* and *Dallas Morning News* had both missed out on winning for their coverage. Instead, the Pulitzer Prize for reporting on the assassination was won by Merriman Smith of United Press International. The *Times Herald* did win a Pulitzer that year for the news photography of Lee Harvey Oswald being shot to death by Jack Ruby, which in itself sent a ripple through Dallas journalism circles. The picture that won the Pulitzer had been snapped by Robert Jackson, a twenty-nine-year-old photographer who was regarded by many of his peers as a trust-fund playboy. Jackson came from wealth, knew racing pioneer Carroll Shelby personally, and drove a Porsche. His photograph caught Oswald with excruciating pain in his face the moment the bullet from Ruby's gun struck him and shows smoke rings floating from Oswald's abdomen up to his eyes. Jackson's shot beat out that of Jack Beers, the chief photographer of the *Dallas Morning News* who had been given a wide berth by other photographers assembled that morning in the basement of the Dallas police station. Taking the best view from which to photograph in the basement, Beers was standing on a railing on top of the incline, giving himself a height advantage of several feet. He later said he had seen sudden movement out of the corner of his eye and then heard Ruby cursing "You son of a bitch!" punctuated by the sound of a gunshot. Instinctively Beers snapped his photograph but too early. He caught Ruby, his .38 caliber Colt Cobra pistol extended toward Oswald who is expressionless. Six-tenths of a second later, Jackson snapped his photograph and captured history.

"The reason Beers shot too soon, in comparison to me," Jackson later said, "is that he saw it easier and quicker than I did. Ruby was more in his vision. I had a better position because I wasn't distracted by Ruby as much. I was still looking at Oswald's face, and I knew I was going to shoot before whoever that was blocking my view."

When the papers came out the next morning, Beers' photograph had the Morning News office ecstatic with his boss, exclaiming, "My God, you've just won us the Pulitzer Prize!"

Jackson's photograph, however, quickly stole the thunder. Inexplicably, though, when Pulitzer time came around, *Times Herald* editor and publisher Felix McKnight, the man who wanted my byline to be Antonio, felt sorry for Beers and lobbied for the prize to be shared. It wasn't, and Beers was devastated by the turn of events. Beers' daughter Darlene Williams later said her father lived the rest of his life "feeling let down. Not by anybody in particular. More by fate, I guess. He always felt like, 'Why have I had to struggle so hard to finally get the picture and then not get it?'"

Life after the assassination was similarly traumatic for many other Dallas journalists. Some were guilt-ridden over feeling they had fumbled a tremendous professional opportunity. Others told stories of reporters who suffered momentary emotional breakdowns the day of the assassination. Stories abound at the *Morning News* of at least a couple veteran reporters who returned to the office that day unable to type or report. Fellow reporters and editors had to pump those shocked reporters with cups of coffee and then interview them for bits of details, names, quotes, anecdotes that could be woven together into sidebar stories.

"Some reporters were never the same after the assassination," said Lew Harris, a former reporter at the *Morning News* and my city editor at the *Times Herald*. "It's part of a sorry history of Dallas no one wants to talk about."

It was an incredible first year for me in Dallas that ended when I was awarded a six-month public affairs reporting fellowship in Washington, D.C. It also signaled the first time I realized my marriage had serious problems. Carrie Leigh didn't want to go. She said she hadn't signed on to be a gypsy traveler chasing dreams, specifically my dreams, which I recalled her once saying were hers as well. Maybe we should have taken a time-out from chasing any dream just to get a reality check on who we were, what we wanted, and if we wanted to be together. But when you're in a love affair that you've always defended as being true, you don't admit doubts, nor give anyone a chance to gloat that they told you so. We were also possibly too young to have the common sense to step back and get some counseling. So grudgingly she went to Washington with me. We had gone from two long years of a young love hidden from public, or at least from Carrie Leigh's parents, to a life of newlyweds that neither of us knew how to handle. In my senior year, I had left the *Waco Tribune-Herald*, anticipating the time when we would make our marriage public. One thing I quickly learned was how fast money disappeared when you are married and not working. So in my final semester at Baylor, I had taken the sports editor's job at the *Temple Daily Telegram*, a half-hour commute from Waco, where I was working nights and not getting home to our apartment until well after midnight. I was away so much, barely seeing Carrie Leigh, that once it had even taken me a couple of days to notice that she had cut her hair so short that I didn't recognize her the first time I saw her with it. It soon became that way in Dallas as well. I was working at the *Dallas Times Herald* from just after dawn until late afternoon. When I played golf after work, I didn't get home until sometime in the evening. Carrie Leigh wasn't home much either, as she had chosen to skip college to work for a medical equipment leasing company. With those kinds of schedules, the only quality time we spent together was on weekends, when we often returned to Waco to visit our families. So the time in Washington soon became the first time we spent getting to know one another without the demands of work and family.

For the two or us, it also meant having long weekends to explore the nation's capital and all its historic sites. Our most moving experience in Washington, though, may have had taken place by accident. One cold snowy day, while walking around Georgetown admiring all its quaint townhouses and charm, we happened to come across a memorable scene we would never forget. It was late afternoon with the winter sun about to go down, and we were in front of a home where we spotted two couples at the doorsteps. An older, aristocratic-looking man and his adorable wife were obviously saying good-bye to a tall, straight-backed man and a radiantly beautiful woman with long dark hair who looked remarkably familiar. Then recognition hit. Ted Kennedy and Jacqueline Kennedy Onassis were leaving this home. Both Carrie Leigh and I were unapologetic Kennedy buffs. The Kennedy family had been American royalty for many of our generation, and we were no different. Then, when your political hero is assassinated less than a hundred miles from your hometown, you feel the unbearable loss that much harder to handle. More incredible still, that afternoon, as they left that townhouse, Ted Kennedy and Mrs. Onassis both made eye contact with us. Passing past us on the sidewalk, the senator nodded and Mrs. Onassis smiled and said hello in her distinctively throaty voice. She looked as elegant as we had come to expect as she walked to a waiting limousine. Down the street, we could see Ted Kennedy getting into the passenger seat of a dark green Plymouth that quickly drove away.

"Did Jackie Kennedy just say hello to us?" a startled Carrie Leigh asked.

"I think she did," I said, too star-struck for it to fully register. "Isn't she incredible looking, more so in person?"

"Okay, I've decided," she said. "If you're ever going to leave me for someone, it has to be Jackie Kennedy."

"Sure, and if you leave me, it can only be for Teddy."

We shared a laugh and kissed deeply. We would never be happier.

We later learned that the home they were leaving belonged to Averell Harrison, the former governor of New York and ambassador, and the woman at the door with him was Pamela Hayward, whom he would marry later that year. This became our favorite memory of Washington together. Camelot. Or what was left of it.

Alone, the fellowship proved to be like a graduate school program on learning how America works. We regularly met with the nation's leaders, policy-makers, image builders, and powers-that-be. There were intensive briefings from the White House staff, Congressional members, and the heads of the various government departments and agencies. We were also meeting the reporters behind some of the biggest by-lines in the country. I was interning at the *Washington Post*, one of the newspapers of my dreams, and this was more than a year before it blew the cover off the break-in at the Watergate complex. Barry Sussman, then a metropolitan editor who would be closely involved in directing the Watergate coverage, took me under his wing to talk about reporting in the nation's capital. Sometimes he would send me to tag along with beat reporters to observe them working. At the office, I sat two desks behind Carl Bernstein, already a veteran reporter who with Bob Woodward would break the Watergate story. In *All The President's Men*, the book and film about their reporting, there is an allusion to editors who wanted to fire Bernstein in the period leading up to Watergate. This was not something made up for the book and movie, as some people have thought. In 1971, while I was at the *Post*, Bernstein was under more scrutiny than any other reporter at the paper from some of the editors who wanted to run him off. I also developed a friendship with one of its national editors, J.D. Alexander, which would lead to me becoming the *Post's* special correspondent in Texas at a time before that newspaper opened a bureau there.

It was a wonderful stay in Washington, but we returned to Dallas when the fellowship ended. Carrie Leigh was homesick. So was I, but mine was a different kind of homesickness. Something wasn't right. Something didn't feel as it should. I didn't want to even consider that it might be our marriage. In spite of our time together in Washington, we had lost something; and I had no idea what it was. I could just feel it. We didn't make love as often as we used to. We quarreled about small things. Worse, there were times with a lot of silence. I would ask if something was wrong and whether she still loved me. I was foolish to ask, she said. We also never once talked about our experience of the past four years. She was sixteen when we met and committed ourselves to a relationship whose existence we were constantly hiding and worried of what could happen if it was discovered. Little of our courtship had been normal. We had been robbed of that, and it was something we could never get back. Some might say that our love, relationship, and marriage had all been borne out of one act of defiance on both of our parts. Maybe it was.

For my part, I was torn between guilt and anger that slowly stewed into hostility. I felt guilty over having placed us in this circumstance. This is what I had long been warned against in those "white girls" speeches, and I hadn't seen it coming. And I was angry, and perhaps petty in being so, over how Carrie Leigh's family had treated me for almost two years. The one important thing that was missing on the night her parents learned we were married was anything approaching an apology or words to the effect that they had been wrong in how they judged me and how they had mistreated me. Maybe their acceptance of me alone should have sufficed as an unspoken olive branch extended my way. It made me question my character, and perhaps the depth and maturity of my love for Carrie Leigh, that I could not get past this. After we returned to Dallas, I found myself increasingly reluctant to return to Waco for visits. More and more I insulated myself in a shell of denial not wishing to deal with what for so long had been gnawing away at me. Of course, I had the perfect excuse. I was always on assignment. I had changed newspapers, going to work at the larger and more prestigious *Dallas Morning News*, and I was busy pursuing a story I seemed to own.

In the wake of La Raza Unida's emergence, the Chicano movement was in full swing in the Southwest, especially in Texas. La Raza Unida had been the brainchild of a group of students who called themselves the Mexican American Youth Organization. Their leader was a brilliant young organizer named Jose Angel Gutierrez, a college-educated son of a doctor from the small, dusty hamlet of Crystal City in South Texas. Protesting in 1969, he had drawn attention when newspapers quoted him vowing to "Kill the Gringo," should it be necessary. Gutierrez and MAYO quickly drew the wrath of the state's small Latino leadership who were part of the political establishment the activists wanted to overturn. But MAYO also gained the admiration and following of thousands of Chicano activists who were clamoring for change. Gutierrez and other MAYO leaders were claiming that their movement would tip the political scales in future elections, and the defeat of Ralph Yarborough stood as a harbinger of what could happen. MAYO also was not without its own support among establishment circles. Behind the scenes of MAYO and La Raza Unida, another charismatic young activist named Carlos Guerra with a gift of gab had charmed two strange bedfellows that wanted to assist their movement: Hispanic Republican leaders working in the Nixon Administration in Washington and the heads of the philanthropic Ford Foundation in New York. Long a supporter of liberal causes and programs, the Ford Foundation funneled money to MAYO for its work as well as for the development of what would become the Southwest Voter Registration Project. Meanwhile, the Republican Hispanics gave Guerra and MAYO entre into their political circles and channeled federal funding to programs friendly to the Chicano activists, programs that could be used to sway local support for President Nixon's re-election in 1972.

In the early 1970s, I was traveling around South and Central Texas reporting the story of the development of the Chicano movement's political party and the rising star it created. His name was Ramsey Muñiz, a former high school football star in Corpus Christi and later an inspiring figure on the Baylor football teams of the early 1960s. A linebacker, Muñiz suffered a serious knee injury in an early season game that required surgery. In the days before arthroscopic surgery, knee operations usually ended an athlete's season and required a year's recuperation. Ramsey, though, underwent major surgery on the knee and to everyone's amazement made a near miraculous return to the playing field before the end of that season.

"That's who I am, a fighter," Ramsey later said when I brought up the surprisingly quick return from the knee surgery. By then he was a law student at Baylor, and I was a freshman. We got to know each other on campus, often talking politics and sports in the student union, developing a friendship that came in handy when he became La Raza Unida's candidate for governor in 1972.

Ramsey was ideal for the part of a Chicano political messiah: Handsome, articulate, charismatic. The *New York Times*, which sent a reporter to Texas to write about what seemed like a romantic political revolt in the state, went so far as to call him a "Chicano Robert Redford." I had not anticipated that covering Muñiz, MAYO, and La Raza Unida would affect me as it did personally. I came to learn that, as with Ramsey, I had more in common with some of the leaders of the Chicano movement than I had thought. I visited with Jose Angel Gutierrez and his family in Crystal City and learned that we had almost similar backgrounds: From intellectual curiosity to the feeling of having the dominant white society around us impose limitations on us that they didn't place on other youths who were not Hispanic. I came away from my visits with Jose Angel troubled emotionally that we were more alike than I had felt with anyone else since my friendship with Dick McCall in junior high school.

What seemed to trouble Gutierrez most seemed to be the relationship between Hispanics and white liberals that too often, he said, acted like Peace Corps workers in some underdeveloped Third World country. It was something that reminded me of my own experiences, personally and professionally in dealing with well-intentioned white liberals who had an agenda of how I should think and behave.

"When the Chicano sees a white, he doesn't see a white liberal," Gutierrez said in an interview. "He sees a gringo, and they react this way because liberal Anglos have a facility for insulting people, especially our people. They can't conceive that we like steak, that we get tired of Mexican food because we eat it every day. They are the ones who buy a *molcajete* [a bowl used to pound spices] and use it as an ashtray. They go to Mexico and say they saw the ruins of the Mayan tombs. Well, that makes me jealous and pisses me off because I can't even go to see my own culture. Here they have it in arts and crafts, they have it laying around as ashtrays. They can't appreciate it. They can only prostitute it. It's the same one that gets turned off when he listens to the *ranchera* [Mexican country] music or the polkas, but they like the Mexican music when it's played by the Tijuana Brass... If they hear the music played by the plain *conjunto* [Mexican combo], it's cheap stuff, but it's great when the Baja Marimba Band plays it in stereo...The liberals haven't done a damn thing for the Chicanos. They have done things for themselves and used the Chicanos. I'm a bit critical, but that's the way I feel. I've gone to all those luncheons – this pisses me off! 'Ah, Jose Angel Gutierrez, I want to shake your hand.' And then they start flirting. I feel like a damn commodity. They don't even know what the hell to say. The 'gringas,' for example, want you on their own timetable, not on agendas. They want to see if you're for real, if you really smell bad for whatever. It's like the *molcajete* ashtray. I'm sure if I was for sale, they would buy me, put me on their mantelpiece and say, 'Look, I have a live Jose Angel Gutierrez.'"

My stories on the Chicano movement and activists like Gutierrez were often prominently displayed in the *Dallas Morning News*, and my own career was similarly on the rise. Early in 1972, the Texas Headliners Club awarded me its top political writing prize, and the same year the national magazine *Saturday Review* published my long account on La Raza Unida. A week later, *Saturday Review's* book division contacted me with an offer: A nice advance payment to write a book. They already had a title in mind – *Chicano Power*.

Carrie Leigh was so thrilled at the news that I had this book offer that she broke out in song lyrics she had made up to music of *Chicago, Chicago*. "Chicanos, Chicanos, those crazy brown bears, Chicanos, Chicanos, I'll show you around, I'll put 'em in my lair..." We took the advance and bought a Spanish styled townhouse in North Dallas, a sailboat for getting away to the lakes nearby, and Cowboys season tickets at the new Texas Stadium. The townhouse had a special built-in nursery adjoining the master bedroom, and it was a big selling point. We had talked about having a baby soon, and Carrie Leigh even had names picked out: Lance for a boy, Chance for a girl. I remember checking on the construction of the house just a few days before it was completed. I looked in on the nursery. Standing there, old memories stirring within, I wondered if Patricia was now a mother herself. It was just a moment, and it quickly passed. Many years later, I would learn that at that time she and her young family were living almost within walking distance of our new home.

The townhouse had a thirty-foot high fireplace sweeping up to a cathedral ceiling, and it was an immediate hit with our families and our friends. I finished *Chicano Power* in the study of that house, and our lives now seemed back on track. Each Saturday morning Carrie Leigh and I entertained my best friend John Tuthill for breakfast, tennis on the complex's courts, chess, and lunch. Sometimes Tuthill stayed for dinner or we went out together with his girlfriend or he would sleep over to continue a chess match.

I called John "Tut," and this was long before the craze of the Egyptian boy king. The son of a law professor at Southern Methodist University, Tut had been born in Washington, D.C., and educated at the Choate school in Connecticut and the University of California at Berkeley. Most people who met Tut were initially intimidated by him because of his height — he was six feet, six inches tall — and his looks. Tut had eyes the color of the Pacific at dawn and, though he was starting to lose his hair prematurely, he could strike the pose of an Olympic god. But I was also intimidated by Tut's mind, which is why I was hesitant to be his friend at first. Tut, however, wouldn't allow me to slide out of his life. A couple of drinks led to several dinners, then some sets of tennis and a Dallas Cowboy game or two. We were fascinated by each other's backgrounds. I enjoyed hearing Tut talk about going to prep school at Choate, where President Kennedy had been educated, and about being at Berkeley during the free speech protests of the 1960s. Tut wanted to hear my stories about growing up in the heart of the Bible Belt, about the identity crisis I was going through, having grown up Latino but being an "Anglophile," as he called me, about being a newspaperman, and the struggles of married life. We often poured out our souls about our dreams and our insecurities. Tut wanted to write but feared he couldn't, even though he had shown me notebooks filled with promising prose and short stories. The most memorable of those stories was an account of how he and his fraternity pals at Berkeley would often skip classes for long drives south to Los Angeles to watch John Wooden's great UCLA basketball teams of the 1960s that featured Lew Alcindor, who later became Kareem Abdul-Jabbar. The story smacked not only of UCLA basketball, but of the free spirit of his youth, a 1960s Jack Kerouac. Tut was the only person to whom I ever confessed the nagging insecurity that I then felt. Despite my own voracious appetite for reading and studying the classics, I felt extremely inferior intellectually among people I would meet from the East. It was a phenomenon not uncommon then for Southerners, I would learn later from Southern writers such as Larry McMurtry and the late Willie Morris. One day Tut showed up at my home with a book by Robert Hutchins, the noted educator who championed a renaissance in liberal arts education in America and the Great Books program at the University of Chicago. Tut insisted I read the book and that I begin re-reading Plato's *Republic*. Over the next months, our weekend games of chess and tennis became backdrops to Socratic dialogs about the books we were reading or re-reading – from Aeschylus to Augustine, from Homer to Hobbes, from Dante to Darwin.

About this time, I had the scare of my life. One evening, just after an early deadline at the *Morning News*, I got a telephone call from a woman who identified herself as our next-door neighbor.

"You need to hurry home," she said, and I had already begun trembling with fear at what her next words were going to be. "Carrie Leigh was attacked this evening. She's here. She's going to be okay, but you need to be here."

Anyone who has ever been in a similar situation in which a loved one has been harmed knows that no matter how much you hurry nor how fast you drive you can never get there as quickly as you would like to. All kinds of fears, worries and insecurities go through your head, as do feelings of guilt and responsibility even though there might have been nothing you could have done. The police were already at our house when I arrived, and they assured me that Carrie Leigh was physically well but emotionally traumatized. While she'd been walking our cocker spaniel, someone had blindsided her and knocked her down.

"I don't think the assailant realized she had a dog with her – and that probably saved her from further harm," one of the cops told me. Candy, our cocker spaniel, had tried to protect Carrie Leigh. She had chased off the attacker, and her barking had gotten our neighbor's attention.

The police advised going to the hospital – that although Carrie Leigh had not been raped, she perhaps should still speak to a counselor. But Carrie Leigh adamantly insisted she would be fine. We spent the night cuddled up under blankets in front of the fireplace. The next morning Carrie Leigh refused to talk about what happened and became angry when I suggested that might not be the wisest course. I didn't now what else I should do. I thought that perhaps in a day or two she would have a change of heart and either talk to me about what had happened or discuss it with someone professionally. I was wrong, though. She never spoke about it again.

I changed my work schedule and tried to be home more, but in September I had to go out of town for several days on an assignment. The *Washington Post* sent me to El Paso to cover the first national Raza Unida Convention, which suddenly had become a national media event in large part because of Ramsey Muñiz's campaign for governor. Muñiz had received widespread exposure on the television network news and had become a sensation on the East Coast. So much so that Sander Vanocur, one of the country's most prominent political journalists, headed a national media onslaught that descended on El Paso for La Raza Unida and Muñiz.. The other big media draw was Cesar Chavez, a darling of the Democratic Party. He was scheduled to speak at a convention of Chicano activists who made no secret about seeking an alternative to Mexican American political traditions. Heightening the tension among the activists was the killing of a Chicano delegate by police just a few days before the convention. It was also the first time that activists from various states in the Southwest attempted to unite, a romantic notion that quickly dissolved under the reality of regional rivalries and political jealousies. Ultimately, the radical elements took control of the convention, and their most important action proved to be both politically naïve and a public relations disaster. They rescinded the speaking invitation to Cesar Chavez, of all people.

It was at La Raza Unida's turbulent national convention that I met another young reporter who was following the Chicano movement. At the time Frank Del Olmo was really the only Hispanic news reporter on the staff of the *Los Angeles Times*. Frank had joined the *Times* right out of college shortly after Salazar's death as the *Times* was trying to decide how it would report on the issues that Ruben had brought to the forefront. I had called Frank just a few months before La Raza Unida's convention to introduce myself and to arrange to meet in El Paso. We were both the same age, from the same socio-economic backgrounds, and virtually alone in covering the same stories. Over dinner and drinks, we also learned we had one other important thing in common:

We were each married to lovely blonde, blue-eyed women. However, as we drank and talked more freely, I came to understand that Frank was troubled beyond belief that he had married a non-Hispanic. He spoke about the disapproving looks he would get, especially from Hispanic women his own age, making him feel as if he had badly depleted the bank of eligible Mexican American men with good futures ahead of them. Didn't I get those same looks, too, he wondered. Maybe I did, I said, but I didn't pay any attention to them. My personal life was none of their business, I told Frank. Neither should his be, but I sensed that Frank's issues were deeper rooted than what people thought of him. I also joked about how I was more concerned about the possible lynch mobs of white men, which he didn't think was funny. Frank, I came to understand, particularly as I got to know him in the years ahead, had no sense of humor on this subject.

"You don't feel guilty?" he wanted to know.

"I don't understand," I said. "Why should there be any guilt. You married the woman you fell in love with and love, didn't you?"

Frank, though, feared there had been some kind of heritage betrayal on our part. By marrying non-Hispanics, he wondered whether we might be engendering an entirely new race of people and diluting the existing Mexican-American bloodlines that had been created from the original *mestizo* process – the mixing of Spaniard and Mexican. We strongly disagreed, and we had words, not kind ones either. It was also obvious that we saw ourselves and our roles as journalists differently. Frank was in the process of organizing a group of Hispanic journalists in California as a kind of informal Chicano journalists union and wondered if I was interested in trying to do the same in Texas. Absolutely not, I said.

"Frank, I don't see myself as a Hispanic or Mexican-American journalist," I said. "I see myself as a journalist, period."

"Well, you're being naïve," he said. "Others see you as that."

"That's their problem," I said. "I can't control that, but I'll be damned if I allow how they look upon me or treat me to affect the way I see myself or the way I behave professionally. You start branding yourself a Chicano journalist, and you've lost. You've allowed those people whose hearts and minds you want to change to get into your own head. This isn't like joining a guild or a union. You do this and you start advocating for something as a Chicano, and guess what? You're not much more than another activist, just one with a byline."

Nevertheless, I actually wanted to share a byline with Frank. *Chicano Power* was becoming an overwhelming undertaking. As La Raza Unida's convention in El Paso showed, the movement was rife with fractionalization and rivalries, not only along state lines but also as to priorities. To do justice, it would require extensive reporting in California, New Mexico and Colorado as well as Texas. Despite our personal differences, I proposed to Frank that he handle the two westernmost states and I would cover Texas and New Mexico, as well as do the writing. But Frank resisted. He didn't like the idea of a book written about the movement from a dispassionate perspective. The issues, he said, were too important not to take sides and get involved. I agreed and, if we were activists, we should jump in without hesitation. But we weren't. I wasn't, at least. I would do the book on my own, getting a tremendous assist from Roy Aarons, the West Coast bureau chief of the *Washington Post*, who to that time had done perhaps the best reporting on Cesar Chavez and the farm workers as well as the Chicano movement in California. Aarons helped open doors with Chavez at his compound in La Paz especially, and guided me through the occasionally hazardous trail of getting to see other movement leaders in California and Colorado.

Meanwhile, little did I realize that our own issues at home related to working on *Chicano Power* were already affecting my marriage. There were long additions to the book, rewrites, edits, and proofs. Carrie Leigh was involved in much of the re-typing, editing, and becoming intimately familiar with all the civil rights and discrimination issues that faced Mexican Americans in Texas and the Southwest. Some of this was unsettling for her. She was having to face the roots of her own parents' attitudes toward Hispanics, which had manifested themselves in their opposition to us seeing each other at the beginning of our relationship. It was an unresolved issue that would hang over our marriage forever. Sometimes we would start talking about this, but it was never a comfortable conversation for either of us.

For a while, our lives were made a little easier when I was hired away from the *Dallas Morning News* by the local PBS affiliate for *Newsroom*, the innovative news analysis program originated by Jim Lehrer. He had gone to public television disillusioned with mainstream news media. The former city editor of the *Times Herald*, Lehrer developed *Newsroom* into an alternative daily, having hired only newspaper reporters to tell stories on the air. The ratings were poor, typical for public television, but the salaries were staggering compared to the pay at the city's two dailies. I took the job knowing it would be temporary until the publication of my book. I hadn't counted on the unusually strong camaraderie on the staff. There was a large baseball fan base at the station, and the Texas Rangers team had brought Major League Baseball to the area in 1972. The station also had a crack softball team on which I played shortstop and whose manager took special interest in Carrie Leigh, or his wife did. She was an independent film and commercials director, and she had seen Carrie Leigh at one of our games.

"She's one of the most beautiful people I've ever seen," she told me one day. "She should be doing commercials or film. She's every bit as beautiful as Julie Christie."

Carrie Leigh, though, only laughed when I told her about the complimentary comparison to the British actress who had won an Academy Award for *Darling* and the hearts of movie-goers in *Doctor Zhivago*. But she wasn't interested in talking to the woman, no matter how hard I tried to convince her. I never understood. She knew she was attractive, and she had a certain vanity about her. However, she seemed uncomfortable whenever someone made a big deal about it and always sought to eschew any limelight.

Around this time I was spending a lot of time at airports, arriving from a flight or waiting for one. I had forgotten how much I loved airports, that is to say, our little one-runway airport in Waco. Without much of a social life when I was in high school, I would sometimes hitch rides on a free Saturday to the airport. There I would watch small commuter and private planes landing and disembarking passengers from the cities, and I would play a game I made up. I put a story to each passenger, made up of course, of who they were, where they were coming from and what they planned to do in Waco. I created my mental sketches based on the clothing they wore, their shoes and handbags, their luggage, and even the men's hats because this was time when a lot of well-dressed men still wore stylish fedoras. Sometimes, if the passengers looked particularly interesting, I followed them out of the airport to check how they were leaving. Was it in taxis or personal cars? Or were they leaving in new dark Cadillacs and Lincolns driven by chauffeurs? Now, grown-up and being one of those people getting on and off planes, I often stared into the crowds and wondered. Was one of them Patricia? I would look for the tallest, most slender of women, the ones who happened to walk as if they might have studied ballet at one point in their lives, and who, of course, were blonde and beautiful. It was only when they got much closer that I could look for the hazel eyes, but I never saw her. I would always end up wondering why she had married. Sometimes I imagined that she really had been a princess, possibly from Austria whose family dated back to the time of the Roman Empire. Had custom forced her to be betrothed as a child and then to marry under pressure before her 20th birthday or risk her family's fortune and existence? Of course, I was a master of avoidance, refusing to accept that maybe she had married so young out of practicality – maybe she had gotten pregnant – or just married because she was so head-over-heels in love with someone. In my dreams, I refused to allow reality to creep inside, and my thoughts would snap back to looking at the people in the airport. At one of those airports, one of those times, a man who looked familiar came up to me.

He was Ed Hunter, the managing editor of the *Houston Post*. He had interviewed me for a reporting job when I was a senior at Baylor, and it had been difficult turning down his offer for the job in Dallas. We were both flying from Washington, D. C., back to Texas, and we arranged to get seated together. During that long flight, he told me of a grandiose plan he had for his newspaper.

"I want to move out the old guard as quickly as is possible," he said. "I want to put together a staff of reporters like yourself who are more sensitive to the changes taking place in Texas and can do the kinds of stories that they're doing at the *Washington Post* and the *Los Angeles Times*. Why should we keep losing our best talent to papers like those when they could be writing those kinds of stories here? I want to put together a staff that reflects Texas and all its people, and, without sounding a little conceited about it, I want to turn the *Houston Post* into the *Washington Post* of the South."

Ed had kept up with my career, and I told him of the book that would be published in just a few months, in mid-1974. He was excited about it. A book like *Chicano Power*, he said, would be landmark in the still-infant ethnic studies field that was springing up in academia. I would do well there, he thought, as well as in the general book buying public in the Southwest. He asked if I would allow him to read any galley proofs or an advance copy and promised that his newspaper would review it. Ed then made me the most incredible job offer that I couldn't turn down. He would pay me at the top of his salary scale and, when I smiled like someone who didn't entirely believe him, promised to show me a list of staff salaries to prove it. He said the tradeoff would be that he wanted me to identify myself as a writer for the *Post* on the book jacket cover and in its promotion. He thought it would help him sell the newspaper to other reporters he wanted to hire. Ed also outlined the kind of job I would have at the *Post*. I could cover civil rights as well as politics all as part of being a special assignments reporter. He would also give me a free rein over my story assignments. I would be allowed to work any story I wanted without being responsible to any other editor other than himself and a protégé whom he had molded to follow in his footsteps. Of course, I was experienced enough to know that there would be a backlash among some members of the editorial staff. No one likes to see an outsider – a new kid in town – coming to a new job at the front of the line. Ed promised to take care of this and to see that the transition was smooth. I also remembered the treatment I received from some of my fellow reporters in Dallas, and I figured they couldn't be much different in Houston. Ed and I talked about this, and he said it was those kinds of people with that type of thinking – "the hick sons of red necks," he called them – that he was trying to get rid of, but that it would take time. The publisher of the *Post*, Mrs. Oveta Culp Hobby, the wife of a former governor of Texas, made me the same promises when I met with her as the paper was wooing me. She had also been the first secretary of the Department of Health, Education and Welfare created under the Eisenhower administration and made the decision to legalize Jonas Salk's polio vaccine. Over brunch and tea in her offices, Mrs. Hobby wanted to know more about me. When I told her of my interest in literature, it sprang an unexpected discussion about two of her favorite authors, Fitzgerald and Flaubert. She offered whatever assistance I needed in relocating to Houston where she said she would consider it a special favor to her if I represented her on the board of the Greater Houston Human Relations Commission. Mrs. Hobby said she wanted to make the changes in her newspaper that would help it to better cover "our new Texas." Old ways and old thinking, she said, were changing, and she was determined to help moving it along. At this point of my career, especially with the book about to come out, I thought it was a gift from heaven that this opportunity had presented itself. So I jumped at the chance.

Carrie Leigh was now a twenty-three-year-old woman who had matured emotionally, perhaps more than I had. The rebellious streak that ran through her when she was young had mellowed. In 1972, she was a Dallas County convention delegate for George McGovern in his quixotic but ill-fated crusade for the presidency, though she was never an activist as such. She was also weary of a husband who spent much of his time away reporting on movements and causes and then coming home and talking about the injustices and inequalities he was witnessing. From her perspective, she had some understandable complaints. I wasn't home enough. I wasn't interested in the dinner conversation of her business friends. I went off and made decisions on my own, like taking the Houston job. And I was reckless with our money. Okay, so I also bought a Porsche.

I thought maybe I could work in Houston and come home to Dallas for the weekends. That way she could keep the job she seemed to love, and we still had our great townhouse. But Carrie Leigh wouldn't hear of it, and I was glad she would join me in Houston. We had begun looking for a new home in Houston even before we sold our Dallas townhouse at a profit. On the day escrow closed, I drove Carrie Leigh's car to Houston, transporting our Cocker Spaniel Candy, while she finished some of the paperwork with the sale of our house. I picked her up that afternoon at Houston's Hobby Airport where she got off the airplane looking almost unrecognizable, though nothing about her physical self had changed. Actually, I liked the look. She appeared more confident than ever, and she wore a short skirt that showed off her tanned legs from an early summer we were getting that year. We had made love the previous night on the carpet of our suddenly empty townhouse where we lit the fireplace one last time.

"I liked last night," she said. "It reminded me of when we were first dating."

"Yeah, but I would think the Mustang had to have been more comfortable than that carpet."

"I miss the Mustang," she said. "I miss those early days."

Then she started singing something I'd not heard since that time."

"We've tried it once or twice
"And found it rather nice
"Roll me over lay me down and do it again
"Roll me over in the clover, roll me over lay me down and do it again
"Oh this is number one
"And the fun has just begun..."

The news flash on the car radio announced that H.R. Haldeman and three other top officials in the Nixon White House had just been indicted. It was a glorious day indeed. Carrie Leigh and I looked at each other for a moment and then burst out laughing.

I had no idea that the move begun that day to Houston was also hammering the last nail in my marriage's coffin. Maybe our marriage wouldn't have worked out even in the best of circumstances. We had both been very young. Little, if much, had been ideal for us. And the thing that glued us together at the start, her parents' objection, was no longer an incentive driving her to me. We had been in Houston only a few weeks when on a May Sunday morning, as I tried to caress her in bed, I sensed that something truly wasn't right. She said she just wasn't happy.

"I don't understand," I said, joking with her. "Is there something wrong? Don't you love me any more?"

The moment I asked was the last moment of whatever happiness we had known, or, more correctly, that I would know with her.

"No," she said, lingering on the word. "I don't think I do. I'm not in love with you any more."

Then, moments later, Carrie Leigh would say to me the words that would make me wonder why we had ever been together at all.

"I'm sick and tired of this Chicano thing," she told me.

This Chicano thing.

Where had that come from? It wasn't like I was some activist on a picket line waving the farm workers' flag, protesting and fist pumping the air, yelling "Viva la Raza!" and "Kill the Gringo!" Who was this in bed with me? What had set off all this pent-up anger and frustration that was being unleashed in my direction? I was dumbfounded and speechless. But it was what she said next that destroyed me. "I don't want to feel with a man the way I feel when I'm with you." That came out of left field. I didn't know what to say or do. Part of what I felt was shock. Part was guilt. Had I driven her away and killed any iota of love she had? How could I ever be this wrong about judging anything or anyone? How did I allow myself to become the selfish ogre I must have been to make someone who once had loved me so much, I thought, to now feel nothing more than utter disgust and contempt?

Ironically, in the coming days, the person now most on my side appeared to be Carrie Leigh's mother, the last person I once would have thought to be my champion. Out of nowhere, too, she threw out a possibility that had never occurred to me.

"Tony, do you think there could be another man who's come between the two of you?" she asked.

"No," I answered, almost too quickly. "No. I can't believe there would be."

I didn't sleep for a couple of nights, at least, wondering at the thought that Mrs. Stanton had suggested. Carrie Leigh was an extremely attractive woman, and there had been no shortage of admirers. But no one had acted inappropriately, although how does someone truly know that. The only instance of anything that might have raised concern was when a man twice her age who had joined her company in Dallas, but Carrie Leigh always portrayed him as a buffoon. He had just returned from California and wore casual attire to the office – patterned rayon shirts open to the sternum with gold medallions hanging from his neck. Carrie Leigh said her boss had mentioned to her that this new co-worker had asked about her availability and that their boss had quickly put him in his place about office romances, especially an extra-marital affair involving a married young woman that many of the men looked upon almost like a daughter. The quasi-California buffoon had transferred to the company's Houston office about the time we moved there, but it was the last person I could see Carrie Leigh having an affair with. On top of the age difference, he was divorced and had kids Carrie Leigh's age

Still, our marriage disintegrated with the same speed that it began. I couldn't stop the momentum of its downward spiral, and I couldn't stand what was happening to us. Carrie Leigh wasn't even home at night until late, so it was impossible to talk. I finally concluded that it would be best if I just left, and so I moved out. The surreal then became very real. A day or two later, I was awakened just after dawn by someone pounding on my apartment door. A process server presented me with divorce papers. I tried to stall the divorce – to force Carrie Leigh to take more time to reconsider and for us to see someone professionally. But she wouldn't hear of it. Even after I got us an appointment with one of the country's leading marriage counselors who happened to live in Houston, Carrie Leigh would only go one session and insisted she would not return. I wound up seeing that shrink on my own. The worst part may have been seeing Carrie Leigh in a couple of meetings alone that we had at the offices of our lawyers. Each time, the look in her eyes became more unbearable. Our dreams were no longer the same, and I wondered whether they ever were. I couldn't even recall what her own dreams were any more, or had I really ever bothered in my own self-centeredness to know what they were? I hated myself enough for what I had done and how I had fucked things up. *Mea culpa. Mea culpa Mea maxima culpa.* I didn't need stares from the woman I loved – and who I thought loved me – making me feel even worse. How wrong could I have been about someone? I thought I had found the woman I would spend the rest of my life with and grow old with, but I'd been wrong. This had been the worst mistake of my life, and I hated to admit that I had known it in my heart from the beginning. How could anything be right when, in order to have it, you had to demean yourself and your own dignity the way I had just to see Carrie Leigh. I had thought it was love. Now I felt it was the ultimate in self-immolation. Suddenly, I no longer felt like an intelligent, confident man. I was a cocky, scared, lonely kid.

I soon allowed the self-loathing to get the best of me. The evening of the day I was served with divorce papers, my lawyer told me to go out to a bar and have some drinks. This was new for me. I had never gone out to a bar on my own. I was still new in Houston and ended up at a joint called the Gibson Girl on Buffalo Speedway. It was a strip bar with young dancers and nothing like the old-style burlesque strippers I remembered from the Colony Club in Dallas that Jack Ruby had once owned. I don't know why, but I kept going back to the Gibson Girl night after night. Soon I was involved in a threesome with a young stripper named Samantha who went by Sam and her girlfriend Elizabeth, an English expatriate. I was working as a reporter by day and hanging out at a strip bar at night, shooting pool for money on their billiard table and sleeping with the help. My lord, I realized one day, I'd become my father without the bastard kids.

One night I looked up from the pool table and saw an old friend's face. It was Carlos Guerra, who especially in a drunken stupor looked like a brown-faced William Shakespeare. Carlos and I went back before the days when I started reporting on the Chicano movement. He had been an undergraduate at Texas A&I University when I was at Baylor, and we first met at a 1967 rally in Austin for support of Fidel Castro's Cuba. I had attended as a reporter from my hometown newspaper and got routed into a meeting for students interested in surreptitiously visiting Cuba through Mexico. In 1963, the U.S. had imposed regulations in its embargo of Cuba that effectively banned travel by Americans to the island. But U.S. citizens continued to travel there, though for reasons other than what they did during the pre-Castro era when Cuba boomed as a tourist and gambling destination. Most of the Americans traveling there after 1960 were students, many of them activists. Carlos happened to be at the same meeting in Austin, along with a handful of others from the fledgling MAYO group. Late that summer, we were among three dozen or so young men from the Austin meeting who flew from Mexico City into a small airstrip outside Havana on a ten-day "information mission," as it was called. Most in the group were from the New Left and the Students for a Democratic Society. All but Carlos, myself, and a Chicano activist from Colorado were white. But it was hard to tell about anyone's ethnicity. Everyone's skin was heavily tanned from the scorching sun, and many of the New Leftists spoke Spanish. It was a watershed period for sympathizers of the Cuban revolution. In those first years after Fidel Castro came to power, more than a million Cubans learned how to read and 50,000 new homes were built. So many new doctors were being produced by the revolution that the country claimed there was one physician for every two hundred and fifty residents – a four hundred percent improvement over the last years before the revolution. Carlos was suspicious of everyone in our travel party, believing that at least several were FBI undercover agents. It made sense. The FBI had infiltrated most of the activist groups of the 1960s. That was to be expected, Carlos said. The trick was to steer clear of anyone openly advocating violence or the overthrow of the U.S.

"I'm just here because I wanted to interview Che Guevara," I reminded Carlos.

"We stick together, *carnal*, and don't trust anyone we don't know," he said.

So we did. We anticipated that there would be a hard-sell indoctrination, but we were wrong. It was like a vacation as we toured farms and nationalized plantations, spoke to peasants, visited schools, interviewed students, and spent evenings eating with local Cubans. This was Cuba only five years removed from the Cuban Missile Crisis and eight years after the revolution of Fidel Castro and Che Guevara had unseated the dictatorship of Fulgencio Batista. The U.S. economic boycott was already in place, but Cuba was still some time away from appearing to be a country whose time had stopped in the 1950s. We had been assured that we would also have a chance to talk to government officials, including some of the leaders close to Castro, and we wondered if this would ever happen. Finally, on our sixth day in the country, we were given a tour of El Capitolio, which had been the pre-revolution seat of government. It was empty and in need of repair, and the guide said it being converted into a Cuban institute of arts and sciences. We moved on to the National Library, to the gray marble tower monument to Cuba's national hero, Jose Marti, in the Plaza de la Revolucion, and then behind the memorial to the offices of Castro himself. I don't know why I thought we would get a private audience with him – that came with some two-bit deputy ministers of education, health, and agriculture – but we met Fidel in what seemed like a long assembly line of visitors, possibly not altogether different than what any head of state must endure with visitors. I thought there would be some reaction from Castro when the aide introducing the guests mentioned my name, especially with its distinctive Spanish pronunciation. Surprisingly, there was none.

"He didn't hear," Carlos muttered as we passed. "He's hard of hearing."

"Are you serious?" It hadn't occurred to me that Carlos was putting me on.

"The price of all that gunfire from the revolution."

I don't know what we were really expecting to see or experience. We weren't revolutionaries, nor did we want to join the Cuban revolution. But in our own way I suspect we were like many who fall in love with the romance of revolution – little of which was to be found in the Cuba we visited.

"*Carnal*, I thought it would be different," Carlos said toward the end of the trip. "Didn't you think it would be different?"

"Well, I came for Che," I said.

"He's not even Cuban, *carnal!*" Carlos shot back.

And Che had not been in Cuba. There had been reports of Guevara in several places, including Bolivia where he would be killed later that year.

Actually, I had gone to Cuba for reasons that had nothing to do with the revolution or politics. I had wanted to visit the legendary Finca Vigía, which had been Ernest Hemingway's home in San Francisco de Paula, where he had written much of *For Whom the Bell Tolls*. The new Cuban government had expropriated the property, though the Cuban officials who led Carlos and me on a personal tour of the property insisted that Hemingway's widow Mary had deeded the home and its property to the Cubans. What we saw was effectively a house that looked as if Hemingway could walk into it at any moment. It was filled with thousands of books and artwork, and the Cubans had already roped off areas where foot traffic was prohibited. The Cubans were aware of its historical significance and were trying to protect it, even keeping Hemingway's forty-foot boat, *Pilar*, off limits and about to be preserved on the property. We were shown the house by two Cuban graduate students who had been hired by the government for the long, arduous task of cataloging its contents, with long-range plans of it becoming one of the country's museum treasures.

"Ernest Hemingway," one of the students said to us, "belongs as much to Cuba as he does to the United States."

I don't know what else I had intended to find in Cuba or if I seriously thought there would be a connection with Fidel. And I came away feeling that we had missed something – that there was an entirely different side to Castro's Cuba and the revolution that had been hidden from us. There really wasn't, I would later learn in studying about Cuba and the Soviet Union and reading the accounts of defectors who usually maintained that all you saw was all there was – that spare parts were almost non-existent and that so much of the threat was little more than smoke and mirrors held together by Band-Aids. Castro and the Russians had had great poker faces, as it were, and for years we were so afraid of the threat of nuclear war that we hadn't had the *cojones* to call their bluff.

It would also be a while before I began to appreciate Carlos' wit and humor, which may have been his most endearing trait – certainly what helped break down the door in the doom and gloom offices of American politicians and corporations. He carried it off looking part academic and half bohemian artiste: Stylish corduroy blazer with patched elbows, rock 'n' roller slim flared leg jeans, British boots, a soft brown leather attaché with shoulder strap, and long hair that, with a high forehead made him appear like an American Renaissance man. In the coming years I came to find Carlos hanging out with lobbyists outside the Capitol Hill chambers of members of the House, in the offices of corporate law firms in Manhattan, and in tennis whites at the Longwood Cricket Club in Chestnut Hill, Massachusetts. He had a charm that allowed him to fit in anywhere he either needed to or wanted to be. In 1972, while La Raza Unida was campaigning to get on the general election ballot, Carlos was working in the primary campaign of gubernatorial candidate Sissy Farenthold, no less the darling of the same Texas liberals who blamed Chicano activists for the painful defeat of U.S. Senator Ralph Yarborough two years earlier. I don't know if the Farenthold people either didn't know or didn't care that Carlos was an organizer of MAYO and La Raza Unida. The

Farenthold team was madly campaigning to regroup the Mexican American vote into the Democrats' old liberal-Chicano-black coalition while Carlos was secretly working to keep Chicanos away from the polls until the general election. Farenthold ended up losing to conservative rancher Dolph Briscoe in what may have been one of the last hurrahs for Texas liberals.

However, in Houston, in the weeks after our re-meeting at the Gibson Girl club, I came to see a different, darker side of Carlos. Sam and Elizabeth had been living part of the time with me in a small townhouse just west of the Galleria that had a swimming pool outside the front door. I don't know why I had two pretty, young strippers there. Maybe I was half hoping that Carrie Leigh would drop by and see me with them. But the only person I knew who dropped by was Carlos who wasn't amused either by the girls in tiny bikinis or their drug dealer friend who happened to be there that day measuring out cocaine on some pricey scales on top of my mirrored coffee table. When I walked in from the pool, Carlos had a big Colt revolver – the kind Cowboys in the movies carried – and he had the girls and their drug dealer with their hands up.

"Tony, I told this asshole," he pointed to the drug dealer – I didn't know his name, "and his chippies to gather their shit and their belongings, to get the fuck out of here, and to never come back."

Sam and Elizabeth quickly stuffed their clothes into a bag. They had their own apartment in Montrose. Just as quickly the dealer had put away his product, undoubtedly feeling lucky that the crazy Mexicans hadn't robbed him. I was as surprised as they were. In that moment, Carlos was a complete maniac, spitting out a stream of English and Spanish obscenities as he stormed back and forth, waving the gun as if he might at any moment decide to use it. The girls and the dealer couldn't wait to escape, leaving Carlos and me looking at each other. Then Carlos slipped the Colt back into his attaché, his demeanor back to the old, familiar Carlos.

"What the hell were you thinking?" I demanded.

Carlos just gave me a long, angry look.

"I just saved your career and maybe your life, *carnal*," he said at last. "Did it ever occur to you that there might be people interested in seeing you found with a guy dealing coke out of your living room? *Carnal*, even if you could explain it away, it would cost you dearly, and I'm not talking money. You'd be discredited. Your book. Everything you've worked for. Is that what you want? You'd be going back to writing about the weather, assuming you ever did that – and that's if you're lucky."

"And where's your wife?"

Carlos was as surprised as everyone who knew Carrie Leigh and me that we had broken up. It was getting tiresome explaining what had happened or what I thought had happened, but he was insistent on dissecting the final months of the relationship. Carlos said he had a theory that when attractive people break up, there is usually a significant third party involved. Over the next few days, he conducted what he called a "marital autopsy," quizzing me on our friends, acquaintances, and close co-workers. He asked questions I would never have considered. About the same time I happened to run into Carrie Leigh with an older man: The buffoon. They had been holding hands, which they separated the moment they saw me. I was devastated and even more crushed when I spoke to a friend of ours, who assumed I was aware of Carrie Leigh's new relationship and asked if I was okay with it. I didn't know what to say, I told Carlos. Maybe it was all just platonic, and this guy was simply a friend offering Carrie Leigh innocent support.

"Bullshit, he's fucking her," said Carlos. "And he's probably been fucking her longer than you think or know about. This isn't good, *carnal*. The question is what are you going to do about being cuckold?"

Cuckold? Was Carlos serious? Did anyone outside of the medieval period even use that word? But had I become the Chicano Cuckold? I didn't know what Carlos might have been on, besides the Corona beer we were drinking like water. We spent the better part of a baseball game at the air-conditioned Astrodome talking about the breakup of my marriage, which seemed to affect Carlos more than I would have anticipated. He said he had looked upon my life with Carrie Leigh in

Dallas as something he would like to have one day soon. If my marriage, which he thought had been ideal, could have such unexpected cracks, what could he hope for?

"Look, *carnal*, do you want me to take him out for you?" I thought I misheard Carlos between something the Astrodome public announcer said. Carlos then repeated himself.

"What are you talking about, Carlos?" Had I heard him correctly?

"Whack him?"

I stared at Carlos, not knowing if he was serious.

"It can be done," he said. "You'd have to be out of town and be seen by a lot of people, and it would never come back to you."

"You mean kill the guy?" I was slow to catch on.

"Well, *carnal*, I wasn't thinking of an alienation of affection lawsuit," he said. "But I guess you could go that way, too."

I couldn't believe my life had come down to discussing the murder of my wife's lover, at the Astrodome, a baseball stadium, for crying out loud, where I had seen Mickey Mantle hit the first home run on the day it opened. There was no one I wanted to see dead more than this middle-age son of a bitch who was screwing my wife, but he wasn't worth me or anyone connected to me being responsible for it. Thanks but no thanks, I told Carlos, but maybe I needed to just get past this as best as I could.

I couldn't read Carlos, and I wondered if he was just testing me.

"Do you forgive them?" It was a helluva test he was putting me through.

"No," I said. "Not at all. I don't think they need my forgiveness."

"You don't want revenge?"

"I want a lot of things, Carlos," I said. "I want Mickey Mantle to make a comeback. I want to see the Yankees in the World Series again. I want to work for the *New York Times*. And I would love to be married to the girl I fell in love with in elementary school. But right now. I'm just angry. But what good would any revenge do? I just wish I could find some love and hope out of all this."

By the end of that summer, the divorce was final.

I came out of the marriage shattered and, fittingly perhaps, with the symbol of my recklessness. I got the Porsche.

PART FOUR:
The Kingdom and the Power

"Sometimes good things fall apart so better things can fall together."

-- Marilyn Monroe

I f I could have envisioned the ideally romantic wedding for Patricia and me when I was young, it would have been like the one at which my other best friend and his wife were married in the winter of 1974. Tony and Julianne Pederson were wed in the lovely country church where she was raised in Nevada, Missouri, on a snowy Saturday evening in a scene out of a Currier & Ives greeting card. As night fell and just before the ceremony began, the drifting snowflakes slowed as if in one of those glass globes we all had as children, and the glow from the full moon sparkled off the tree branches and rooftops as if God himself had come down from heaven to light the sky as well as bless their union. Now, *this* was the way it should be, and I hoped that Patricia's wedding had been more like that of Tony and Julianne,

248

a bit more memorable than Carrie Leigh's and mine had been in Waxahachie, Texas, with a felon in handcuffs looking on.

I was Tony's best man, and we were looking ahead to our lives with our wives in Houston. He was a sportswriter for the *Houston Chronicle* and would eventually rise to become that newspaper's executive editor. He was also Carrie Leigh's friend and neighbor from childhood – she had been the first girl he kissed – and I had met him through her. Our lives could not have been scripted any better, or so we thought, until that summer. A friend's broken marriage is a terrible imposition to place on any newly wed, but that year he and Tut took turns checking in on me to make sure that I didn't do something stupid. I didn't. I couldn't fully understand why Carrie Leigh had fallen out of love with me. But I knew I was culpable for being an ambitious, selfish bastard who had taken her for granted. I also knew I should never have married. I wasn't ready for marriage. I had been trying to get over a terrible heartbreak and a loss that needed to be mourned. I don't know if, because she resembled Patricia so much, that I had looked to Carrie Leigh as a quick fix for replacing her in my life. It would be something I would have to wrestle with in the years ahead. If that had been the case, it was an unpardonable sin against Carrie Leigh. I hoped it wasn't. Nevertheless, I was miserable. I had come to love her dearly and I wished that I had had the wisdom and character to have gotten past all that I could not. I should have, if I loved her as I proclaimed, and all of that would be on me.

We all make mistakes, I had learned, and we all pay a price.

My cost was a long tab of emotionally empty soirees at nightclubs, bars, and parties, not to mention the strippers and the cocaine. Not long after the strippers came a collection of eccentric women from Houston's inner social circle, among them: An oil tycoon's debutante daughter who drove her Ferrari into the Houston Ship Channel; a former Miss Houston with a five-figure backgammon gambling addiction; the social queen ex-wife of a Duke who kept a stash of secret recording equipment in her bedroom. Years later, when the *Houston Chronicle* fired a reporter who covered society news for being a stripper on the side, I was surprised by the firing, but not that a stripper could fit in so properly with Houston's social elite. My introductions into the world of Houston society came through the *Post's* own society page mavens. Many of the social hostesses, they said, were always asking them to be on the look out for straight single young men, for this, the mid-1970s, was a period when many previously eligible young men were coming out of the sexual closet. Many of the discos and clubs of that time, places with such unimaginative names as After Dark and Elan were crawling with beautiful young men on the prowl for other beautiful young men, much to the chagrin of many of the city's beautiful young women. Never let it be said that Houston, Texas, for that matter, didn't have its own Lost Generation. I wasn't sure what to make of it, and I was too busy guzzling Chivas Regal to think of being its voice. I left that to a young debutante from River Oaks who introduced me to eating Tacos Al Carbon from Ninfa's, a Mexican restaurant on Navigation, whose food she would sneak into the Rothko Chapel, a non-denominational meditative sanctuary displaying fourteen of the artist's paintings.

"Isn't this like a Texas Sistine Chapel?" she asked me on our fifth visit.

"I don't see it," I said, "but then I've never been to the Sistine Chapel."

I also couldn't imagine Michelangelo painting anything as dark as the black canvasses adorning Rothko Chapel and calling it religious art. But I kept going back, each time with a bag from Ninfas stuffed into a briefcase. I finally came to the conclusion that I didn't understand what I was looking at. I didn't understand art. I didn't understand life. I didn't understand much about the world.

In 1976, I was awarded a Nieman Fellowship to Harvard. This was not how I had once dreamed of getting there. When *Chicano Power* was published, a month after Carrie Leigh and I separated, I wanted to disown authorship. I equated the book with the demise of our marriage – the "Chicano thing," she spoke of. Maybe writing the book had changed me. I didn't know. If she felt it had, who was I to question?

No one else knew me better. When the publisher sent me off on a book tour of the Southwest and other major cities, I did it grudgingly. I was speaking at colleges and universities that now had sizable Mexican American student enrollments, and I wasn't enjoying any of it. I was even oblivious to the fact that the book was getting unusually positive reviews. *Publishers' Weekly*, the bible of the industry, called it "brilliant... a valuable contribution to the understanding of our time." In Washington, D.C., several influential journalists who reported on civil rights hosted a dinner and reception in my honor, all because they also thought the book important. My friend J.D. Alexander, a national editor for the_*Washington Post*,_said I had succeeded in what he thought I needed to do when I set off to write the book. "Re-interpret whitey's understanding of the Chicano," he had suggested.

One of those journalists, Jack Nelson, a Pulitzer Prize winning reporter and Washington bureau chief of the *Los Angeles Times*, was especially interested in my work. To say I was flattered was an understatement. Any reporter, in the South especially, who had covered the civil rights movement was familiar with Nelson. In 1960, while a reporter at the *Atlanta Constitution*, Jack won a Pulitzer for a series of articles that revealed inhumane practices at a mental hospital in Milledgeville, Ga., including the use of experimental drugs on patients without their permission and surgeries performed by nurses when doctors were absent. In the mid-1960s, while with the *L.A. Times*, Jack became perhaps the country's leading civil rights reporter. Among the injustices he uncovered involved violence in Orangeburg, S.C., in 1968. Three students were killed and two dozen wounded when more than one hundred National Guardsmen and local police fired on students protesting a racially segregated bowling alley. Jack went straight to the local hospital and introduced himself as "Nelson, with the Atlanta bureau. I've come to see the medical records." He never said he was with the FBI, but the ruse worked. Those records proved that sixteen students had been shot in the back and others wounded on the soles of their feet. The FBI began to investigate, but Jack didn't leave the story there. He reported that the federal agents were eating, drinking, and sharing hotel rooms with the state troopers they were investigating.

Jack had learned that I was going through a painful divorce and offered some advice from his own personal experience: Keep working and stay busy. Jack also made me aware of my name appearing on one of the numerous "enemies lists" of the Nixon White House that had surfaced. Apparently members of the 1972 Nixon re-election Hispanic team, in retaliation for what they had viewed as unfavorable stories I wrote about the campaign, circulated a memo aimed at stopping me from getting a reporting job in Washington. Now, more than a year since Nixon's resignation, that memorandum had surfaced in documents of the House Judiciary Committee's files obtained during its impeachment investigation.

"I'll get you a copy of that memo," Jack said. "Take it and frame that mother!"

Jack got me involved as a founding board member of the Reporters Committee for Freedom of the Press and began paving the way for a Nieman nomination at Harvard, even though I was much younger than anyone who had previously been awarded the fellowship.

Chicano Power also led to a contract for a follow-up book about the "Chicano experience," a tale about growing up Chicano. My New York-based publisher wanted a book about my rite of passage, imagining a manuscript about growing up without a pot to piss in, disadvantaged, and downtrodden in some rat-infested, inner city San Antonio barrio. They had great expectations based on nothing more than the fact that I was Chicano and had written for them a Chicano civil rights book that had been profitable. I hadn't been involved in writing the promotional material for *Chicano Power*, and I had been put off with the premise in the book's dust jacket saying that "Tony Castro's own Mexican American heritage helps him get an inside view of the Chicano movement." It was something the editors assumed and obviously led to their disappointment with the growing up Chicano manuscript I submitted. I had written too much about what it was like to grow up in Texas, they said, and not enough about what it was like to grow up Mexican. In their minds, I'm sure, they had come to the conclusion that their Chicano author was too vaguely Hispanic for the book they wanted to publish, as if some white guys living east of the Hudson who had never been to Texas would know, right? As always, I was too Mexican for some and not Mexican enough for others. But I wasn't that upset by the rejection. I hadn't liked the book idea anyway. Shouldn't I live more of my life to be able to reflect on it with some wisdom and hindsight? The selection committee at the Nieman Foundation loved the anecdote, though, and at least somebody was falling in love with me.

When I finally arrived at Harvard, it was not as I had once envisioned it being nor was I completely certain that this was what I wanted at this time of my life. Sir Edmund Hillary once wrote that reaching the top of Mount Everest had been exhilarating as well as empty, empty because there were no higher mountains to climb. My dream had been to go to Cambridge as an eighteen-year-old undergraduate, full of idealism and unspoiled by working in the real world. But I had now come to Harvard a decade past those youthful expectations.

I was immediately thrown off my first night on campus. I was walking around Harvard Yard late in the evening when I came across the statue of university founder John Harvard. In the shadows I could make out the outlines of two male students who had climbed on top of the statue. As I approached, I saw that one of the students was urinating on the statue, and I laughed, figuring it must have been two Yale students defacing the figurehead of their Ivy League rival. Imagine my surprise the next day when I mentioned the incident to one of the professors I had already met, and he said there was a longstanding tradition of Harvard undergraduates urinating on the statue at night. The statue, I was told, was known as "the statue of three lies." Lie 1: There was no known image of John Harvard when the statue was made, and the likeness is of a student who was used as the model. Lie 2: Although the statue identifies Harvard as the founder, he was not that but only a contributor. Lie 3: The statue says the university was founded in 1638, but it actually was founded in 1636. Perhaps, as a teenage undergraduate, I might have had a better appreciation of the rebelliousness and de-mystification. As someone returning to an academic environment in his late twenties, I wasn't amused. Leonel Castillo, a Houston politician with some familiarity of the Ivy League, had taken me aside shortly before I left for Massachusetts. "Too much Harvard," he cautioned, "can be like eating too many tamales."

The Nieman Foundation was a perfect anomaly. It was established in 1938 by a huge gift from the widow of the founder of the *Milwaukee Journal* "to promote and elevate the standards of journalism" at a university that had no interest in establishing either an undergraduate journalism school or a graduate school of journalism. So Harvard decided to use the money to annually select about a dozen journalists who were in the middle of their careers for a yearlong sabbatical, ideally to allow them to do intensive study in their area of expertise and improve their future work in the process. But realistically, for many, the Nieman experience becomes a year of reflection, of giving your head a break from deadline pressures and allowing it to go mushy. There are no finals for fellows. They are only required to audit any courses they choose to take. Some fellows have even been known to disappear for weeks or months during the year. The author Larry L. King, himself a recipient of a Nieman fellowship, once wrote that the year was so much fun he'd like to go back and do it again – sober. A lot of booze does flow freely in that year, but that's not the point of the fellowship, nor is it whatever studying that does get done. During my year, one of the friendships I struck up was with the sociologist David Riesman, who poignantly pointed out that the Nieman experience was a validation. He said these men and women who came to Harvard as good, already illustrious journalists in their own right with a year to spare were, in that short time, imbued, as if by magic or decree of the king, with designation of suddenly being better than they had been and elevated above their peers.

"You become the princes and princesses of journalism," he said. "And the quid pro quo is that Harvard gets served in the process."

For many, the validation of Harvard would lead to better jobs, higher profiles, greater respect, and a quantum leap in their careers. Many of us also walked away with Rolodexes full of professors and experts to call upon to deepen the understanding for our readers of our future stories with the insight of noted specialists, who, of course, are identified as practicing their craft of knowledge at Harvard University.

The Nieman fellowship also brings the attention of politicians, who are always trying to ingratiate themselves with journalists they believe are on their way up. In Washington, Representative W. R. Poage, the longtime congressman of my home district who wanted to appoint me to West Point or the Naval Academy, hosted another dinner for me and invited several other members of the Texas delegation, among them Congressman Henry B. Gonzalez of San Antonio. Gonzalez was a gregarious political old-timer who had quarreled with the Chicano activists and liked that *Chicano Power* had not been, as he put it, an apologist's book on their behalf. But it hadn't been a book siding with the political establishment either.

Gonzalez toasted me as the youngest person to be awarded a Nieman, and the first Mexican American given such a fellowship.

"We are making history," he said.

"No, congressman, you make the history," I said. "I'll just report it."

All in all, the Nieman and all the surrounding attention might not have been a bad trade-off for anyone, especially someone trying to understand a love gone wrong. In those first days I tried looking for answers in the Chivas Regal I had learned to drink. When I was drunk enough, I would pull out a letter I carried with me from Mrs. Lucile Weldon Teague, my third grade teacher. She had written to me after reading that I had been awarded a Nieman Fellowship, and she took it as a sign of her own personal contribution to my growth.

"I knew when you were my third grade pupil in Gurley School that you would succeed in whatever line of work you chose, if you continued to apply yourself with the enthusiasm and zeal you exhibited then," she wrote. "I'm certainly not surprised that you are in the field of journalism. You could express yourself so well in writing in the third grade that your stories then would have done credit to a high school student. I can still see, in my mind's eye, the happy, bright-eyed eager boy you were then. I wish I had a copy of one of your stories you wrote that year. I especially remember the story of Columbus finding America – perhaps because that was near the first of the school year, and I found out then how well you could write and what a memory you had. You wrote five, six or maybe more pages on that and on every other story during the year. What a joy it was to have you as a student!"

I didn't know how to answer her. No one from my early years, which are always so important to a youngster, had ever written such kind, glowing praise about me. I remembered her as a nice lady who, along with Miss Taylor, had taken a personal interest in me at a critical time; and I sometimes wondered what would have happened if they hadn't invested that care. Perhaps the best way to thank them was to continue that search for knowledge and enlightenment that they had helped develop. At Harvard, one of the Nieman perks was a blank check at the Faculty Club, a restaurant and lodge tucked amid the Harvard landmarks and holding perhaps the biggest collection of Harvard memorabilia in the world. You could entertain anyone you wanted, ideally active or retired professors but I would learn that no one ever checked on whom you wined and dined. That year I spent considerable time talking to and studying under Robert Fitzgerald, a classics professor and author of acclaimed translations of *The Iliad* and *The Odyssey*, and the Mexican writer, poet and diplomat Octavio Paz, a visiting professor and author of *The Labyrinth of Solitude*, a telling book about the Mexican mindset.

On several occasions, I also entertained Professor Riesman, who had been a Harvard undergraduate many years ago and was among the longest-tenured professors at the university. He was the author of the sociological classic *The Lonely Crowd* about the disconnection of people in society. "I always tell students who come to me complaining that they don't feel they belong or are worthy of Harvard, not to worry," he said in one conversation. "They're not alone. No one, even the most qualified of people who have matriculated through Harvard, feel that they belonged here. I felt that way myself my first day at Harvard, and I still feel that way today."

All that brain-power and knowledge was self-congratulatory, as if by connection being part of what David Halberstam had called *The Best and The Brightest,* his great book about the Ivy Leaguers who advised President Kennedy. However, the person who may have had the biggest impact on my life that year was the wife of a Harvard professor who will have to be known only as Gabriela. I met her and her husband at the welcoming reception for Nieman Fellows the first week of the semester where I was inundated with questions about my being from Texas. Why didn't I speak with a Texas twang? Did I own a horse? Was I a gun-owner? Would they be seeing me in cowboy boots? Then there was Gabriela, who I was almost certain felt up my butt when she approached me from behind. She had dazzling blue eyes, which were was the first thing you noticed, along with a flawless ivory complexion, and black hair that she wore back on one side, exposing an ear with a dangling pearl earring and a long elegant neck. She looked like no one I had ever seen. She wore a dark suit fitting of a professor's wife, and, though not petite, looked fragile as she stood on tall stiletto pumps that didn't look like what a professor's wife would wear. She introduced herself and wanted me to meet her husband, Ackley, who was in the history department. I couldn't tell Gabriela's age. She could have been in her early thirties, or she just as easily could have been in her early forties. I thought the latter when I met her husband, a studious, professorial-looking man at least in his mid-fifties, if not older.

A few evenings later, I was a guest for dinner at their home, not far from Harvard Square and the Law School. It was a charming house, and Gabriela delighted in showing it to me. It was a Mansard Victorian built in the 1870s with seven bedrooms, bay windows, fireplaces with marble mantels, ten-foot ceilings, and enchanting gardens that were on *The Secret Gardens of Cambridge* tour. She served Coquille St. Jacques, an elegant way of describing seafood on a shell, in a rich cream sauce with mushrooms and a wine I had never heard of. Oh, I had heard of Perrier, the water, but not Perrier Jouet Fleur de Champagne. It was soft, slightly sweet, and heavenly to taste. At dinner, we went through three bottles by the time a man about my age arrived. Gabriela's husband excused himself, and I figured the young man who had come to see him was a graduate student or teaching assistant. Minutes later Gabriela took my hand and said she wanted to show me the wine cellar, which turned out to be a small winery lined with Perrier Jouet Fleur. She gave me two bottles to take upstairs and then planted the softest, deepest kiss I had ever had, or could recall because it had been a long time since I'd kissed anyone. I almost dropped the bottles when she told me she wanted me.

"I don't think I can do that," I said. "I mean, you're married."

She let out a laugh. "Are you a Baptist?" she wanted to know. "Is this some kind of Texas morality coming out?"

"I just can't," I said. "Look, I was brought up to believe not to come between a husband and wife."

"Well, you know, if you did, it would be the first thing that's come between Ackley and me in our entire marriage!"

She saw that I didn't understand.

"Oh, my God, you haven't figured it out, have you?" she said. "Ackley has no interest in women."

The thought hadn't really crossed my mind. Everything about him suggested blueblood breeding and impeccable manners, and he was a tenured Harvard professor, for crying out loud.

"No," I said. "No, I thought he was just, you know, a bit eccentric."

"Eccentric!" Gabriela let out a loud laugh. "Our late French poodle was eccentric! Ackley thinks he's the goddamn Radio City Rockettes!"

It wasn't my place to judge. I was just a little slow letting this sink in.

"Ackley's a flaming queen!" Gabriela said.

"He's..."

"He's queer, as you would say in Texas," she said. "That's his latest who came to see him tonight. There's nothing between Ackley and me except a big front he needed when he came up for tenure. Don't get me wrong. He's a good man and a brilliant professor. Just a little different. And I was having trouble raising two kids on my alimony from my ex. Ackley's been a wonderful stepfather and the only reason my kids are able to be in fancy boarding schools today. So do you think you can get off your moral high ground and enjoy what Harvard has to offer?"

Put that way, well, of course. I had an apartment across the street from the Nieman House, but I spent much of the time that year at Gabriela and Ackley's. There were actually two master suites, and she and I lived in one and Ackley in the other on the far end of the house. The only rule we had was discretion, of which I was an old hand. Gabriela's two children were in their teens and well aware of her and Ackley's arrangement, so they didn't have any problem with me being there when they came home. It also didn't interfere with my Nieman responsibilities, which were minimal: Show up at wine and cheese functions held almost every week day, and attend an occasional night event. My study plan, like that of most other fellows, had long bit the dust. Any publicity the foundation sent out said that I was studying third world nation-building and political economy. But when I wasn't in one of Professor Fitzgerald's classes, I was in a seminar with Professor Paz. Once, maybe twice a week I was also treating them to long lunches with a lot of booze at the Faculty Club. Once, while I was dining with Paz, we ran into Gabriela. Paz was smitten, and, with her permission, I had to clue him in.

Early in the semester, Paz had said he didn't think I should be in his exclusive seminar. He had asked all the prospective students to fill out a note card with some biographical information. On my note card, I included the footnote that I also aspired to be a novelist one day. After class, he took me aside.

"Señor Castro," he said. "If you want to be a writer, the last place you should be is in a classroom. You should be out in the world experiencing life."

I reminded him of that conversation.

"Professor Paz," I said, "That's what I'm doing with Gabriela: Experiencing life."

He laughed and said we should get drunk, so I showed him Gabriela's wine cellar. Here was a man whose work I had long admired, a man who later would be awarded the Nobel Prize for Literature, getting drunk with us, while explaining to me what he meant about the Mexican and his masks. In *Labyrinth of Solitude*, he wrote: "(The Mexican) passes through life like a man who has been flayed. Everything can hurt him, including words and the very suspicion of words. His language is full of reticences, of metaphors and allusions, of unfinished phrases, while his silence is full of tints, folds, thunderheads, sudden rainbows, indecipherable threats... He builds a wall of indifference and remoteness between reality and himself, a wall that is no less impenetrable for being invisible. The Mexican is always remote, from the world and from other people. And also from himself." As a result, he wrote, the Mexican retreats and hides behind masks that shield him from the world - and from himself.

In the years ahead, I would have the good fortune of staying in touch with Paz, though it was not without discomfort at times. I also came to know another of Mexico's literary giants, Carlos Fuentes, though not as well and eventually feeling wedged between the two men in what can truly have been called a Mexican standoff. Their feud, if you can call it that, stemmed from both being great men of letters and rivals as symbols of a nation that both had transcended but still wanted to elevate into the cultural world which made each of them wealthy and famous. In 1988, Paz's literary magazine *Vuelta* published a blistering critique of Fuentes' work that destroyed a friendship that at the time was already tenuous as they engaged in an ongoing literary dance for the ultimate crowning honor that they both wanted, the Nobel Prize for literature. Paz, who could be arbitrary and contentious, had a way of sometimes tweaking people just to get a reaction. He had originally turned down my request to study under him, but a couple of days later he called me to say that he had changed his mind.

"I'm always suspicious of people who say they are writers or want to be writers," he said. "I feel as though what they want is to spar with me intellectually as if I'm Manolete, Pelé, or Muhammad Ali, and they want to take me on."

In the months ahead that year, I once asked him about Fuentes, and I recall him taking a long, almost exaggerated breath. In the long conversation that followed, Paz seemed to be most critical of Fuentes not about his work but over his politics, especially his early championing of Fidel Castro and any kind of revolutionary activity in Latin America. He called Fuentes *"un gran novelista, pero un mediocre político."*

Paz considered himself the consummate liberal and a "responsible leftist" but he couldn't abide the politics of Fuentes, nor of Gabriel García Márquez, for that matter. Those were surprising words coming from a man known as much for being a diplomat as a literary icon, and I suspect the same may have been at play when his magazine made its vituperative attack on Fuentes' work, even questioning the depth of his Mexican identity. I wondered how much of the criticism had stemmed from literary jealously. Paz was a brilliant essayist, and *The Labyrinth of Solitude* is a classic study of Mexican identity and thought. But as a creative genius, there was no comparison with Fuentes whose novels captured the complex, convoluted essence of Mexico as never before.

It so happened that just three years before the *Vuelta* magazine attack, Fuentes' novel *The Old Gringo* had become the first book by a Mexican novelist to hit the bestseller lists north of the border. The novel, about an American writer who disappeared during the Mexican Revolution, was made into a Hollywood film starring Gregory Peck and Jane Fonda. It also vaulted Fuentes into the world of celebrity, cementing him as the literary voice of Mexico and placing him alongside such great Spanish writers as García Márquez, Mario Vargas Llosa and Julio Cortazar. Some thought that *The Old Gringo* would also elevate Fuentes to the coveted goal of the Nobel Prize ahead of Paz.

But in 1990, it was Paz who was awarded the Nobel Prize for Literature, laurels that I sense left him with some personal discomfort. In the early 1990s Paz and I had corresponded on some personal matters on which he was assisting me, and in one of those letters he asked if I would be so kind as to relay a message to Fuentes with whom I was also corresponding.

"Tell Carlos I am extending the olive branch," he said, obviously seeking to mend the friendship that dated back to the early 1950s.

I relayed the message and got an earful from Fuentes about Paz a year later over dinner in Mexico City.

"He asks you, his student, to do what he should do," Fuentes said. "It's up to him to do it."

Paz died in 1998 at the age of 84. He and Fuentes, who died in 2012 at the age of 83, would never speak again.

The Octavio Paz of 1976 struck me as less stuffy and less secure than the one I knew later, or perhaps that was what Harvard did to all people. It was also a time when Harvard was diversifying itself with students from all racial and ethnic minorities as well as from all walks of life. One of the Nieman responsibilities was to meet with any group wanting our attention and for me that included the Harvard Radcliff Chicano Association, which was made up of dozens of the several hundred Hispanics at the university. This was a time when the backlash against affirmative action programs had gained footing at campuses across the country, and many of this group's Hispanic students were feeling the brunt and understandably upset about it.

"Many of us were valedictorians and salutatorians of our high school class, with four-point-zero-plus grade point averages who are more than qualified to be here," one of those students told me at one of our meetings. "But all we hear from the white students is that we're only at Harvard because of affirmative action. It's not fair. We're all being characterized as being nothing but tokens."

A student named Barbara Cigarroa, the brilliant daughter of one of the oldest and most influential families in South Texas, would wind up graduating Summa Cum Laude from Harvard. All together, Barbara's siblings boasted twenty Ivy League degrees among them. Her father was a prominent cardiologist, but it was the mother, also named Barbara, who was the driving force driving all her ten children to excel. Young Barbara and I became friends after she read some of my fiction and compared my writing to the Mexican writer and philosopher Jose Vasconcelos, which stumped me. I had to run over to Widener Library on campus to find out who he was and why she would make the comparison. I never saw it. But what I did see was a troubled young woman. One night over coffee she told me the story of the day she was stunned by a reception at the Harvard house that was her home at the university.

"I was carrying my tray to a lunch table," she recalled, "when I heard someone say, 'Here she comes, Miss America Alien."

I felt for Barbara and all the other Hispanic students and sympathized with their anger and frustration. Perhaps we all could have used a shrink, or someone to talk to like Paz. Discussing the Mexican and his fears with him opened a window to a part of me I had long denied. Confront that side of myself, Paz said, and I would find some answers, though perhaps not the ones I wanted. Was I willing to gamble and try?

I was game. Maybe I wouldn't if I was alone, and perhaps that's why Gabriela had come into my life. To get to another stage of my life, I needed to forget: Carrie Leigh, Houston, and Texas for that matter. I needed to start life anew without the baggage of the past. I needed to go back to the beginning. I needed to dream. I needed Patricia. Not the way I needed her in the past, wanting her in my life, to share it. No, I needed the dream she represented. I needed to touch what was true and good and honest about myself because those had been the things that the dream of her had brought out in me. I needed to believe in something that would help make me a better person.

Gabriela didn't know about Patricia, but she knew there was something or someone I needed to find. More importantly, she knew I just needed the distance of time from all the hurt. Over the months I was in Cambridge, she didn't demand, she didn't question, and she didn't probe. She just lived life and allowed me to string days of forgetfulness together. I introduced her to baseball, taking her to New York for games three and four of the Yankees' 1977 World Series humbling by the Cincinnati Reds. She showed me New England. We made love on the shore of Walden Pond. We helped crew a big sailboat one weekend off Nantucket. Another weekend, we stayed at a lighthouse in Maine. She was a ballet aficionado, so I escorted her to the Boston Ballet and another time to New York to see Gelsey Kirkland and Mikhail Baryshnikov dance *The Nutcracker* with the American Ballet Theater. We spent several days together in New York just before Christmas and again in the spring. By then, my Nieman experience was in full bloom. I was spending free time at the Kennedy Institute of Politics, participating in discussions about the New Politics and The New South, ideas that had been spawned by the young presidency of Jimmy Carter, the former governor of Georgia.

Among the luminaries who came to participate was John Connally, the onetime Texas governor who had become President Nixon's Secretary of the Treasury. I had interviewed Connally on a couple of occasions, but I came to know him a little better after the publication of *Chicano Power*. I had been at the *Houston Post* offices early one evening when I took a telephone call from someone with a deep baritone voice looking for me and identifying himself as Connally. Anyone else, and I would have suspected a prank being played by one of my fellow reporters. But the Connally voice, almost a deep bellow, was so distinctive, I knew no one on our staff, who might have wanted to play a prank, had the talent to imitate it. He was calling, he said, to thank me on how I had portrayed him in the book - fairly, I thought, though much to the chagrin of activists, including many of my friends.

In 1966, as the farm workers movement was attempting to make the same kind of statement in Texas as it was doing in California, Connally stole the activists' thunder as they marched from the Rio Grande Valley in South Texas to the state capitol in Austin. Connally did it doing little more than leading a small group of officials in confronting the marchers near New Braunfels, roughly halfway between San Antonio and the capitol. With a Catholic priest shoving a crucifix in the governor's face, Connally told the marchers he would not accept their invitation of meeting with them because he would not be in

Austin, and wouldn't meet with them even if he were there because of the fear of violence. The march continued, but the steam seemed to have been taken out of the campaign, with the confrontation with Connally stealing the headlines. The farm workers movement never achieved anything close to the success that it had in California, though for entirely different reasons. But many activists blamed Connally for the defeat, as the governor was riding the crest of his popularity in the years after the Kennedy Assassination in which he had been critically wounded.

By 1974, when *Chicano Power* was published, Connally's life had changed, almost dramatically. He had become treasury secretary for President Richard Nixon, led a group of Democrats campaigning for Nixon's re-election in 1972, and finally changed parties to become a Republican. On the day he called, Connally and his wife Nellie also invited me to dinner at their River Oaks home where the former governor regaled me with stories of Lyndon Johnson who had died the previous year. Connally had known Johnson since 1938, and he talked about one day possibly writing a book about his relationship with the late president but apparently never did. Over the next two years I was an occasional guest at the Connallys, even after he was indicted for allegedly taking a bribe in a milk price scandal. I attended his trial in Washington the day that Jacqueline Kennedy testified as a character witness on Connally's behalf, which was perhaps a tipping point in how the trial would go, at least it was for me. How do convict a man on meager evidence when he is vouched for by the widow of a slain president?

Connally's fortnight stint at the Kennedy Institute of Politics in early 1977 was one of his first trips outside Texas since his acquittal as he sought to show the country another side of himself. There was talk, too, that he was thinking of running for president as a Republican, so the visit to the heart of liberal America took on national significance.

The Connally visit was also the first time Gabriela, Ackley and I had ventured outside their home together. Connally and I reacquainted ourselves before the discussion session, and I introduced him to

Gabriela and the professor, who had appeared to be on an academic cloud nine. Ackley was not without a strong reputation in his own circles and well known at the Kennedy Institute. So he was given a wide berth after the discussion to continue talking to Connally about LBJ and about his time as a lawyer for the Texas oil tycoon Sid Richardson, with many in the audience hanging on the words of both men.

Late that night, we ended up leaving the Kennedy Institute with Connally in tow back to Gabriela and Ackley's house. Connally seemed to love the adoring attention and, though an avowed tea-totaller, he didn't abstain from the Perrier Jouet Fleur. He told us more stories of LBJ, many with which I was familiar with in Texas but some that I had not heard, specifically about the period in Washington when Connally was Secretary of the Navy in the Kennedy Administration. The governor had an engaging way of telling stories with a twinkle in his eye and an imitation of the LBJ Texas twang that took you into what behind-the-scenes life at that level of political power must have been like.

This was also the first time I had seen Ackley in his element. A New Englander who had known Kennedy from the time he was a young congressman, Ackley probed as gently as he could for reminiscences that Connally might have of the early days of JFK's administration, leading ever so gingerly to the topic the former governor rarely spoke about – Dallas 1963. Gabriela had mentioned early on that Ackley was working on a Kennedy book, and for the evening he had hit the mother lode. I also watched Gabriela's face, hanging on Ackley's curiosity with a wife's pride. Whatever arrangement they had, it was obvious that she loved him dearly in her own way.

At one point, I did catch the governor, as everyone called him, looking at Gabriela and me holding hands while she popped blackberries in my mouth as we sipped on the champagne. Ackley and Gabriela had been introduced to Connally as professor and wife, so he must have wondered what *our* arrangement was. Finally, as Ackley opened another bottle of champagne, the governor looked over at me and winked.

"There's no place like Texas, wouldn't you agree, Tony," he said. "But it sure as heck is great to be away every once in a while, ain't it?"

About this same time, I had received a disturbing phone call from a reporter and friend at my newspaper in Houston. Ed Hunter, the managing editor who had hired both of us for his dream of a "new *Houston Post*," had suffered a debilitating illness, my friend called to tell me. It was still unknown when he would recover enough to return to running the paper, if he even could. In the meantime, my friend said, the direction of the paper had been taken over by the very people that Ed said he was hoping to get rid of. The bottom line was I might not have a home when I returned from the Nieman, or, at least, the home I thought I would have. My only regret from that time may be that I didn't take Ed Hunter's declining health as a signal to move on. I had promised both him and the Nieman Foundation that I would return to my newspaper. There was always a fellow or two each year who didn't return to their previous employment. I would not have had a problem breaking my word to the Nieman program, but I didn't want to let Hunter down. I also couldn't see the *Post* reverting to whatever paper it had been before the changes Hunter had instituted.

As the sabbatical was winding down, Gabriela and I made one last out-of-town trip together, visiting Washington in May for the Robert F. Kennedy Foundation awards dinner. I was on the awards selection committee that year, and one of the perks was spending a long weekend with the extended Kennedy clan at Hickory Hill, Ethel Kennedy's home in McLean, Virginia. The Kennedys' touch football games on lazy Sunday afternoons were legendary, and Gabriela insisted on playing. She was an incredible sport, even after spraining an ankle. Ted Kennedy himself wrapped her sprained ankle with an Ace Bandage that she had him sign for Ackley. It was a fitting end to a memorable, glorious year. Yet it was an end neither Gabriela nor I were looking forward to. We had promised each other that whatever developed between us would not be serious, but still, those are words lovers often live to regret. She would be possibly the only thing I would miss from the Nieman year. Perhaps if I had attended Harvard as an undergraduate, I would have had greater affinity for the school and the area, but I didn't. And Boston had failed to grow one me. It was, as Joni Mitchell had sung of England, "too old and cold and settled in its ways." Anyway, if I were going to work in the East, it would be in New York or in Washington, somewhere where I felt a personal connection, like my beloved Yankees or the hated Redskins. But I knew that Gabriela likely would never leave Ackley, and I wasn't going to ask her.

Besides, Gabriela had already helped me find my way to understanding perhaps the most important lesson about love and life. When you find love, you needed to place it and the person you loved above all else, especially above a job – and even above yourself. I realized that I had felt that way about Patricia. There would not have been anything I wouldn't have done for her, sacrificed for her, and put far down on my priorities for her, had we ever been together. In being honest with myself, I had to concede that I had not made that kind of commitment to Carrie Leigh, who hadn't been a wishful dream but someone who had actually loved me and been in love with me at one point. I was guilt-torn beyond belief. Why had I failed to hold her above all else? Would I have done the same had she been Patricia? Would I do the same to someone else once outside my sanitized existence in Cambridge and in the real world?

But maybe you can't change who you are and how you feel, no matter how much you try. One day I arrived at Gabriela's to see an unusual looking woman saying good-bye to Ackley at the door. She saw my car and asked if she could sit inside of it for a moment. It was an innocent enough request, and the Porsche was still immaculate.

"I envy you," she said.

"Thanks, but it's just a car," I said.

"Yeah, but you know what?" I didn't, but she was going to tell me. "I used to be a dude like you. But in the last year, I spent almost forty thousand dollars for a sex change to become a woman thinking it would make me happy. And if I had to do it all over again, I'd take the money and buy a Porsche instead."

Happiness, I was learning, was as elusive a jewel as there is.

Gabriela and I agreed not to have any teary farewells. She had long planned to spend the summer seeing Europe with her children, and I had a commitment to the Nieman program to tour Japan that June with several other fellows. Our parting was a long good-bye kiss at Logan Airport where Ackley dropped her and her kids at one terminal from which they were leaving for Rome and then leaving me at another terminal where I was bound for Tokyo.

If ever there was the perfect salve to ease myself from Cambridge, it was getting away to somewhere foreign an exotic. And I hadn't counted on just how culturally distant Japan would be, possibly because of my own unexposed innocence as a world traveler. The Nieman fellowships, though, had baptized me well. In the winter, our program had taken us across Canada for a two-week immersion into that country and its politics. The centerpiece of that experience had been Quebec City, where we were snowed in for several days and got the full measure of the Quebecois, a movement of national sovereignty for the province of Quebec and secession from Canada. It paralleled the dreams of some of the Chicano activists who were advocating a separate state in the southwest they called Aztlan. I had several interviews that winter with activists from the Quebecois movement, and it felt like I was back in Texas with La Raza Unida. The most poignant moment for me that came out of the Canada trip, though, was a lunch conversation one day with Jack White, a Nieman Fellow who worked at *Time* magazine. Jack was African American, and Canada was the first time we had spent long enough together to know one another. He was headed to Nairobi for *Time* after the fellowship, and his personal life was as much in chaos as my own. I learned that Jack was as bothered as I about the way he was viewed professionally. He was not an African American *Time* correspondent, he felt, but a *Time* correspondent who happened to be African American. He also knew, however, the reality of race in America and that no one questioned white journalists who were Niemans about whether they had been chosen because of their qualifications or their race, as they did those who were black or Hispanic. Maybe we had just had too much Chivas Regal on the long trip or maybe it was just thinking out loud. One day, as we ate a big buffet lunch, Jack pointed to several of the white Nieman fellows who were with us on the trip and who were eating together at another table.

"Can you believe that their great-granddaddies or great-great-granddaddies could ever have been smart enough as to get the upper hand on ours?" he said, shaking his head in disbelief. "For the life of me, I can't."

Jack, unfortunately, was not with us on the trip to Japan. Besides, there would have been too many distractions in Japan to gloat on the racial history of America. There also were no comparisons in Japan to anything in Texas, not even the baseball where fans reminded me more of the soccer fanatics I had read about in England. We were supposed to be participating in meetings with government officials while in Japan, but all seemed lost in the decorum and formalities. For most of us, our visits were vacations in which we soaked in the most important aspects of Japan – its people, its customs, its culture, and its heritage. I couldn't sleep much, so I spent nights and the wee hours of the morning in the Ginza nightclub district or in the all-night bars and restaurants at the New Otani Hotel where we stayed in Japan.

I asked only two things of our Japanese hosts. I wanted to see Nara, which had been the country's capital in the eighth century and where Gabriela said she had lived as a child. Her family lived there while her father, a Far East Studies professor, researched a mythological god who, according to legend, had arrived in the city on a white deer. Gabriela talked about how tame reindeer historically had roamed through the town. I also wanted to meet and interview Sadaharu Oh, the Babe Ruth of Japanese baseball who had recently broken Ruth's all-time home run record. Oh played for the Yomiuri Giants, considered the New York Yankees of Japan, and I was allowed access to Oh during a home game. Even with a translator involved, the interview proved to be one of the most genteel experiences I could remember with Oh extending courtesies no American player would even consider and speaking graciously about Ruth and his place in the game worldwide.

But then there was Hiroshima. Its significance was not lost on any of us, but perhaps to emphasize its importance, we were taken to the Hiroshima Peace Memorial Museum, a gut-wrenching experience if there ever was one. In documenting the devastation caused by the atomic bomb dropped on the city in World War II, the museum spares little in graphic details. Displays show actual burned clothing, hair, watches, and other personal items worn by the victims. Other exhibitions offer a glance at what happened to wood, stone, metal, glass and flesh from the heat. Most moving of all are the life-size enlargements of photographs of Japanese men, women, and children grotesquely brutalized by the radiation. As a human being, you can't help but be moved by the savagery. As an American, even as the son of a soldier seriously wounded in Germany who lost relatives in the war, you can't help but be struck by a sense of horror and guilt. A couple of the Nieman Fellows I was with stood jaws agape, as did I. We looked at one another and then felt uneasy. We looked around and saw a large room full of Japanese school children staring at us. They were there on a field trip and most likely looking at us because we obviously were foreigners. But a part of us also felt that it was the *way* they were looking at us. Perhaps we were imagining it, with our sense of guilt getting to us. We left as quickly as we could and walked into the nearest restaurant where we ordered Saki after Saki to get drunk.

I returned from Japan severely jet-lagged and laden with Kuniyoshi wood block prints, an ancient wedding kimono, incredible material that my mother requested, several strings of pearls, a newfound appreciation of sushi, and an incomparable experience. There was also tremendous apprehension over what I dreaded in returning to Texas and to my old job. A part of me wanted to say screw it - I'm not going back. If Ed's not there, I quit. It would have made my life easier in moving on to another newspaper. But part of the Nieman commitment was that fellows were obligated to return to their old jobs. Otherwise, newspapers might be understandably hesitant to support future applicants if they thought the Nieman year was just a way station to a better job. A few fellows never went back to their old jobs, but most did. No sooner had I returned from Japan, however, before I got a call from the *Washington Post's* Dick Harwood, an editor on the paper's city side staff, who offered me a reporting position. I should have taken the position, resigned from my paper in Houston, and moved on. However, I felt a do-gooder need to tell the Nieman program curator, Jim Thomson, of what I was thinking of doing. It turned out to be a bad decision on my part, and I picked an equally bad afternoon to do it. Born the son of missionary parents in China, Thomson was an Ivy League Far East Studies specialist who had been sidetracked into heading up the Nieman program and was generally credited with opening it to minorities. I didn't know Jim well, and I had forgotten I had heard it was best to catch him early in the day to have a serious conversation with him, before he had started drinking. From personal experience with my father and with Mantle, I should have also known better how you dealt with someone unwilling to admit his problem with alcohol. Maybe Jim would have reacted the same way early in the morning, but disturbing him late afternoon at his favorite French restaurant just off Harvard Square obviously colored his usual wit with surprising ethnic sarcasm. When I informed Thomson that I was likely going to the *Post*, he exploded.

"Are you slow or don't you understand what you're doing!" he said, raising his voice. "You have been granted one of the highest honors of distinction in your profession, coming to this institution where all the doors have been opened to you for the rest of your life, and you want to do this! Well, if you do this. If you don't go back to your newspaper and you take his job – a job you could easily have a year from now – you'll be turning your back on your word, and you know what they'll be saying? They'll be saying that you *are* just another Mexican."

That I am just another Mexican.

I was going back to Texas for all the wrong reasons, but I was going back. In a few days, all my things had been boxed up and shipped back to Houston except a suit, a blazer, some shirts, my portable typewriter and the growing up Chicano manuscript. Those I was taking back with me in the Porsche. I had a week to get back.

The day I planned to leave Cambridge, I was running last minute errands and enjoying a sunny New England summer day with the sunroof off. The car was tuned up and running great, and it always drew admiring looks. It was a Porsche, for God's sake. I had just turned into Harvard Square when I noticed a young couple staring at the car and waving frantically at me. I tried to recognize who they were with nothing registering in my brain until another car pulled up alongside, with the passenger screaming.

"Get out! Get out! Your car's on fire! Get out!"

In the rearview mirror, I saw flames shooting up from the rear engine in the car and immediately slammed on the brakes. Suddenly all I could smell was gasoline and burning rubber, even as I jumped out of the car. At that same instant, the blaze engulfed the interior compartment, and the Porsche exploded. It seemed to jump into the air for a moment before settling on the street, on flames as if it were a bonfire.

I stood on the side of the street in front of the Harvard Coop watching as the car turned into a charred hull. People kept walking up, asking me to sit down and move away. But the scene was hypnotic, like watching my own life go up in flames. The paramedics said I was miraculously lucky to escape with no more than singed hair and some bruises. But everything else I had in the car – the manuscript and my clothes – had gone up in smoke. All that remained was me and my thoughts.

I am alone.
If that's not death,
I wish to know what it is.

If it is not,
If loneliness is not death,
If sounds are never shared,
If thoughts cannot be bared,
If love has empty arms,
If tears are never seen,

Then silence fills the mind
And blindness guides the heart.

I am alone.
If that is life,
Then must I be reborn?

There was no reason for Ackley to have helped, but he did. Everyone else I knew had either left for the summer or gone back to their newspapers from the sabbatical. The Nieman House was closed, so I had called Gabriela's home hoping Ackley was there. He was alone in their house for the summer and rushed over to pick me up.

"You should see a doctor," he said.

"I have," I said. "And they've seen me."

"What did they say?"

"They gave me a shot, some antibiotics, and Valium," I said.

"Valium? What's the Valium going to do for you?" Ackley immediately got me a glass of his champagne once we got back to his home. "Do you want me to call Gabriela? Maybe you could talk to her."

"Where is she, do you know?"

"Versailles," Ackley said.

"No, don't ruin it," I said, remembering that she loved to study the age of the French Revolution. "You know how she is about Versailles."

"Oh, yes. *Berceau-de-la-Liberté!*"

Ackley called the airlines and got me a one-way ticket to Houston. The insurance people said it would take a week, at least, to investigate the fire and to either replace the Porsche or pay me its value. Ackley said he would handle that, too. Finally he drove me into Boston to a great men's store he knew to buy a blazer, slacks, a couple of shirts and shoes until I could get my things unpacked in Texas. I could just imagine my next American Express bill, which had ballooned in Japan.

"You know, Gabriela's in love with you," Ackley said the next day as we waited for my flight to board. "Are you in love with her?"

"Yeah, Ackley, I am."

"I wouldn't stand between the two of you, if that means anything," he said.

"I appreciate you saying that, Ackley," I said. "But Gabriela's life is here. I have no idea where mine is, and that wouldn't be fair to her. I feel like Icarus, you know, having flown too close to the sun and now flying through the sky with no wings."

"The price for being reckless," he said. "It comes with the territory."

"Yeah, but I think I need to know myself a little more before I complicate Gabriela's life or anyone else's. I hope she understands."

"I think she wishes she didn't," he said.

"I know you'll take care of her," I said. "You're a good man."

Just as I got ready to board, Ackley tugged on my arm.

"You know, Tony," he said, "it would go a long way in this journey of yours, if you could find it in your heart to forgive yourself."

Indeed, and it was a monster that laid ahead.

It would also take a while to get to it. In Houston, I first had to take my lumps. Ed Hunter was no longer in charge, and those who were made it clear right away that I was not welcome back. Why was I not surprised? That first day back, I was assigned the agate weather report – the long one-column, small-type listing of all the highs and lows in cities in the country and the world. It reminded me of Carlos Guerra's warning that reporters who blew out their careers wound up reporting on the weather. The second day I walked out of the office to attend some club luncheon meeting they wanted me to cover as punishment – these things were rarely, if ever, taken seriously enough to send a reporter. It was an assignment from which I never returned. Why would I want to? Maybe if I had been born the hick son of rednecks, as Ed once called them, and thought wearing ties fashioned out of the Confederate flag was appropriate, I might have fit in at the new *Houston Post*, but those kinds of rebels belonged draped in the white robes of a by-gone era of which I wanted no part.

Jack Nelson, who had confronted real Klansmen of his own, laughed when I told him the story. I was free to take a job in Washington or New York, if he could help. But summer is the wrong time to look for newspaper jobs on the East Coast. Editors are gone, if not on vacation then for the entire summer. I regretted playing by the Nieman rules and not having taken the job at the *Post*. Gabriela had urged me to look for a job on the East Coast all spring, and she became slightly miffed when I hadn't. It was the only time she had shown disappointment in our time together. I was an outlaw, she had told me, and I should know that I shouldn't - and couldn't - play by the rules. Any time I tried, she said, it would go against me. She had been right.

"Go home, see your family," Jack advised. "Get some rest, and see if you can make up with your ex."

"Jack," I said. "She's remarried."

In 1976, Carrie Leigh had married the buffoonish man almost twice her age - the guy with the California tan and chest exposed in a rayon shirt unbuttoned down to the sternum showing off cheap costume jewelry. I had a hard time imagining it, and I'd learned about the actual marriage in the oddest way. I had sent her some old photographs of herself that I found in some of my belongings. She called to thank me.

"Are you angry with me?" It was the first time since we had split up that she had bothered to ask.

"What makes you ask?"

"You addressed it to Carrie Leigh *Stanton*," she said.

"Yeah?" How else would I address it?

"You didn't get my announcement?"

"I haven't gotten anything in the mail from you in a while," I said. "Announcement for what?"

"I remarried," she said.

I had suspected that one day she would. However, even seeing her with the buffoon that one time hadn't convinced me that she was with someone else. I didn't want to believe it, even though her mother had alluded to the possibility of it. But to finally have to admit it to myself, and to learn of her remarriage from the woman you thought - that you would have sworn on your own life – would love you into eternity, well, I wasn't prepared for that. But if losing Patricia taught me anything, it was that if I could deal with knowing she had married someone else, I wasn't going to allow the loss of another love to destroy me. So when Carrie Leigh finally told me she had remarried, I wasn't surprised when she told me what her new married surname was. Years before, after Carrie Leigh's parents had forbidden her to see me, her mother had written me a letter reaffirming their opposition. And she had said something prophetic: "A relationship that is built on deception, in the end, will be destroyed by deception." Why hadn't I listened to my gut? Why hadn't I listened to her mom? The lady had been smarter than I gave her credit for being.

"Kid, roll with the punch," Jack said. "You have all the time in the world."

Everyone was full of knowledge for what would suit me best in my future, including my ex-wife. We saw each other a few times before I left Houston for Cambridge. At one point, I even baby-sat Candy, our Cocker Spaniel, who now belonged to her and her new husband whose own Cocker Spaniel had mated with Candy. Oh, how symbolic. It was in one of those last meetings that Carrie Leigh and I finally parted ways in some reasonable facsimile of understanding.

"You always thought you need me more than you did," she said. "You thought you had to be white to make it in the world."

"I can understand how you would think that," I said. "But I needed you because I loved you. More than you knew, and much, much more than you loved me."

"Then I hope the next woman you love deserves you more than I did," she said. "I just didn't want our final words to be angry ones."

I was learning, though, that sometimes it takes less than death to kill a man.

In the fall of 1977, after walking out of the *Post* and hanging out exploring Martinique, Washington, New York and Boston, I returned to Waco for the first time in years. It felt strange being at my parents' home without having to go to school, without having a job, without having any kind of responsibility since the start of kindergarten. I was thirty years old and my youth was gone, but I'd never felt more like a child. I watched kids' cartoons on television. I ate cereal several times a day. I stayed in my pajamas from morning until night. One day my parents handed me a business card of a doctor they insisted I see. It was a shrink.

As a favor to our family doctor, the psychiatrist had blocked out a couple of hours late one afternoon just to see me. Our session lasted into the early evening. I don't know why I found myself being so candid. Perhaps it was because I knew my parents didn't believe in shrinks. They ordinarily would have sent me to see their parish priest. So this had to be extraordinary on their part to fear that their son, their pride and joy, had gone mad enough to turn to a psychiatrist.

Depression was an easy diagnosis. But there was far more: The self-destructiveness that seemed to have begun with learning of Patricia's marriage had now manifested itself in other ways. I wondered if I hadn't been solely responsible for ruining my marriage. I had turned Carrie Leigh away in much the same way I had other friends and family members who tried to help or befriend me. I had turned my back on the best friend of my youth, Dick McCall. Even in my pursuit of Patricia, I had sought to do it alone, when I now realized that I easily could have turned to others for advice, counsel, or assistance. I had lived selfishly, too often acting as if I had certain princely entitlements. I was my own enemy.

I told the shrink about the craziness of the day when I was served with divorce papers and about how I had ended up with the two strippers: Sam and her girlfriend, Elizabeth, who were both gorgeous, in their late twenties, and ex-cons who had done time in women's prisons for drug possession, armed robbery, solicitation, and prostitution. I wondered if this poor shrink in Waco had ever heard anything this sordid. Was what I experienced what it felt to be Mick Jagger? A lot of crazy sex, drugs, and rock 'n' roll? I lost much of my good judgment, and I became complicit in some other stuff in their lives that went on. Sam and I were especially close emotionally, and that created friction with Elizabeth. Still, I think they also saw a guy who was especially vulnerable and yet quite open. I think I once asked them why they were so kind to me and why they hadn't taken advantage of someone in my situation. They each told me that I made them want to be better people than they had become, and I wound up crying uncontrollably. Nevertheless, I was curious about them, and I'm a pretty good snoop. I checked on Sam and learned she had been at the University of Colorado when, as an eighteen-year-old, she accompanied a boyfriend on a drug buy that turned into a bust along with a shootout with police. Lizzie, as Elizabeth was called, had a lot of legal paperwork with her – immigration documents, probation reports, psych exams – and I worked with her on a book she was trying to write.

They found my naïveté about everything they knew in life charmingly refreshing. They also took pity on me when they saw how devastated I was about the divorce. They cooked, cleaned the apartment, and wouldn't take any money from me to buy groceries or even to pay the rent. They had all kinds of cash flowing in. I would find rolls of hundred-dollar bills in the kitchen cabinets. On the days the club was closed, they would treat me to movies in the afternoon and evenings and late dinners at some of Houston's fanciest restaurants. Elizabeth, who had studied acting in England, spoke with what she told us was a "received pronunciation" that she said she picked up in her training. So when she spoke in that manner, it was amazing what tables we could get in a city striving so hard for a sense of culture and class, even if it was feigned. I told the shrink how Carlos had chased them away, but how they had returned a few days later. When they left Houston that fall to work the more profitable exotic dance and burlesque circuit on the East Coast, they said they could take pride in leaving me better prepared for the life of a worldly bachelor. Of course, their newfound pride didn't last long. The following spring, heartbroken over another love affair gone bad, Lizzie blew out her brains. Sam I lost track of.

The shrink said he would hold off on medication for the time but insisted that I see him again. That weekend my parents also forced me out of the house to attend a family reunion, something I'd not done in almost twenty years. I hardly recognized anyone except some uncles and aunts. There were cousins and extended relatives whom I neither knew nor had seen since they were children.

"Who are you?" one of them came up to me and asked.

"I'm Tony," I said.

He searched his brain for a Tony. No one else in my family was named that.

"Are you Aunt Emma and Uncle Antonio's Tony?" he finally guessed.

"Yeah."

"Man, you don't look like him," my cousin said.

"Don't feel badly," I said. "I don't recognize myself half the time."

"No, man, you're supposed to be big," he said. "All the things that you've done. I thought you'd be a big guy. But, man, you're puny. I don't understand."

Like most of my relatives, he knew me, or knew of me, through the photographs in my parents' living room or the certificates and awards that lined a hallway of their home. I always sent them those. They always felt empty to me. They had not been the prize I had long sought. Photographs never give you any sense of true proportion, and trophies always distort any achievement into something grander than it is. My relatives also knew me from the way my mother kept my bedroom, almost as it had been when I lived there, like a sad museum, lined with books and mementos. She had scrapbooks of my clippings from the newspapers I sent to them. The only thing no longer there was my extensive baseball card collection. She said I had thrown all the cards away when I moved out, but I would sooner have died. She didn't have the heart to tell me what I had been told by another cousin. He had ratted out yet another of our cousins who apparently had squirreled away hundreds of cards under her clothing every time she visited her Aunt Emma. These included valuable cards of Mantle, Mays, Aaron, and all the greats from the 1950s and through the mid-1960s. It also included Mantle rookie cards from 1951 and 1952, including two

Bowman's, not in the most mint of conditions, but still valuable. My Uncle Frank had handed them down to me from his own collection. Coincidentally, the cousin who took my baseball card collection later opened her own collectibles store in a suburb of Dallas. Ah, what we do, wittingly or not, for our loved ones. So if my relatives didn't know me, perhaps it was my fault as well.

"This is me," I said to my cousin at the reunion. "Everything you heard was wrong. I was always the one getting beaten up."

"Nah, I don't believe that," my cousin said. "I've seen and read what you've accomplished. We're proud of you, guy. How did you accomplish what you've done? You grew up one of us. It seems like it would be impossible to do some of those things coming from where we did. Wasn't it hard?"

"Well, it wasn't easy."

"I knew it had to be hard," my cousin said. "So what's the trick to doing it?"

I wasn't sure, and I thought about it a moment. "The trick," I said, "was not minding that it was hard."

My cousin laughed. "Let me get you a beer, guy."

We shared several beers, and he kept hammering away looking for better answers, as if I truly had some secrets instead of just having muddied through an uncharted course. There was no magic elixir as far as I knew. Perhaps if there was any fix, it was something within, an inner drive or blind ambition that was fueled by an almost neurotic need to succeed. The era of the civil rights movements had produced the cries of the need for role models, black or Latino symbols who could be inspirations to minority youth. I didn't know how much of this I bought into. I'd certainly had no particular role models in Waco in the 1950s or 1960s, and I didn't know of any of my white friends who spoke openly about wanting to follow in someone's footsteps unless it was the jocks who wanted to be like their favorite big league baseball stars. The role models I found were those in the books I grew up reading: the self-educated Abraham Lincoln overcoming a lack of money or social standing; the struggling journalist Ernest Hemingway who found his voice as a novelist; Jonas Salk, the son of marginally-educated Russian Jewish immigrants who discovered the vaccine for polio; Helen Keller, the first deaf-blind person to earn a Bachelor of Arts degree and go on to become an author and political activist. I wasn't looking for a Latino Lincoln, a Hispanic Hemingway, a Mexican Salk, or a Chicana Keller. For that, maybe I had my father to thank. He had lectured me against being marginalized as a Mexican as well as about not using my ethnicity as an excuse. My aunts, uncles, cousins, and family friends had often praised my parents for the way they had raised me, but I don't think it ever occurred to them that perhaps the greatest gift they had given me was instilling in me that I was as much a part of God's chosen as anyone else – and that, if I was a child of my race, it was of the human race and not some arbitrary nationality.

I wished I could have said all this to my cousin, but it would have taken much more time than either of us had that day. My cousin kept going back to the courage it would take, and I wondered about the circumstances that must have beaten him down.

"How did you have the *cojones* to even think you could do some of those things?" he wanted to know.

I laughed to myself and thought my cousin would have made a great interviewer. He was a bulldog at seeking some truths that I could not give him.

At last, I gave him the truth.

"I did them for a girl," I said.

My cousin spit up his beer and broke up laughing. He found that hard to believe. And I suppose he would never have understood my chivalry, if that's what it was, that came from a bygone era. "Come on, man, you did it for a girl? What girl could get a guy to do those things?"

"A girl," I said. "A girl in my dreams."

At least, I had my grandmother Doña Concha I could talk to. I told her that the previous year, fittingly the country's 200th anniversary, I found a memorial marker dedicated to Don Juan de Miralles Trailhon, our distant relative, at 242 South 3rd Street in Philadelphia. The inscription on the marker described Miralles as "the first Spanish diplomatic representative to the United States of America." I showed her a photograph of the marker and of the New Jersey cemetery where Miralles was originally buried. I told her of some of the documentation I found while researching Miralles at the Library of Congress and Widener Library at Harvard, but she just kind of smugly laughed me off.

"You didn't believe your *abuelita* and had to find this out for yourself," she said. "When will you start listening to me?"

I kissed her cheek and allowed her to ruffle my hair the way she used to when I was a child. Then she said something that made me sadly realize how old she was, and how I, too, if she remembered me at all, was also just a distant memory.

"Now, *hijo*," she said, "you're Jaime? Or are you Tony?"

I was a total stranger to my family, I realized. Some of my relatives had no idea who I was beyond those photographs in my parents' home, pictures that apparently bore little resemblance to what actually I looked like. I couldn't recall when exactly it had been that I had effectively severed ties. It hadn't been something conscious. At least, I didn't think it had been. But if I had to date it, I suppose I had started pushing away around the time that my Mexicanness – the color of my skin and my heritage – started getting in the way of being acceptable to the society that would judge and accept someone like Patricia and me together. I had taken and channeled my anger and frustration to all those around me. That's how I had lived, day by day, doing what I did. I'd wake up thinking of Patricia, angry at the world around me, and trying to find a way out. I blamed the dominant white society around me for imposing those kinds of feelings and restrictions, but I think I also – in my own ill-founded thinking – faulted my fate. My family and my heritage bore no responsibility for the discrimination I had faced in my life, but what youth doesn't rebel at who they are and who brought them into this life? I was as much a product of the rebellious nature of the times in which I came of age as I was of my family and my background.

I was also a stranger to my parents, who weren't exactly thrilled to have me home for any extended time. It wasn't good that I wasn't working, they said, and that I wasn't continuing to make a name for myself. Translated that meant that they preferred the role of proud parents of a son who was away from the small town writing stories about big name politicians and winning newspaper awards. They loved having a son they could brag about more than a son who wanted to be at home near them. One evening after dinner I said what was on my mind.

"I just want to feel that you'll be just as supportive of me when I fail," I told them.

"But you've never failed," my dad said.

"I've always been afraid to fail," I said. "I've been afraid to see the disappointment on your faces. I knew you wouldn't be behind me if I did fail. Look how you two reacted when my marriage broke up."

"Because it was your fault," he said.

"See you have no idea what happened," I said, "but you assumed I was the one who messed it up. I'm your son, but you took her side."

I picked up a framed photograph of Carrie Leigh that they still had on a sofa table in the living room, and my mother snatched it from me, thinking, I suppose, that I might smash it.

"She's so beautiful," my mother said. "She was my other daughter. How could you have hurt her?"

"Mom, it wasn't like that," I pleaded. "How can you take sides when you don't know why the marriage broke up. *I* don't know why it broke up."

But my mother lived in utter denial. All you had to do was look at her photograph albums. Many of the pictures of my sister with her boyfriends or of me with my occasional dates, like to my proms, existed with the image of the former boyfriends and dates completely cut out or, worse, with their faces removed. Her reasoning was that these people in our pasts should not exist and, heaven forbid, ever be seen by our current spouses. This was her way of editing our pasts, not by compartmentalizing them in our memories but by physically erasing them from sight. My father could be a bit less radical in how he viewed the past, but not by much.

"We know how you are," my dad said. "You close off people. You don't let them get near to you."

How could I win with parental support like that? I couldn't. But it became an exchange we had to have, not with the anger and recriminations of past arguments but with the measured words and tone of trying to help my parents see a part of them they had long overlooked. I shared with my father how truly insecure and frightened I often found myself in my work no matter how much confidence I projected. I didn't tell him about Patricia by name, but I did confess about there being a long love for someone I had known as a youngster and the hurt and heartbreak of being told that there were places for people and that mine would never be at her side. He told me that he felt at times he had not been the father he should have been, but I wouldn't hear of it. I had not been in his shoes, I said. I knew how difficult it was to get along in life with the advantages I'd been given. I couldn't imagine how hard it would have been at another earlier time and place.

One afternoon I finally got him to talk about any involvement he might have had with the OSS. He genuinely seemed to have no first-hand knowledge about the agency or its work, though he said he met several wounded officers in the hospital when he was convalescing. A couple of those officers, he said, might have been in intelligence.

"They had letters and notebooks written in Spanish," he said. "And their Spanish was awful."

"So did you help them? Translate for them."

"I did a few times. Some of it didn't make sense - I told them that," he said.

"What didn't make sense? The Spanish or the messages?"

"It's been so long ago, it's hard to say. A lot of it was like *tonterias*," he said. *Tonterias* was Spanish for nonsensical.

"Like puzzles? Or codes?"

"Maybe," he said. "I would just translate it and give it back to them and tell them it didn't make any sense."

My father said he was at the hospital for almost half a year, an unusually long stay, because of infections he continued contracting. His wounds had been extensive. He had one wide scar that began at about his sternum and extended down around his belly button and continued to his groin, something you would imagine to see on a bullfighter who had been gored.

"Was this where you met that nun mom was always giving you hell about?" I asked.

He laughed, recalling all those times my mom had pulled out the photograph.

"She was a nurse," he said. "She spoke Spanish, and she tried to help make heads and tails out of those documents they kept showing me?"

"How many documents did those officers ask you to help them with?"

"Oh, I don't know," he said. "A lot."

"A lot like dozens?" I asked. "Or a lot like hundreds? How often did they ask you to translate?"

"Every day," he said. "I didn't mind. There was nothing else to do except smoke cigarettes, play cards, eat, sleep, and see the doctors sometimes."

"Dad, were you working for the OSS and can't tell me you were or what?" I said. "Because this sounds like you were doing intelligence work. There's nothing wrong with that. I'm just curious about what you did in the war."

"I was a soldier," he said. "I did what soldiers do. I obeyed orders and did what I was asked."

We went round and round until late in the evening. I got nowhere conclusively, nor would I. In the coming years, I made no fewer than half a dozen requests to the Defense Department about any intelligence work my dad might have done for the Army or any agency of the government, including OSS. The most I ever received were the honorable discharge papers detailing his service, documents we already had. In 1992, my father suffered a series of strokes that left him in a delicate condition. Curiously, although these strokes seemingly had nothing to do with his war service, the government changed his disability status. He had been classified fifty percent disabled since the war. He was reclassified as one hundred percent disabled. The difference meant tens of thousands of dollars in increased benefits dating back years. When he died in the VA Hospital in Temple, Texas, in 2004, the cause of death was complications related to the strokes. He was unable to eat, and doctors were unable to successfully implant a feeding tube in his stomach. Within a day of his death, though, the government reclassified the cause of death as being from his injuries while wounded in action at the Battle of the Bulge. The reclassification meant another significant increase of tens of thousands of dollars in benefits to my mother. Not that that proved anything. It just made it curiouser.

Our conversation in Waco in late 1977 was also the first time my dad and I had talked this freely and the first time we drank together. I wasn't a beer drinker, and I had to disappoint him.

"Dad, I hate to piss in your beer," I said. "But your Coors tastes like lukewarm milk in summer."

I went to the vegetable bin of the refrigerator where I had been hiding my own stash. I had several bottles of Corona, not the greatest beer in the world but a far cry better than anything domestic. I was surprised he had never tried it.

"Do you trust Mexican beer?" he wanted to know. "I've heard they piss in it."

"Dad, do you realize how silly that question sounds?" I got him to laugh. "You know they had this at the Harvard Faculty Club last year just to please Octavio Paz."

"He drinks beer?"

"Yeah, from a champagne glass. We should try it."

We went out that afternoon and bought champagne flutes. Then I took my dad to the only mall in Waco at the time. At a store called

Goldstein-Migel, the closest thing to a Neiman-Marcus in town, I bought him a three-piece pinstripe navy suit that he first refused to try on when he saw the price tag.

"It's too expensive," he said.

"Think of it this way, dad," I said. "It's the only suit you'll want to wear the rest of your life."

He looked at himself admiringly in the long fitting room mirror.

"Now, one last thing, dad," I said. "Stop coloring your hair."

"That's you mom," he said. "She wants me to do it."

"Yeah, but with this suit, the gray hair will bring out the chalk in the pinstripes. The other way you look like a used car salesman."

He took the suit. He said he would stop coloring the gray. Then we went home and had the rest of the Corona.

Maybe it was that my father was getting on in years, though a part of me likes to think it might have been the Corona, but he opened up to me that day in a way he never had before. Apparently he was guilt-torn over something that had happened more than twenty years earlier, when we had gone to San Antonio at the height of Davy Crockett mania to see the Alamo. I had begged for weeks, and visiting that old Spanish mission was the pinnacle of my year in the third grade.

I spent an entire day touring the Alamo – the chapel, the museum, the rebuilt fortress, and the grounds – and I did it all on my own. While my mother used the day to shop in downtown San Antonio, my father spent the entire time chain-smoking on a bench just outside the Alamo entrance. No matter how many times I tried to get my father to join me in my sightseeing, he refused to enter the historic site.

"I visited the Alamo once when I was a boy," he now told me, much to my surprise.

"Why didn't you ever tell me?" This was something I would have loved to have known back then.

"It was a long time ago," he said. "It was a different time. My father took me and your uncles to the Alamo, but we never went inside."

"You're kidding," I said. "You went all the way to San Antonio? You went all the way to the Alamo, but didn't go inside? That doesn't make sense, dad. What happened?"

"There was a man at the door who stopped us," he said. "He was white, and he told us they didn't need any more Mexicans coming to the Alamo."

His words hung in the air like a bad odor before I could say anything.

"Oh, dad, why didn't you tell me?"

"I didn't want you to know," he said. "I didn't want you to ever think you couldn't do some of the things I couldn't. I didn't want you to ever think that there were doors that would be closed to you."

We both had tears in our eyes.

"Fuck them, dad," I said at last, some of the Corona going to my head. "Fuck them all. Fuck the Alamo. Fuck the Daughters of the Republic of Texas."

"Don't blame those people, son. Times are changing." My God, the man had more forgiveness in his heart than I ever would.

"No, dad. Times won't change until all those people and their sons and daughters are dead and gone," I said. "The hate those people preached is alive and well today."

My dad shook his head. "I didn't raise you to feel that way," he said. "When you talk like that, you're a stranger to me."

Then perhaps I was a stranger everywhere. Everywhere except my lifelong love for Patricia and in the eyes of the man who had tried to help me in fulfilling it, Uncle Jesse. Despite my promise to Doña Juana, I had never stopped longing for Patricia. Hardly a day passed when I didn't think about her and wonder about how her life had turned out. I wrote down thoughts that I hope I could one day share with her.

I would love to fall asleep in your arms.
I would love to kiss your forehead
And every part of your face.
I remember once seeing you bite your lip,
Gently, as if you were trying to piece
Something in your head you'd forgotten.

I wanted to kiss that very spot you were biting.
I also used to study your mouth when you spoke.
Has anyone ever told you that you appear to be
Smiling when you talk, almost giggling and
Appearing as if you know a secret we all don't?
I wanted to walk up to you and take your hand
The way I did when we waltzed together and to ask
You to pull your hair back as if in a ponytail
And to promise to wear it that way when we made love.
I was so bold in my imagination.
I was so unflinching in my dreams.
And you were the gorgeous princess.
You still are.
You are the center of my universe.
You are all I have ever wanted.
You are the heart and joy of my soul.

My Uncle Jesse was also back in Waco at this time. He had fallen on hard times. Something about the feds and a crackdown on the home improvement industry. But he was making a comeback, he said, in Spanish music of all things. I don't think I had ever heard him speak much Spanish except with my grandmother and with my own mom. In the entire time I spent with him and his family in Dallas, I don't think a word of Spanish was ever uttered. And Spanish music? That's not what Jesse played on his eight-track tape player of his El Dorado. But he had discovered a market for eight-track tapes of Spanish music, especially Mexican *conjuntos*, in South Texas, and he was prepared to exploit it. Still, I felt badly that, financially, he had been forced to retreat to Waco. I offered him the money I was getting for the Porsche, as payback for all the things he had done for me, but he wouldn't hear of it. Wouldn't you believe it? A week later he was trying to buy me another Porsche until I told him I wasn't staying in Texas, and that a sports car might not be my best transportation in Washington or New York. He made me promise, though, that I would let some time go by before I made any commitment to leave.

The next day I left for Corpus Christi where an eccentric old oil wildcatter was setting up a weekly as an alternative to the city's daily. David McHam, my old professor from Baylor, and my reporter friend Tommy West were involved in developing the weekly. The wealthy wildcatter was pouring in several hundred thousand dollars into the newspaper, and he was housing all of us in hotel rooms at the Corpus Christi Hilton along with providing leased cars and full expenses. He hired me to write a multi-part sequel to *Chicano Power* as well as to add to the new paper's prestige, mostly the latter. I was told I could write my stories from anywhere – back in Waco, if I wanted – and to do whatever I wanted to do. At this time, Carlos Guerra was also back in his hometown of Robstown just outside Corpus Christi, so I quickly got him involved. Carlos wanted to be a journalist, specifically a columnist, and he would later become one in San Antonio. At this time, though, Carlos was trying to distance himself from a gubernatorial campaign that turned not just badly but disastrously horrible. In 1974, he had been campaign manager of Ramsey Muñiz's second run for governor, which hadn't fared as well as his first run. Muñiz had failed to arouse the quixotic urgency that had made his campaign so novel in 1972, and La Raza Unida didn't make any of the local inroads that many activists expected. Ramsey also found that he couldn't raise the money of the first campaign that had allowed him the freedom to travel around the state. So he had turned to alternative means of financing the campaign that would eventually bring Muñiz personal doom.

According to Carlos, Muñiz called on drug contacts he knew and began importing airplane-loads of marijuana that, for him, became the mother's milk of politics. Carlos said he had opposed the idea. Knowing Carlos and how he had reacted to the drug-dealer in my apartment, I believed him. But Ramsey was hard-headed. I knew that personally from having worked with him one summer during college on a Model Cities program in Waco where he was briefly in charge. Ramsey didn't like following all the boring minutiae required of federal programs, and he loved taking shortcuts that would meet the same ends.

"Ramsey was greedy, and he didn't need to be," Carlos complained. "He didn't want to skimp. He insisted on doing it the same way he did it two years earlier, and he didn't need to. He wanted to be on the campaign trail every day, even when he didn't need to be. And to do that, he needed more money than we could raise."

At one point, Carlos recalled, Muñiz's reliance on financing his campaign with marijuana sales reached the level of absurdity. On a trip on which he accompanied the candidate, they flew into Mexico in a small, low-flying rented plane to avoid radar, finding the drug contact waiting with several tons of marijuana.

"I knew there was a problem immediately," Carlos recalled, "and I tried to bring it to Ramsey's attention, but he was so wired, he didn't want to listen to anything. All he wanted to do was to pay for the load, get it on the plane, and get out of there. I kept telling him, 'Ramsey, man, we've got a big problem,' and he kept saying, 'God dammit, Carlos, I know what I'm doing! I've got this! I'm in charge! So shut the fuck up!' So I did and just let him find out for himself. They packed the plane with as much weed as they could get inside, and that's when Ramsey finally realized he had a problem. Almost half the marijuana he had bought was still on the ground. Can you believe that? Damn it if Ramsey hadn't rented a plane big enough to carry the load he'd bought. And he had already paid them the money for all of it! So then he's asking me, 'Carlos, why don't you tell them we're only buying what we loaded up and to return the rest of the money?' I said, 'Ramsey, are you fucking crazy as well as stupid? You tell these guys you want half your money back, and they'll blow us away. Look at all the rifles they've got.' I think that's when Ramsey realized how much danger he was playing with, and that he didn't know what he was doing."

Muñiz should have taken that as a warning, but he continued his involvement in illicit drug activity even after that campaign. In 1976, he was charged with federal felony drug conspiracy charges that were only the beginning of a series of criminal prosecutions. Ramsey eventually would be sentenced to life in federal prison. Carlos was never charged in any of the cases, but he was understandably concerned in the aftermath of the first prosecution against Muñiz and was laying low. I told him I was headed to Los Angeles and urged him to relocate with me.

"I can't, *carnal*," he said. "My heaven and hell are both here."

It was also nearing the holidays, and I returned to Waco where I spent the coming days and weeks revisiting places I had known growing up. I revisited Gurley, walking in the old playground to the exact spot I where I had stood throwing a ball when I first saw Patricia, and then went to the location where she had turned the pirouette that changed my life. None of that had changed, but the garden at the front of the school where I had photographed her had been razed and was now only a memory. I spent time at the bear pits at Baylor, but the university had expanded so much that I no longer knew my way around the campus. I visited my grandfather's old neighborhood on South Second Street, but all the old housing had been torn to the ground for a new renewal project adjoining the Brazos River. The ballpark where the Waco Pirates had played and which Ruth had once graced was also gone, and South Junior had been shut down as a school and looked almost unrecognizable.

Of course, I also took a ride to Patricia's house. The O'Neals no longer lived there, I was told by a neighbor, and whoever did wasn't home. As he had promised to do, Ackley had sent two cases of Perrier Jouet Fleur to my parents' home, and I had taken a bottle and two glasses with me to Patricia's just on the one-in-a-million chance. My gambling luck, of course, hadn't changed. On a late winter afternoon, I sat on what had once been Patricia's porch and sipped the champagne from both glasses until it was gone. I kept hoping it would rain and that a rainbow might appear, as it did that one day, but do rainbows ever appear on cold winter days. The Perrier Jouet, though, was in fine spirits.

The sad lesson of coming home had been that it all could have been so easy.

I'd come home wiser
than I left for life's dream kingdom,

293

and all the poorer with a wealth of knowledge.
I'd come home to the snowflakes I never saw
and the ice-capped mountains that never grew.
But most of all, I'd come home to be able to move on.
You are my Juliet at the costume ball
and I, disguised and masked, have stolen all those dances,
though you never noticed.
And now night's shadows sleep at peace,
and I want to lead you in the morning sunlight.

The thought of being grown up
confuses my sense of time
where a clock never ticks
and where I count years on broken watches.
I only wish I'd acted sooner.
Or that I'd been a Nutcracker in a dream's ballet.
Still, I wonder even now if this be fantasy,
and if I've not awakened for a single night
to later drift back to my cotton-stuffed self.
Can't Nutcrackers live in their dreams
and keep away the stroke of midnight's change.
Oh, I pray – and I also know:
If any dreamer can, it is I.

A few days later, Jack Nelson called with good news and bad news. The bad news was that it might not be until the middle of the next year before a job I would want might open up in Washington or New York, not just any reporting job but one covering civil rights and politics from a national perspective. There would be retirements coming at that time, including one in his bureau. The good news was that there was this one great job coming up after the start of the new year, but it would be in Los Angeles.

"Ah, man, Jack, I'll die in Los Angeles," were my first words.

There was a pause. "You mean because of what happened to Ruben?"

"No, Jack, it has nothing to do with Ruben," I said. "I'm not worried about that. But did you see Woody Allen's latest movie? He has a line in there about how L.A.'s only cultural advantage is being able to make a right turn on a red light."

He laughed. "L.A.'s not that bad."

"Jack, if it's not that bad, why are you in Washington for the *L.A. Times* and not in L.A.?"

"Good point," he said. "But this would be a good opportunity for you. My friend Jim Bellows – he used to be editor of the *Washington Star* – has just become the editor of the *Los Angeles Herald Examiner.*"

Bellows also wasn't without his own stellar reputation. He was known in the industry as having been the last editor of the old *New York Herald Tribune*, which many journalists considered having been the best written newspaper in America in its heyday. At the *Trib*, Bellows groomed writers like Tom Wolfe, and he converted Jimmy Breslin from a sportswriter into a news columnist regarded by many as the voice of New York newspaper readers. He had also reworked the paper's Sunday supplement into *New York* magazine, which quickly became home to the so-called New Journalism that emerged in the late 1960s and 1970s. But the *Los Angeles Herald Examiner?* Everyone in the business knew that it had become the target of what was ultimately the longest newspaper strike in the country's history. One journalism review had even rated it one of America's ten worst big city newspapers.

"Jack, isn't that paper on strike?" I asked. "Or almost dead?"

"It's no longer on strike, and Jim's been hired to revive it back to the way it once was," Jack said. "Jim's gonna call you and offer you a job as a columnist."

"A columnist? Jack, I haven't been a columnist since high school," I said. "I'm a reporter."

"Well, you can do that, too," he said. "Look, do it for six months. A good job will open up back here by that time, and Jim knows you don't plan to be there long. But this will get you working again, and it's L.A. You've got all that sun out there, and you're single. In six months you probably won't want to leave."

"I wouldn't bet on that," I said. "But for six months, expenses, and a car, yeah, I'll do it."

Finally, I was leaving Texas, away from all the bad memories and the terrible work environments, for a job where I'd be wanted and a place at the end of the world almost, where ultimately you could be whoever you wanted to be and make of yourself whatever you could. That was what I had read in some Raymond Chandler novel, anyway.

I had only a few weeks and the holidays to count down in Waco.

For some time I had also wanted to see my longtime family doctor to learn what he could tell me about my dad and the OSS. After all, Harry Provence had alluded to how my family doctor had known something about my father in the war. I figured the easiest way to start a conversation with him would be to see him for a checkup. He had known me since I could remember, watching me as a little boy come to his office dressed as Roy Rogers, Davy Crockett, and Mickey Mantle, decked out in chaps, boots, coonskin cap, suede jacket with fringe, and a Yankee pinstripe uniform with number seven on the back. He had seen me in almost all my costumes except the Atomic Man. On this visit, though, for no apparent reason, Dr. Franklin asked me to dinner at his home that evening. I sensed a great opportunity to gently ask him more about what my dad did during the war, but it didn't take long to understand that my doctor had an ulterior motive of his own for his new hospitality. His youngest daughter Meredith, who was my age, now lived back home. She was divorced with two small children and, undoubtedly, bored out of her mind not only living with her parents but in Waco of all places.

Meredith didn't remember me at first, but we had met once, years ago when we were juniors in high school. I had broken out in acne for the first time in my life and had gone to her father to ask him if he would prescribe tetracycline, the antibiotic many of my friends were taking for their skin problems. It was an expensive medication, Dr. Franklin told me, but that he had months' worth of samples at his home that I could have. He sent me to an address on Austin Avenue lined with multi-story homes, many of them mansions that belonged to some of the wealthiest people in town. Meredith answered the door, bringing me the samples of tetracycline, and out of the clear blue she asked what high school I attended. She was at Waco High, and for half an hour we sat on her front steps talking about each other's schools and the people we both knew like Dick McCall and Patricia. It felt odd talking to my doctor's daughter, and I sensed a line that I didn't know if I should cross. When I left, Meredith gave me her phone number, and we agreed to talk again but we never did.

Dr. Franklin, I discovered to some surprise over dinner, had followed my career closely. He had a copy of *Chicano Power* that he had me sign for him, and civil rights became our big topic of conversation over dinner. A big admirer of Eleanor Roosevelt, Mrs. Franklin had long been active in social causes and was even on the board of the local chapter of the NAACP.

"So why didn't you call my daughter way back then?" Mrs. Franklin playfully demanded.

I thought she would understand and appreciate the story, so I told her and her family about all the "white girls" speeches I got as a kid and as a teenager. It had all borne out, I said, in what had happened with the girl I eventually married in secret. Mrs. Franklin and Meredith were shocked.

"I wish I had known," Mrs. Franklin said. "Maybe we could have done something."

"Mrs. Franklin," I said, "I don't think there's anything anyone could have done. I mean, how do we read people's hearts? How do we know that the person who is the most open-minded individual on most issues will balk at seeing their daughter with a man of a different color or a different background?"

"Still, this is 1977," said Mrs. Franklin. "We've gone to the moon. We've seen hate kill some of our best leaders. How do God-loving people still judge someone by the color of their skin?"

"Mom," begged Meredith. "Waco's that way. I wish none of us lived here."

That evening was one of the most memorable nights of my adult life in Waco. I learned that Dr. Franklin had become my father's doctor after he and mom moved to Waco after the war. During World War II, Dr. Franklin had served in a mobile tent unit similar to the M*A*S*H units of Korean War fame. He later worked at a military hospital in Italy where one of the wounded men in whom he took great interest happened to be my father. He had sustained massive internal injuries from shrapnel that had required extensive abdominal surgical procedures. After his discharge, my father suffered several setbacks that forced his hospitalization at the VA hospital in Temple, Texas. There, once again, he crossed paths with Dr. Franklin, who was about to go into private practice in Waco.

After I was born, Dr. Franklin became my doctor as well. He reminded me of my own extensive hospitalization when I was a child. I was suffering from what was originally diagnosed as a gastro-intestinal infection, he said, but numerous tests failed to locate the source.

"We had to have you fed intravenously, I seem to remember, but we couldn't get the fever down, and we couldn't control the cramping and diarrhea," he said. "You had us worried."

"So what finally cured me?" I asked. "Tons of antibiotics?"

"You don't remember?" He seemed puzzled that I didn't know.

I didn't. I must have wiped the memory out of my mind.

"It was that aunt of your father's," Dr. Franklin said.

"Doña Juana?" Could it have been?

"I think that's what they called her," he said. "She did some strange folk medicine ritual. That night she came you showed some improvement. The next day you were almost good as new."

Meredith took it all in with genuine interest. Of course, I knew I was there for her, and she was easy on the eyes. She was a longhaired brunette with hazel eyes and an even tan she said she worked on by swimming in their backyard pool several hours a day. She had the help of a nanny and was working on a master's degree in psychology at Baylor.

"I'm trying to understand myself and some of the things that have happened to me," she said. "Does that sound crazy? Like why is it that I don't want to belong to any club that would have me as a member?"

"Woody Allen," I said, remembering the line from the final scene of his latest movie. "*Annie Hall.*"

"Yeah, actually, it's..."

At the same time we both said, "Groucho Marx!"

Late that night, she and I went to the movies to see *Annie Hall* again, and Meredith turned out to be a big fan of Woody Allen films, as I was. A week later we drove to Dallas to see *Play It Again, Sam*, which was showing at a festival, along with *Casablanca*, the classic film that had inspired *Play It Again, Sam*. Dr. and Mrs. Franklin made it easy for us. They doted on their grandchildren and were all too eager to watch them so that Meredith and I could spend time together.

We had long talks about our lives and about the unexpected things that change our plans. She had gotten pregnant her sophomore year at Southern Methodist University, and her boyfriend, who had recently graduated, proposed to her. Then, while still nursing her first child, Meredith became pregnant again. After he graduated from law school, they were living in Dallas and had just bought their first home when her husband turned her life upside down. He announced he had fallen in love with a co-worker and wanted a divorce.

"I can't believe it to this day?" she said. "Why would he do that?"

"Did he marry her," I asked.

"No, they live together," she said. "I think they'll probably get married, though."

Meredith's daughters were in elementary school, and it was obvious she was a great mom. Both girls were exceptionally bright and curious with wonderful imaginations. We started taking them with us to dinner sometimes, and we would regularly read to them at night. One Sunday we all drove to Dallas to see a Cowboys game, after which the girls announced that when they grew up they wanted to be Cowboys cheerleaders. Surprisingly, a part of me started wondering whether I couldn't extend my time in Waco a little longer than I planned. I didn't know where any of this was going, but it was certainly giving me a new perspective on my hometown. The only person in the Franklin household who wasn't sold on me was Rosa, the Mexican housekeeper who had been with the family since Meredith's early childhood. She was understandably over-protective of someone she had come to see as her own daughter.

"*Yo lo conozco,*" she said once when she caught me alone. She knew me, she said, though I didn't know from where. "They say you have a bad reputation with girls. You cannot have your way with *señorita* Meredith."

"Rosa Maria," I said, using both her names. "She's a *señora*, isn't she?"

She conceded she was.

"But I will conduct myself as if she were a *señorita*," I said. "As for whatever people have said, I'm not the bad guy here. All I can tell you is that I've never done anything to a girl like what Meredith's ex-husband did to her. When he comes here the next time on one of his visiting days, why not be as bold with him as you are with me?" Rosa softened up after that. It may have also helped that I started bringing her books and magazines in Spanish, including one of Paz's books of poetry.

When my parents learned I was seeing Dr. Franklin's daughter, they quickly expressed their displeasure. My mother even went to see Dr. Franklin to confirm my story that it had been he who had invited me to their home and that both he and his wife approved of me seeing their daughter.

"Dr. Franklin said he thought your intentions toward his daughter were honorable," my mother said when she got home. "What *are* your intentions?"

"I have no idea, mom," I said. "But whatever they are, they're a whole lot better than those of her ex-husband who left her with two kids to chase after another woman."

As fate would have it, the next day I happened to be at the Franklin house when Meredith's ex-husband Greg arrived to pick up the girls on one of his days to have the children. It was awkward and quickly became even more so. As we waited near the entry for Meredith to come downstairs with the girls, he exchanged pleasantries with his former mother-in-law and kept eying me, not with an intimidating stare – he wasn't going to intimidate anyone in that household – but with a look of apparent recognition.

"Reicher Catholic High School, 1965," he blurted.

But I couldn't place him, and we'd had an extremely small class.

"State drama that spring," he said. "We competed in dramatic interpretation. We both did *Hamlet*. I was at Dallas Jesuit."

I remembered that someone else had also performed the same soliloquies at that competition.

"Yeah, I remember," I said, recalling his performance but not his face. "You were great."

"You were better," he said.

Oh, man, had I come home to have a dick-measuring contest with a guy from the past? And Meredith's ex, at that?

"That Irish accent you used," he said. "It won it for you."

"Welsh," I said. "It was a Welsh accent."

"It caught everyone off guard," he said. "You had the judges salivating."

"What do judges know?"

"I always wondered," he said. "Where did that accent come from? You don't look like you're... you know?"

"I know, I've had an ethnic-change operation since then," I said. "I thought I could get further ahead in life being Mexican."

He didn't know what to say, and Mrs. Franklin quickly jumped in.

"He's joking, of course, Greg!"

He seemed relieved. But I wasn't going to tell him that I'd spent two months back then listening to old 33 1/3 rpm recordings of Richard Burton's *Hamlet*, memorizing each inflection and intonation, until I could mimic it almost perfectly. A classmate even made an audio tape-recording of my soliloquies. I didn't think I captured what I was shooting for at all. It sounded too "sing-song" and guttural and not as melodic as I wanted it to be as the tone went up and down. I had

301

Burton's speech pattern down, I feared, but not the dignified baritone. But I suppose in Texas, with Greg as our witness, who was to know a Welsh accent from an Irish accent?

"We had a Welsh priest at Reicher," I lied. "He helped me with it."

"You also did something with your hands..."

"When we have shuffled off this mortal coil," I said, doing a circular motion with my hands in a manner Burton had in his 1964 *Hamlet*.

"Yeah, that thing," he said.

"A bit hammish, I know."

"So, what do you do now?" The man sounded like he was hoping I could relieve him of any alimony and child support he was paying Meredith.

"Greg, I'm kind of between jobs," I said.

"Rubbish!" said Mrs. Franklin. "Tony's a very successful journalist. He just finished a fellowship at Harvard... what do they call it, Tony?"

"A Nieman Fellowship," I said.

"And he's soon going to Los Angeles where he's going to write a column for the *Los Angeles Times*." The *Herald Examiner* wasn't quite the *Times*, but I was enjoying her buildup. "Meredith's talking about us going out there to visit him and taking the girls to Disneyland."

Just then the girls bounded downstairs. They gave their father kisses and hugs, then ran to me.

"So don't forget," the oldest one said. "Tomorrow you're teaching us how the knights attack."

"I won't forget," I said.

Greg looked puzzled, so the younger one explained. "Tony's showing us how to play chess. Yesterday we learned how to castle."

"Yeah," said the older girl, "and today we learned how to pin pieces with the bishops."

Greg's jaw didn't drop exactly, but it did when he saw Meredith grab my hand to lead me out the door to try to make the movies on time.

Of course, nothing makes a man more insecure than thinking he has lost his family to someone else, even if that isn't what's happened. But what Greg had seen was his ex-mother-in-law bragging about the new man in Meredith's life who was also showing interest in his children. I didn't think any of this had been staged, though the Franklins visiting me in L.A. and going to Disneyland caught me by surprise. Greg, though, was a world-class idiot if he was going to throw all this away, and in the coming days this must have occurred to him as well.

Wouldn't you know it, not long afterward, Greg begged Meredith to take him back. He had left the woman he dumped Meredith for and had already gotten a place of his own. Even more, he was telling Meredith that he would move here with her and leave his law firm in Dallas for one in Waco, if she wanted to remain closer to her parents and continue attending Baylor. He was a man after even my own heart, and how do you compete with that? No matter how well you think you know a person, or have started to get to know them, what goes on between a man and a woman who have been married – and especially if they have children – can be as mystifying as anything known to mankind. I knew something wasn't right between us on the day when Meredith called and insisted that I not come over to her house and that we meet instead at the Elite Café on The Circle.

When she showed up, Meredith had raccoon eyes, obviously from a lot of crying and soul-searching, and she broke the news to me as I held her in my arms. I was a little surprised but not devastated, though maybe I should have shown a bit more emotion in my disappointment. I guess I just accepted it as another sign that there was nothing for me here in Waco and that I should get on with what I had planned all along.

"Don't hate me," Meredith said. We were standing in the middle of the restaurant parking lot with traffic all around us, and I was numb from the cold and the news. "Please, say something."

My head was racing to think of something clever, anything that would keep me from crying. I didn't know what to say. I wondered if there was much I could say beyond good-bye, and yet I didn't want to sound bitter and hurt. What good would that accomplish?

"I'm no good at being noble," I began at last, hoping it sounded even remotely like Bogey. "But it doesn't take much to see that the problems of three little people don't amount to a hill of beans in this crazy world."

"No! Stop that!" Meredith screamed angrily, pulling away. "It's us. You and me. We've been too honest with one another. We've bared our hearts and souls to each other. My God, Tony, I've been falling in love with you, and I think you've been falling in love with me. You're the man I had always wanted to meet. You're funny. You're witty. You're not demanding. You're patient. You love my girls, and they love you. We'd be perfect. It's just that Greg and I, you know? I mean, there's the girls, and we're here and you're going to be so far away. So talk to me, just us: Meredith and Tony. We mean more to each other than cute dialog."

"Meredith, I don't know what to say," I said. "I've never done any of this right. I don't even know where to start. I'm terrible at love. I've never said the right thing at the right time. I've never been successful in winning the girl. Not really. You and I were barely getting to know one another. I care for you. You care for me. I'm not sure I know what love means any more or what it is, if I ever did. You deserve much more than someone just telling you they love you because they don't want to lose you."

Meredith started crying, and I wasn't far behind. But I sensed that the decision right now was entirely hers and that not much I could say would change things. Did she want me to offer a competing marriage proposal? That might have been the most romantic thing to do, and maybe I was right. Maybe I was just terrible at these things because they never seemed to work out.

"This time we spent together: It's got to count for something," I said. "I would have loved if we'd had a chance to see where we were going. But that's not going to happen, it looks like. I can't tell you not to go back to your ex-husband and to marry me because we would still have a long time to get to that point. And I'm not going to jump into anything blindly like I did in the past. That's when the people you love the most get hurt the greatest. I care too much to do that to you. This has to be your decision. If you say you're not going back and want to see where we go, I'll love that. If you say you have to give your marriage another chance, I'll live with that, too. So you ask me not to hate you. How could I? How can anyone deny someone a chance to save their family? You need to do what's best for your children and for yourself. Not what's best for me or what's best for your ex."

"Oh, God, this isn't easy, is it?" Meredith's teeth had begun chattering, and I held her tenderly for possibly the last time.

"No," I said, "and I think the last thing you want is regrets."

"I wish we had met sooner," she said. "Why didn't you call me back then when we were kids?"

"Believe me," I said, "I've been asking myself the same question."

"We could have made it," she said. "You've seen my parents. They wouldn't have objected. They're crazy about you."

"Yeah," I said. "But it's not your parents that I have to win over now, is it?"

"I know." Meredith appeared torn and not altogether certain of what she was doing. Who could blame her? "Please don't give up on me."

"Look, take care of yourself and your girls," I said. "But tell that husband of yours that someone who has grown to care about you is waiting on the on-deck circle, so he better not screw this up this time. And tell him that I'm as patient as Job."

Meredith was going back to her ex. I didn't want to tell her, but I wondered how much of this was about him wanting her back and how much of it was his fear of possibly seeing his daughters moving to Los Angeles or Washington or New York. When kids are involved, it's always about the kids. What did surprise me is that she took out a folded piece of paper that she held out to me.

"Remember that you asked me if I knew where Patty O'Neal was?" she said.

"Yeah?"

"You know, she's married, don't you?" she said.

I nodded.

"Well," she said, "a friend who knows her was able to get her address."

I stared at the paper for a moment, wanting to take it and see where Patricia lived, but I remembered my promise to Doña Juana. She had died not long ago, just days after my last visit when she asked if I had kept my vow. I had, I told her, and I would continue to. But standing there, oh, how I wanted to read that note. But I needed to keep my promises, just as it had become even more urgent that I move on. If anything, what had happened with Meredith was an omen that it was time. I also had no idea what I would do if I took that note, except that I knew that at this moment, I had to do the right thing.

"Meredith, that was really nice of you," I said. "Thank you, but hold on to the note, okay?"

We kissed one last time and wiped away some tears.

"Okay," she said. "You can always call me for it."

"No," I said. "If I call you, it will be for you."

She smiled and started to leave, then she turned back.

"You didn't say so," she said, "but you really cared for Patty, didn't you?"

She saw the answer etched on my face.

"You must have loved her a great deal."

"Yeah, I did," I said. "I still do. I guess I always will."

"I'm so sorry," she said.

The traffic beat on around us, and it was starting to get even colder. Suddenly I couldn't wait for the promise of all that sun in Los Angeles and even the right-hand turns on red lights. I was learning that in life, maybe there is never a mistake. There's what you do and what you don't do.

"I'm sure it's all for the best," I said, unconvincingly. "I'm told that, anyway. But you know what they say about heaven, don't you?"

"No," she said, "tell me."

I looked at her one last time.

"They say that, if you're good down here on earth, in heaven, when you get there, you'll get another chance at love."

"You really believe that?"

Of course, I did. I recalled that day when Patricia had pirouetted into my life. So much had changed for me that year, much of it that spring. So I had come to associate so much of what started going right in my life with seeing her that first time: A beautiful, magical, mystical vision brought to life in what I now imagined a summer evening sky filled with fireflies, a gull in flight, sunlight sparkling on water, a great painting and music that haunted - maybe she would tell me one day she was a sap for flutes - all under majestic trees with lush lawns and a fairy ring of toadstools. In her mind, she could see herself that simple, a small town girl. In some people's minds, though, that was no less than a fairy tale princess - and what else is there?

I believed in her. I believed in destiny. I believed in love. Time had not eroded how I felt about her. Lost loves and lost hopes would not destroy it. I didn't send roses every day, not the kind cut from my mind and soul the way I wrap the petals of my heart and send to you, Patricia. And I would go on wondering if kissing your lips would be like your soul's caressing touch. I dare to think, and suspect, that it would be more. Would anything ever change the way I felt? No. Absolutely not. There is a place in the hearts of romantics where lovers don't disappoint and where dreams, images, and illusions about those you love are never ruined. It's a place where those dreams are always the truest.

Believe in happily ever afters.

AUTHOR'S NOTE

M Y FATHER NEVER said so, but I always got the impression that he wished Henry Cisneros had been his son. Henry and I grew up at the same time in Texas in the 1960s, each of us attending Catholic schools in our respective hometowns and sometimes competing against each other in interscholastic league speech and drama contests. The only time my father attended one of those competitions, I believe he saw Henry deliver an interpretation of one of Abraham Lincoln's addresses — the one appealing to the better angels within us — while I did two soliloquies from Hamlet using a Welsh accent I nailed from listening to a recording of Richard Burton.

My father was blown away — by Henry's performance.

When he learned Henry had enrolled at Texas A&M, my father asked me to reconsider my choice of colleges. In the 1950s and 1960s, A&M was the place all Mexican-American military veterans wanted their sons to attend. It was the school where they could join the corps, graduate as second lieutenants and serve their country as officers.

"Dad, Henry's the son of a general," I said, lying. I had no idea what Henry's father did. "He'll be an officer. Heck, he'll probably be president one day. I'm the son of an enlisted man. I can't lead men on a football team, much less on a battlefield. I'm a rebel and an outlaw. You said so yourself."

My father had once said writers were all rebels and outlaws, and I wasn't about to let him forget it. All this came back to me years later when I read about Henry having prostate cancer. I prayed and hoped he would beat it. But what that news about Henry did was shake my foundation of well-being and forced me, for the first time, to seriously confront the mortality not only of someone so close to my dreams as a youth but also of myself as well.

Over the years, Henry's life and mine have passed each other in Texas, Washington, Los Angeles and anywhere there were political conventions of any significance. I've interviewed Henry on occasions and, in our own ways, we've praised each other on our successes as well as consoled one another on our falls from grace, personally and professionally. People who grow up together invariably have nicknames for each other, monikers that we use behind their backs. I don't know what Henry's was for me, if there was one. I've heard them all from other friends and I imagine it might be something similar. Mine for Henry was Manolete, the Spanish bullfighter who rose to glory in the years after the Spanish Civil War. I called him Manolete because I have never seen a picture of Manolete smiling. He always seemed so serious, almost sorrowful and tragic. Henry struck me that way, even when he was smiling, as if something very sad was going on in his life. I've never thought of myself as a playboy; but, in contrast, you would have thought I was the life of the party.

"Henry, it's only words," I recall saying to him after a high school debate tournament. His team hadn't won, but neither had mine. Henry, though, wore that game face, as if blaming himself or as if he were facing a firing squad or some fierce 2,000-pound animal in a bullring. "You're a great debater. You'll win the next competition."

I think we all sensed that Henry was destined for true greatness, if anyone we knew ever was. He became mayor of San Antonio and the rising Latino star of the Democratic Party for his time. In 1984, Democratic Presidential Nominee Walter Mondale considered Henry as a running mate before choosing Rep. Geraldine Ferraro. In 1992, Henry finally made it on to the national political landscape when President Bill Clinton named him to his Cabinet. We all have our secrets, however, and Henry's doomed him. He was found to have lied to the FBI about a mistress, hush payments to her, and a sordid affair that destroyed his dreams.

My father kept up with news reports of the investigation as if... well, as if Henry were his son. My father learned that a journalist in whom Henry had confided about the affair had betrayed him, and you would have thought I had been that writer who ratted him out.

"You work in a profession full of sons of bitches and Judases," my father said to me at the time.

"And rebels and outlaws," I reminded him.

A few years later, as my father lay on his deathbed, I wasn't sure what else to say. We had made our peace, what we could anyway. I just wanted to say something more that would ease his final hours.

"Dad," I said. "I'm sorry I wasn't more like Henry Cisneros. I'm sorry I couldn't fulfill your dreams. If it's any consolation, I haven't fulfilled my dreams either."

My father shook his head, as if to protest. He had tears in his eyes, and I thought we would just sit there for a while longer.

"I don't care about Henry," he said, finally. "I care about you and what you did or tried to do. A father's dreams for his son are never fulfilled. They're just that — dreams. The important thing, and what I'm proud of you for, is that you had the courage to chase your own dreams. Your dreams — not someone else's."

And dreams really are what life is about in America, isn't it? What would we be if we weren't dreamers – and believed that those dreams could come true?

As an eleven-year-old fifth grader in 1958, I believed in two things: Patricia O'Neal and Mickey Mantle. They were intertwined in my consciousness – my great love and my great hero. Fittingly, when I spoke to her again more than half a century later, I had to tell Patricia that someone said that reading about her in a rough draft reminded him of the first line of my Mickey Mantle biography: *If Mickey Mantle hadn't been born, he would have had to have been created.* So, too, for Patricia. As I have written about her, no one would have believed she existed. For that reason, with her permission, her real name was of paramount importance in the book. Patricia O'Neal. The name resonates in memory and in life even today.

The book itself has its genesis somewhere in my foggy memories of the 1970s. It began as a growing-up-Chicano story that my publisher at that time wanted as a follow up to *Chicano Power.* But the publisher's perception of the experience it expected in the book and the reality of my life until that time were not the same. That rite of passage book was never published; and most, if not all, of the manuscript went up in smoke when my Porsche blew up in the middle of Harvard Square at the end of my Nieman Fellowship in 1977. I kept thinking I would get back to that book some day, but quite honestly my heart was never into doing that. I'm not sure why. I suspect I was either refusing to be honest about some of the things that happened in my early life or simply didn't wish to face them. I had never told anyone about not being allowed to dance that special waltz with Patricia in our elementary school year-end show, nor my embarrassing demotion to performing as the Atomic Man, and the reasons behind that. It wasn't just the pain of that loss. It was the humiliation associated with it, that the color of your skin or your heritage made you unworthy in the eyes of the people in position of power. I think I would have rather faced a more overt kind of discrimination than the kind of inequality that profoundly affects matters of the heart.

It was more than half a century before I ever revealed this secret and all the "white girls" speeches that teachers and other adults delivered in those formative years. And, in being forthcoming about that, I finally told someone about my first love and the undying affection and devotion for her that I carried all those years. For helping me get past making such a private matter so public, I owe deep gratitude to the least likeliest of confessionals for a kid who grew up deeply engrained in Catholicism -- the social networking phenomenon of the 21st century, Facebook. In the spring of 2010, after some prodding from friends and co-workers, I at long last signed up for Facebook. Among the "friends" that I made on that social network was a real friend of many years ago. Linda Dunwody had been a classmate at South Junior High School, and reconnecting with her turned out to be a Godsend. Over several Facebook message exchanges, the comfort of speaking to an old friend returned, along with a newfound openness made easier by the passage of time. I happened to mention to Linda my fear of incurring the wrath of teachers and other adults should I have tried to take an interest back then in her or in Judy Wammack, another friend of ours, because they were white. She was shocked with disbelief. So I began telling her about the "white girls" lectures I'd been given, all beginning with my early infatuation and obsession with Patricia O'Neal. Linda knew Patricia. We all had been in our junior high school's Press Club, which produced a bi-weekly mimeographed newspaper.

When I started telling Linda about Patricia, the emotional floodgates opened. As I recounted the story and heard her profound interest, I realized I had kept an entire side of my life secreted away inside - and, with it, a powerful window to understanding the time I grew up in and how it had shaped me. That night I went back to writing my rite-of-passage story.

Months later, with the manuscript in full swing, I decided to reach out to Patricia, to whom I had not spoken in almost fifty years. I had a terrible fear she would not remember me, or, worse, that she would see me as a stalker, which I suspect many of us in journalism sometimes happen to be in the pursuit of a story, a source, or an interview. About this same time, I happened to catch the romantic youth comedy *I Love*

You, Beth Cooper on HBO. Toward the end of the film, the kid who is in love with Beth Cooper expresses out loud to his best friend his fear of being mistaken for a stalker. To which his friend says something to the effect that "it's not stalking when you love her." Emboldened, I called Patricia, and we soon struck up the friendship via iPhones that we failed to develop when we had gone to school together many years earlier.

Today, she goes by Tricia and lives in Northwest Arkansas. She has been happily married since her sophomore year in college, and she is now a grandmother to two lovely tweens. Today we both realize we grew up at a special time in America, but a time that was seriously flawed by its past. I am indebted to her not only for her friendship but also for her assistance in this book. Patricia unselfishly offered her own memories and the knowledge she had both of her family and of the lovely Victorian home in which she grew up in Waco, as well as photographs of herself and her family from that period. When she told me something that I would have never suspected – that the row of wood-frame cabins in the back of her house had been slaves quarters in the 1800s, Patricia opened up a new window into our hometown that suddenly gave me a different perspective on Waco.

Another dear friend from the past with whom I fortunately renewed ties in recent years is Barbara McBride Smith, who kindly shared her memories of her teen years, especially her time as a cheerleader at South Junior High School. Babs was also generous in allowing me access to some priceless photographs of her and her friends at that time. She is now an accomplished writer and a storyteller in Tulsa, Okla., where she lives with her husband Dennis Edwin Smith, who is also from Waco. I cannot thank Babs enough for reading my manuscript through its various stages and taking the time to offer insights based on her own remembrances as well as much-need encouragement. Babs knew Patricia at South Junior as well as at Waco High where they were both actively involved in the school's drama and speech activities. Dennis attended West Junior at the time we were at South Junior, and he later was a star on the Waco High School football teams that I wish I could have played on. Dennis was also splendidly gracious in recalling his own memories from junior high school of Jerrell Marshall, the person whose friendship both Babs and I shared at South Junior. That was important in understanding that Jerrell's football heroics when we were kids extended beyond our school and were known and shared elsewhere, as was that remarkable haircut none of us could ever duplicate!

My junior high acquaintance Dolores Mendoza is another with whom I reconnected after four decades. Lola, as I've always called her, was vice-president of the Student Council at South Junior and both involved with and part of the increasing Hispanic clique at that school that I never understood nor befriended. We viewed each other with suspicion and confusion. I look back on that with some sadness. Now, many years later, Lola has assisted in helping me finally coming to terms with a part of my past that was as disturbing as anything I knew at that time. I know Lola has done an incredible amount of soul-searching, as have I, in seeking some understanding of our differences at that time. We both wish things had been different back then.

My cousin Jimmy Duarte has been an invaluable friend and ally throughout our lives, and he was again in this project. He was especially helpful in helping me remember a part of our maternal grandmother, Concepción Rivera Segovia Veracruz, that I had forgotten. Jimmy was also with me the last of many times I spoke at length with our uncle, Jesse Segovia. When he was already approaching the late stages of Alzheimer's, Jesse sat with us in his home for hours as we gently guided his mind back many years to recollections of the Segovia family, as well as of the Castro family.

This book would not have been possible without the love and patience, and countless stories, from my late parents. They were unhesitating in sharing everything they knew about our ancestors and their formative years, even when they didn't want to be as open as they were and especially since they knew their admonitions about family privacy would go unheeded. This book is generously seasoned with their love as well as the same failings that are typical in almost every American family, and that is what they sought to be, after all.

Who ever truly understands their parents? Or knows them beyond what they are allowed to see in family settings. Perhaps I should have tried harder, but I eventually stopping trying to get to the essence of who they were, not because I didn't love them but because each answer seemed to come with several more questions. Ultimately, I came to accept them for who they were, no more, no less. Two questions about my father did nag at me, and continue to. The first was the second family he evidently had with a girlfriend named Jerri. He would not talk about it, at least not with me, and neither would Jerri. I tracked her down and visited with her on a trip to Waco in the early 1980s. She was friendly and even generous with her time. She talked to me about my father but refused to confirm or deny that either one or two of her children were my father's. She also steadfastly denied that my father had been involved in her husband's violent death. However, she was kind enough to allow me to see several photo albums of her children. The son in question resembled my father even more than I remembered. The daughter I wasn't so sure of. The second question involved my father's involvement with the Office of Strategic Services during World War II, at least according to what Harry Provence told me and which was confirmed by our family doctor who had told Provence of his own OSS ties and that of my father. It would have been ideal to have gotten an official confirmation from the Defense Department or the Central Intelligence Agency, but numerous attempts failed to get anything substantive from either. According to the Archival Research Catalog of the National Archives, tens of thousands of files, including thousands relating to OSS personnel, that were made public in 2008, are redacted, incomplete, or not available. A California congressman who is a friend also tried to learn of my father's role, if any, in official intelligence gathering during and after the war but could get nothing conclusive. The work of many civilians and military on behalf of the OSS may never be fully acknowledged, according to my friend. It raised eyebrows with him and other officials, though, to learn that at two critical times in my father's medical care in later years that his disability level was increased after almost half a century and that his death was officially attributed to wartime wounds. Both instances resulted in significant increases in financial benefits for him and then for my mother, his widow. A soldier's sendoff if ever there was one.

To my extended family, I ask their understanding and indulgence. Over a number of years, having known I was working on a book related to our family, their mistaken impression has been that it was to be something akin to a favorably edited coffee table Bible loaded with an extensive family tree and extolling the virtues all families see in themselves. It was never going to be that, though there is a great deal about my family woven into the story of growing up in the 1950s and 1960s in Waco and Texas against a backdrop of the racial and ethnic divide of that time. I would hope for their understanding that this book is far more meaningful as it is, honestly felt and with no holds barred on who we are as a family, than it would be as an insincere but lovely valentine. I had not meant to recreate my family as the multigenerational and dysfunctional Buendía clan of the Gabriel García Márquez novel *One Hundred Years of Solitude*, which is how one friend has described the book. I am humbled if it resembles that great work even in the remotest of tequila induced fantasies. My apologies, Gabo!

In addition to Patricia's, I have tried to use the actual names of most of the people with whom I interacted during my life in Waco. Of course, there are a few obvious instances where changing the names was the wisest course to take for numerous reasons, some personal, a few legal.

I am also indebted to my agent, Mike Hamilburg, for his years of patience, advice and labor on projects over more than two decades, as it was for this. His counsel on the manuscript and what I wanted for this book have been both as an agent and a friend, and I am enormously grateful.

Writing the book that this became would not have been possible without the gracious assistance of a number of people. Foremost among them are the wonderful research staffs at the Waco Public Library, the Baylor University Library, and the *Waco Tribune-Herald*.

They were remarkable in their diligence when confirming everything from historical anecdotes to details about old neighborhoods in Waco that no longer exist but were important in my life or in the city when I was growing up there. The research staff of the *New York Times* kindly assisted in researching the slavery history in Texas and Waco, as well as the atrocity that was committed against Jesse Washington in my hometown. I am also indebted to the assistance of the Widener Library at Harvard University, the Library of Congress, and the University of Texas Library. Finally, I wish to thank the editors and staff at Voxxi. com, where personal anecdotal parts of this book appeared in a slightly different form.

Throughout my work on this book, the individuals who have contributed the most are those closest to me, without whose love and devotion this would never have been possible. When Lincoln talked about "the better angels of our nature," he must have meant my loving wife Renee, my *raison d'être*, who put up with my neurotic behavior of recent years as only someone from heaven could. My boyhood dreams were just that, and they were the driving force that ultimately led me to her, the love of my life. My sons, Ryan and Trey, know their father as an absent-minded man-child who at least can keep some of his thoughts together in print. I appreciated their review of the manuscript, their editing suggestions and their comments. And my black Labrador Retriever, Jeter, has been as noble a muse and inspiration as his New York Yankee namesake.

Finally, there are some people who have provided meaningful contributions of one form or another over the years leading to this book: They included but are not limited to: Vicki Saffle Adams, Richard Alatorre, J.D. Alexander, Tommy Anderson, Jim Atkinson, Sallie Baker, Ronnie Barber, Sandra Barnard, Penni Barnett, Carolyn Barta, Simon Barzilay, Kamran Behbehani, Ray Bell, Jim Bellows, Hollis Biddle, Mike Blackman, Sandra Blankenship, Roy Bode, Warren Bosworth, Ronnie Bradford, Jimmy Breslin, David Broder, Jerry Brown, Christy Turlington Burns, Roger Butler Jeanette Cagle, Barbara Callaway, Doug Calmelet, Dave Campbell, Lou Cannon,

Buff Carmichael, Lloyd Carll, Robert Caro, Jimmie Carpenter, Sylvia Cortez Carrizales, Gary Cartwright, Judy Cartwright, Frank Casado, Lucy Casado, Patricia Casado, Ruben Castaneda, Leonel Castillo, Matilde Castro, Linda Chavez, Laura Chester, Barbara Cigarroa, Henry Cisneros, Pam Vardeman Compton, Robert Compton, Carlos Conde, John B. Connally, Diane Copeland Mitchell, Sylvia Cortez Carrizales, Elba Covarrubias, Paula Cozart, Richard Ben Cramer, Mimi Crossley, Micah Daily, Teo Davis, Rod Decker, Rhoda Dellinger, Dominique de Menil, Ann Salisbury Donen, Debbie Dickerson Donnelly, Dee Dee Dwyer, Zvi Dor-Ner, Arlen Dunham, Judy Elfenbein, Charlie Ericksen, Jim Ewell, Ginger Faulkner, Janettte Sherill Finley, Robert Fitzgerald, Cathie Flahive, Frances Flores, Robert Flynn, Luke Ford, Don Forst, Jeanie Francis, Paul Francis, Paul Francis Sr., Shirley Franks, Doug Freelander, Glenn Frey, Barbara Zuanich Friedman, Arthur Fuentes, Carlos Fuentes, Chris Garcia, David Gardner, Chris Gilbert Mikal Gilmore, Aaron Glantz, Carole Player Golden, Betty Goodwin, Carlos Guerra, Jose Angel Gutierrez, David Halberstam, Donald Hale, Jack Hale, Denis Hamill, Dana Harmon, Don Harris, Lew Harris, Jack Harwell, Jickey Harwell, Don Henley, Larry Henry, Frank P. Hernandez, Gracie Hilton, Oveta Culp Hobby, Fred Hofheinz, Joe Holley, Ken Holley, Joy Horowitz, Michal Ann Horst, Jaquine Hudson Bly, John Huerta, Chuck Hughes, Ed Hunter, Carolyn Hurry, Jackie Holdbrook Ivie, Molly Ivins, Alex Jacinto, Barbara Johnson, Kathryn Johnson, Caroline Kennedy, Terry Kliewer, Sam Kinch Jr., Larry L. King, Sally Taggert Klein, Doug Krikorian, Mary Nell Walker Jones, Christina Kahrl, Ron Kaye, Mike Kennedy, Preston Kirk, Robert A. Kraft, Su Zann Lamb, Linda Smith LaRoque, Christine LaSalle, Jean LaSalle, Lisa LaSalle, Donnie Laurence, Lynette Wade Leber, Jim Lehrer, Mickey Leland, Gay Lynn Lieb, Jules Loh, Angelina Lopez, Carmen Lopez, Dolores Lopez, Elva Lopez, Hank Lopez, Robert Lopez, Gary Luft, Larry Lynch, Rodney, Lynch, Ralph Lynn, Cassie Mackin, Diana Macias, Molly Maloy, Ivonne Malaver, Theresa J. May, Bob Maynard, Mickey Mantle, Merlyn Mantle, Jerrell Marshall, Tony Martin, Dolores Martinez, Rene Martinez, Barbara Matusow, Garry Mauro, Margaret Mayer, Judy Mayr, Bill McAda, Abner V. McCall, Dick McCall, Julie McCullough, Sue McDonald, David McHam, Dave McNeely, Ardie

Meeker, Diane Copeland Mitchell, Kevin Modesti, Sharon Moline, Jeannette Monahan, Ricardo Montalban, Hilda Montelongo, Gilbert Montemayor, Lidia Montemayor, Dave Montgomery, Jim Montgomery, Linda Thompson Montgomery, Susan Moore, Mike Moran, Louis F. Moret, Willie Morris, Georgette Mosbacher, Jeanie Holdbrook Moss, Connie Moss Guinn, Dwain Moss, Jimmy Moss, LaVerne Moss, Lawrence Moss, Mike Moss, Jamil Mroue, Dennis Mukai, Ramsey Muñiz, Bill Murchison, Barba Holdbrook Muse, Jack Muse, Ramsey Muñiz, Yolanda Nava, Jack Nelson, Laura Nelson, Carolyn Neuwirth, Donna Oliver-Leep, Bill Orozco, Eli Osorio, Gloria Castro Palacios, Sister Karen Patrice, Darwin Payne, Octavio Paz, Julianne Pederson, Tony Pederson, Larry Pendley, Bob Pettit, John Robert Pharr, Walter Pinkus, Billy Bob Pittman, George Pla, Jim Plunkett, W. R. "Bob" Poage, Billy Porterfield, Ella Wall Prichard, Sister Karen Patrice, Harry Provence, Harold Purvis, Henry M. Ramirez, Bernard Rapoport, Monica Reaves, Judy Wammack Rice, Mike Ritchey, Mike Robins, Tom Robbins, Gregory Rodriguez, Penny Rosalez, Ed Roybal, Ruben Salazar, Carlos Sanchez, Emilio Sanchez, Dutch Schroeder, Darlene Scott, Blanca Segovia Fajardo, Jesse Segovia, Mario Segovia, Modesta Segovia, Mike Shannon, Charlie Sheen, Blackie Sherrod, Peggy Millender Shinkle, Ambrosio Silva Jr., Joe Silva, John Silva, Dennis Edwin Smith, Isaac Martinez, Jose Martinez Soler, Jon Standefer, Sandy Gottlieb Steigerwald, Ben Stein, Randy Stewart, Gracie Stringfield, Gary Stratton, Patsy Swank, Gay Talese, J. Randy Taraborrelli, Lucile Weldon Teague, Bob Terry, John Terry, Paul Teske, Jimmy Tighe, Joe Tighe, Reies Lopez Tijerina, John Tormey, Art Torres, Don Trull, Johnny Tusa, John Tuthill, Marianne Tyler, Chase Untermeyer, Hennie Van Deventer, John Vasek, Debby Veracruz, Bob Vickrey, Antonio Villaraigosa, Lynette Wade Leber, Mary Walsh, Don Wanlass, Bob Wendorf, Don Wendorf, Tommy West, William Wheatley, Jack White, Tom Wicker, Apala Wilson, Tom Wolfe, Clare Wood, Bob Woodward, Eddie Wright, Lawrence Wright, Russell York, Lynn Wyatt, Richard Zaldivar, Mary Anne Zoul.

ABOUT THE AUTHOR

Tony Castro is the author of two critically acclaimed books, the civil rights history *Chicano Power: The Emergence of Mexican America* (E.P. Dutton) and the biography *Mickey Mantle: America's Prodigal Son* (Potomac Books). He is a graduate of Baylor University and was a Nieman Fellow at Harvard. Formerly a staff writer for *Sports Illustrated*, he is currently working on a biography of Ernest Hemingway. Castro lives in Southern California with his wife Renee LaSalle, their sons Trey and Ryan, and their black Labrador retriever Jeter.

Tony's Website: TonyCastro.com